NONE SO BLIND

NONE
SO
BLIND

A Personal Account of the
Intelligence Failure in Vietnam

George W. Allen

Ivan R. Dee, Chicago 2001

Library of Congress Cataloging-in-Publication Data:
Allen, George W., 1926–
    None so blind : a personal account of the intelligence failure in Vietnam / George W. Allen.
        p. cm.
    Includes index.
    ISBN 1-56663-387-7 (alk. paper)
        1. Vietnamese Conflict, 1961–1975—Secret service—United States.   2. Indochine War, 1947–1954—Secret service—United States.   3. Vietnamese Conflict, 1961–1975—Personal narratives, American.   4. Allen, George W., 1926–   I. Title.

DS559.8.M44 A45 2001
959.704'38—dc21   2001028244

To my dear wife, Dola,
who waited and kept the hearth warm

Contents

Preface

THE BOOK is written in response to the urging of friends, former colleagues, journalists, and historians that I put on public record the unique experiences and perspective I gained as an intelligence analyst who worked for almost twenty years (1949–1968) on the Vietnam problem. Three of those years were spent in Vietnam, including a half-dozen visits to the area, each two to twelve weeks in length, between 1954 and 1968, and a two-year tour with the CIA station in Saigon (1964–1966). I saw how the French were fighting their war in Vietnam, Cambodia, and Laos in 1954, and how the United States fought its war in twenty-six of South Vietnam's forty-four provinces.

My work in Washington included a dozen years in the Pentagon with army intelligence and the Defense Intelligence Agency, and seventeen years with the CIA. In these assignments I absorbed intelligence reports from a wide variety of sources and produced innumerable intelligence summaries, situation reports, studies, and assessments of developments in Indochina. I also had the benefit of discussing intelligence issues with countless Vietnamese and American military and civilian officials of all ranks, from junior officers and noncommissioned officers in the field, to staff officers, generals, ambassadors, and cabinet officers in Saigon and Washington. My work also frequently involved representing the CIA in interagency working groups dealing with Vietnam, including both formal and informal presentations to key policymakers. All of this gave me more access to more intelligence on Vietnam over a longer period than most other Americans, and afforded me unique insights into our involvement there.

A first draft of this book was prepared shortly after my retirement more than twenty years ago. It was based on my recollections at that time, supplemented—and refreshed—by a reading of open literature, including the *Pentagon Papers*. (I had accumulated no "private" cache of official documents and records during my career.) My involvement in the CBS-Westmoreland litigation refocused my attention on Vietnam and brought me into association with many former colleagues, most of whom urged me to publish my manuscript, which had been subpoenaed to become part of the trial record. Since then I have read extensively in the historical literature on Vietnam and have studied much of the declassified material released by the CIA and other agencies. Much of this work was related to my development of graduate and undergraduate courses on intelligence in the Vietnam wars which I presented for the Defense Intelligence College in the early 1990s.

Thus when I finally succumbed to entreaties that I publish on Vietnam, it was possible to rework the original manuscript, updating it and adding more perspective. My intent in publishing is not to provide the "final word" or the "ultimate truth" on the trials of the intelligence community in its efforts to inform the policymaking process in Washington on the situation in Vietnam. Rather, my hope is to contribute to the reader's understanding of the complexities of that process. America failed in Vietnam not because intelligence was lacking, or wrong, but because it was not in accord with what its consumers wanted to believe, and because its relevance was outweighed by other factors in the minds of those who made national security policy decisions. When this occurs—when political and ideological factors dominate the decision-making process—there is little the intelligence community can do about it except to stay on course. On balance, I believe the record demonstrates that the CIA as an institution (and also the Department of State's bureau of intelligence) performed both credibly and creditably on Vietnam.

In his *mea culpa* on the Vietnam War ("we didn't know . . . we didn't understand"), Robert S. McNamara decries the lack of area knowledge and expertise on Indochina available to guide the "best and the brightest" in their decision-making during the most tragically futile of America's wars.* In fact there was no shortage of Southeast Asian specialists in the foreign affairs and intelligence arms of the U.S. government who *did* know and *did* understand. Their knowledge and comprehension of the situation in Vietnam were readily available to McNamara and his high-level colleagues, but they were rarely consulted, and their written assessments were consistently dismissed or ignored. Their substantive expertise was never effectively brought to bear on the formulation and execution of American national security policy as it related to the war in Vietnam.

Many authors, in tracing the evolution of America's efforts to "stem the tide of Red aggression in Southeast Asia" from 1950 through 1975, have correctly noted that the views of the intelligence community on Vietnam were usually at odds with those of its consumers, the people who utilized intelligence. The leaders responsible for formulating policy on Vietnam were aware that saving that country from Communist domination was a dubious proposition, and they desperately sought solutions that would avert defeat. But intelligence estimates and studies consistently made it clear that the odds were heavily stacked against the achievement of America's declared objectives in Vietnam. Policymakers knew but rarely acknowledged this as they resolutely led the nation ever deeper into the Vietnam quagmire, repeatedly "reinforcing disaster," as one of my military colleagues so aptly described our policy. Many of our leaders simply "damned the torpedoes"—the negative and pessimistic intelligence estimates—as they forged ahead. The historian Walter Laqueur was on the mark when he judged that American "intelligence" was essentially irrelevant to policymaking in Indochina.[†]

Vietnam was never a rewarding "account" for the professional intelligence analyst. It did afford more opportunities than most other assignments for analysts to learn their trade quickly, to gain exposure through

---

*Robert S. McNamara, *In Retrospect: The Tragedy and Lessons of Vietnam* (New York, 1995).

[†]Walter Laqueur, *A World of Secrets: The Uses and Limits of Intelligence* (New York, 1985).

the continuing production of reports and studies and the presentation of frequent briefings, and thereby to win early promotions. But these analysts also experienced gut-wrenching frustration, heartache, and disillusionment with the decision-making processes of our executive branch, over a longer period, than those who dealt with any other intelligence issue.

I spent fourteen of the first twenty years (1949–1968) of my intelligence career working full-time on the Indochina problem, and the area was in my sphere of professional responsibility during the remainder of that period. Even after I officially left the Vietnam account at the end of 1968, the situation there never disappeared from my professional horizon until after the capture of Saigon by the Vietnamese Communists in 1975.

Acknowledgments

I AM GREATLY INDEBTED to my early colleagues and mentors in army intelligence, and particularly to Evan T. Sage, Lieutenant Colonel Don Husman, and Bob Kinney, who introduced me into the arcane art and craft of military intelligence analysis. Much is also owed my colleagues from other agencies in those years, especially Dave Gaddy, Paul Kattenburg, and Jack Kelly, whose generous collaboration contributed so much to my professional development. It was also my privilege to work with, and learn from, scores of people in army intelligence; noteworthy among these were the exceptionally able members of the army attaché office in Saigon during the French War, especially Lieutenant Colonel Bob Taber, Major George Rheuark, and Captain Al Percival, all of whom "maxed the course," and Brigadier General Ed Doleman, who headed the intelligence staff at the army's Pacific Command in Hawaii in 1959–1960.

I am grateful to Dick Lehman, whose extended hand brought me into CIA "from the cold," and also to Ed, Molly, Jack, Jim, Stan, and the rest of the Southeast Asia gang of CIA's Office of Current Intelligence, who made me feel so much at home in the analytical trenches at Langley. It was a pleasure also to know and work with Hal Ford, Jim Graham, and Bob Layton of the Office of National Estimates, and with all the folks in the Vietnamese Affairs Staff, including Don Blascak. All of these people contributed much to my professional growth, as did Russ and the other capable members of the "herd" in 1964.

The people in the CIA's Saigon station in the mid-1960s were uniformly helpful and cooperative, as were Phil Habib and others of the embassy staff. My relationships with Major General Joseph McChristian, Colonel Bob Crosson, and Lieutenant Colonel Gaines Hawkins of MACV's intelligence staff in Saigon, were, I trust, mutually rewarding. Colonel Ted Mataxis, the very capable senior army adviser to the Vietnamese II Corps headquarters at Pleiku, contributed a great deal to my understanding of the grim situation in 1964 and early 1965.

Finally I am grateful for the efforts of the CIA's publication review board in expeditiously processing my original draft of this manuscript in 1980, and the extensively expanded version which I submitted in September 1990, in accordance with agency regulations. The board's clearance of the text for publication in no way reflects agreement with its substantive content.

Many people over the years have urged me to put my story in writing. The historian Lloyd Gardner tipped the balance late in 1999 by putting me in touch with his publisher, Ivan Dee, whose keen editorial efforts deserve credit for whatever coherence and focus this account possesses. I am also grateful to Vicki Hsu and all the others in Ivan Dee's editorial and production staff for the professional quality of their contribution to this project. I, of course, take full responsibility for any errors or misstatements of fact, and the judgments expressed herein are my own and should not be construed as those of any agency of the U.S. government.

G. W. A.

Williamsburg, Virginia
May 2001

Rigorously objective analysis is vital to the development of a foreign policy which properly serves the security interests of the American people. . . . But decision-makers must be willing to accept its results. In the issue of Indochina they were not. . . .

—Paul Kattenburg, *The Vietnam Trauma in American Foreign Policy, 1945–75*

U.S. policymakers could have acted more wisely, and might have had more success in Vietnam than they did, had they been more receptive to more of the bold facts and probing interpretations CIA analysts gave them along the way.

—Harold P. Ford, *CIA and the Vietnam Policymakers*

The disaster in Vietnam was not the result of impersonal forces but a uniquely human failure, the responsibility for which was shared by President Johnson and his principal military and civilian leaders. The failings were many and reinforcing: arrogance, weakness, lying in the pursuit of self-interest, and, above all, the abdication of responsibility to the American people.

—H. R. McMaster, *Dereliction of Duty*

NONE SO BLIND

1

A Taste
of War

I DON'T BELIEVE I was programmed from birth to be an Indochina specialist, but my family background, military experience, and education certainly pointed me in that direction. An "army brat," I was born and raised on coastal artillery posts ranging from the harbor defenses of Boston to those of Manila Bay, with tours also on Fisher's Island in Long Island Sound, and in Honolulu and San Francisco. This environment imbued me with a keen sense of patriotism and a lifelong affinity for military matters. The coastal defense focus brought me an intense interest in international affairs, diplomacy, and the issues of war and peace.

The two years our family spent on Corregidor (1929–1931), the brief stops in China and Japan on the way home in the early 1930s, and two memorable boyhood years in Hawaii in the mid-thirties heightened my interest in the Far East and Pacific regions. This interest continued during our six years in San Francisco, where we lived until I volunteered for the Navy on my seventeenth birthday in early 1943, fifteen months after Pearl Harbor.

This burst of youthful enthusiasm and patriotic zeal brought me stunningly face-to-face with the brutal realities of war nine months later at Tarawa. As Navy radiomen five days after the invasion, we stumbled into the aftermath of one of the most bloody struggles of the Pacific war. It was only weeks later that we learned we were destined to be part of the naval

3

air base communications component. The island had been declared "secure" two days before we landed, but mopping-up action was still under way and would continue for another thirty days. During our first two weeks ashore, however, we were diverted to the grueling and gruesome task of recovering and burying the rapidly decomposing remains of the 1,000 Marines and 4,700 Japanese who had been killed on the square-mile of hell that Betio Island had become. The equatorial heat was stifling, drinking water was scarce and carefully rationed, and no other water was available for washing, shaving, or bathing. I became inured to the stench of the rotting dead we handled for two weeks.

Betio Island had been thoroughly devastated before and during the four-day battle. Every above-ground structure—barracks, warehouses, workshops, pigstys—had been demolished, except for the concrete blockhouses and stoutly built coconut-log bunkers and bombproof shelters, and many of these had been damaged. The island looked—and smelled—like a huge garbage dump; it was littered with crumpled sheet-metal roofing, shattered vehicles, and the debris of battle-broken and abandoned weapons, half-empty cases of rations, grenades and ammunition bandoliers, and scattered personal belongings of the garrison. Everywhere there were bodies and bits of bodies: heaps of Japanese who had been machine-gunned while running between blockhouses, then seared by flamethrowers; groups of dead Japanese in blockhouses, weapons emplacements, bomb shelters, and in huge bomb craters and shell holes; U.S. Marines in their twos and threes in some places, and in their dozens lying along the beach line or floating just offshore.

Such was my soul-searing introduction to the character of war. After cleaning up Betio, where the battle had been fought, a number of us were sent off on Christmas Eve to a neighboring isle—Buota—where navy Sea Bees had built a second air base from scratch, and we set up the communications facilities that would be required to support the operations of well over a hundred navy and army air force aircraft based there. These planes—mostly B-24s and B-25s—were busily engaged for six or seven weeks in bombing raids to soften up the Marshall Islands. By the end of February, the Marshalls had been taken, and most of our aircraft moved on to new bases there.

At the end of March 1944, I was sent back to Betio for duty as the communications clerk on the staff of the Commander, Gilbert Islands Sub-Area, with added duties as clerk for the staff intelligence officer. This gave me my first exposure to the heady world of "secrecy." I found myself responsible for controlling the circulation and storage of classified publications dealing with ongoing enemy activities, and of plans for future Allied operations in the Central Pacific. My access to these fascinating documents, combined with the off-duty opportunity to study again in detail the scene of the battle on Betio, kept me intellectually engaged.

I had become deeply interested in issues of strategy and the nature of war, and absorbed with the question of why nations couldn't find better means of resolving their problems than resorting to the seemingly wanton slaughter of each other's youth. I had ample occasion to study the battle scene at Tarawa and to contemplate the character and consequences of war in general. I also explored, many times over, the remnants of the fortifications manned by the island's tenacious defenders. One could only wonder at the courage of the Marine riflemen struggling over the reef through several hundred yards of armpit-deep water in the face of intense automatic weapons fire. And of those huddled behind the coconut-log wall fronting the beach, who ultimately had to go over the top.

In late June 1944, I returned to Pearl Harbor for assignment to an amphibious command ship, the *USS Mt. McKinley*. Aboard her I observed two full-scale amphibious assaults on the Palau Islands, east of the Philippines. By this stage of the war—only ten months after Tarawa—our forces in the Pacific had refined and perfected the techniques of amphibious warfare, the most complex of military operations. Our amphibious group, carrying the landing force, included about a dozen large attack transports, a half-dozen attack cargo ships, two dozen tank landing ships, and another three-score assorted amphibious vessels, together with accompanying minesweepers, patrol craft, and escort ships. Another task force, comprising some half-dozen battleships, a similar number of cruisers, and a score of destroyers, battered the island with shellfire for several days before the assault, and provided continuing gunfire support to the troops ashore after their landing. Still other task forces with carriers, stationed beyond the horizon, provided massive air support for the entire operation.

These ingredients combined to present an awesome display of American military power at its height in the last year of the war. In the landing at Peleliu, I was struck by the realization that, though some of the battle-ships there had been resurrected from the bottom of Pearl Harbor, most of the other ships, and all the landing ships and craft, had been built in the thirty-three months since that disaster. Similarly, the hundreds of partici-pating aircraft and virtually all the arms and equipment being put ashore had been manufactured since Pearl Harbor. And the vast majority of the men manning the ships, and of the Marines and soldiers assaulting the is-lands, had—like me—been civilians two years before. Now we were em-ploying these ships, weapons, and equipment in a highly complex activity with some semblance of professional competence. This display of what the industrial might and organizational ability of a fully aroused and de-termined America could accomplish made a vivid, profound, and lasting impression on me.

A month after the Palau assaults, I returned to Pearl Harbor and to a month of home leave before assignment to the *USS Ancon*, another am-phibious command ship. I boarded her in late January 1945 and sailed for Saipan, where the ships of our task group were gathering for the assault on Okinawa. Our task force received the first kamikaze air strikes on land-ing day at Okinawa. Just after dawn, a troop ship immediately behind us was badly damaged when struck by a piloted, rocket-propelled bomb. The low-flying twin-engined bomber that had released the "baka" bomb went on to crash into an LST farther back in the formation.

At Okinawa we took over the command and control communications links for Admiral Spruance, who commanded the Fifth Fleet. We acted as the communications center for more than twelve hundred naval vessels in the Okinawa area. We remained in the main anchorage for forty-two try-ing days, enduring seemingly endless kamikaze attacks, before leaving in early June for the Philippines. At Subic Bay we boarded the *USS Blue Ridge,* the worn-down command ship of Admiral Daniel Barber, for the voyage back to Pearl Harbor, where the ship was to be refitted and refur-bished in preparation for the invasion of Japan. It was at Pearl that we learned of the Japanese surrender.

On V-J day proper, several of us were checking in for temporary duty at the naval radio station at Wahiawa when we heard President Truman's formal announcement of the end of the war as it was broadcast over Armed Forces Radio. We were indoors, lounging about in the personnel office when the radio music was interrupted for Truman's statement, which was followed by the playing of the "Star Spangled Banner." We rose to our feet and stood at attention, with tears rolling down our faces, joyful that we had survived while mindful of those who hadn't lived to see the day. Since then I have never been able to sing the words to our national anthem; its stirring strains always take me back to that moment, raising a solemn lump in my throat.

2

The French in Indochina

MY WARTIME EXPERIENCES sharpened my interest in world affairs and led me to pursue an intensive study of political science, international relations, and history at the University of Utah. The GI Bill of Rights made this possible. I wanted to understand the factors that influenced nations' conduct of their affairs with one another, the processes of diplomacy, the determination of national goals, the basis for international rivalries, and the sources of national power. Deeply moved by my experience on Tarawa, I hoped to contribute in some way to public understanding of such matters and of the issues that would confront our country in the postwar era. I knew that America had interests that must be protected or advanced, and that the prevalence of war throughout history demonstrated that conflict between nations would inevitably occur. My hope was to participate in the development of rational and "realistic" policies and strategies that would enable our country to pursue its aims and interests in ways that might avoid the destructiveness of war. I recognized that we could not determine the actions and policies of other nations, but I believed that sound and just policies on our part would help bring about an international climate in which all countries might be encouraged to pursue their interests without resorting to war.

I had little interest in pursuing academic research or a teaching career, and I did not wish to criticize the conduct of our foreign policy from the sidelines. Rather, I concluded that government service might enable me to participate somehow in the development of sound foreign policy decisions.

Although I was initially inclined toward the diplomatic service, the announced creation of the Central Intelligence Agency in 1947 persuaded me to equip myself for a role in intelligence. I saw this as a means of ensuring that our government acted with an understanding of the challenges and opportunities facing us in the developing cold war. I was already focusing on Russian language and area studies, having concluded in 1946 that the Soviet Union would probably be our principal adversary during my lifetime. I also maintained a military connection as an active participant in the naval reserve, finding my way into a unit involved with intelligence duties as a means of complementing my academic studies.

My postgraduate life began in June 1949 with a thirty-day training assignment as a reservist at a naval intelligence activity in Washington. There I had an opportunity to apply my Russian language skills and discovered that I enjoyed intelligence work. My hopes of parlaying that training opportunity into a permanent job somewhere in Washington were almost scuttled by the 10 percent cut in the defense budget decreed that summer by Secretary of Defense Louis Johnson. The defense-wide hiring freeze was almost airtight, but I lucked into an exception to the freeze which permitted the army's Assistant Chief of Staff for Intelligence (ACSI) to fill one vacancy for a much needed clerk typist in its Far East section. Under the circumstances, a foot-in-the-door in a subprofessional position seemed to me preferable to returning to graduate studies for a nonexistent job market. As it turned out, the clerk-typist job led me into an almost career-long association with the Indochina wars.

Despite my apparently menial work, I viewed my position as an opportunity to observe and learn about the intelligence profession from the bottom up. The job involved a variety of clerical functions, including assistance to analysts responsible for studying the structure and composition (order of battle) of the Chinese Communist Army and other military forces in the Far East region. Of course I also typed all kinds of intelli-

gence summaries, reports, briefings, and studies, so I soon became familiar with the formats of such papers, the writing styles that would pass
muster with editors and reviewers, and the inner workings of the relationships between intelligence and its consumers. I also learned how the analysts did their work, noting particularly the techniques, work styles, and
intellectual processes of those who were more successful. Few analysts
joining the government were afforded a comparable apprenticeship before
having to assume professional responsibilities.

The Korean War ended all restrictions on hiring for years to come.
ACSI expanded chiefly by recruiting from outside sources, and thus overlooked me. But when I reluctantly gave notice of my intent to accept a job
offer as an intelligence analyst with the air force, the army promptly promoted me, and I was assigned analytical duties in October 1950.

This change in my responsibilities coincided with large-scale Communist attacks on French positions near the China border. Since December 1946, French military forces had been fighting the Communist-led
guerrilla forces of Ho Chi Minh's Democratic Republic of Vietnam.
These rebels, known as the Viet Minh, were fighting for Vietnamese independence from France. They had achieved a strategic stalemate, with the
French holding most of the major towns and cities, and the guerrillas in
de facto possession of much of the surrounding countryside. After the
Chinese Communists extended their control down to the Indochina border in 1950, the Viet Minh sent a number of regimental-sized formations
into China, where they were re-equipped and trained in more conventional military tactics. These new "main force" units were intended to enable the Viet Minh to break the strategic stalemate and move the struggle
into a new phase of mobile warfare. In October 1950, in a series of powerful attacks, they overwhelmed French forces of more than 3,500 men at a
number of strongpoints guarding the principal approaches into northeast
Vietnam, thereafter permitting the Chinese to pour arms, ammunition,
and other supplies into Tonkin to support the Viet Minh struggle.

ACSI's Indochina desk was covered at that time by an integrated
British army major (the United States and Britain had reciprocal arrangements for such assignments in those days). Since it appeared that the
Indochina war was likely to draw increasing interest, I was assigned to
help with the crisis posed by this major French defeat. Having gained

some familiarity with the situation in Indochina while performing my earlier duties, I was able to be more immediately effective than any of the newly recruited analysts who might otherwise have been available for the job.

When my naval reserve commitment expired, I was commissioned in the army's military intelligence reserve. I immediately began a three-year training course in combat intelligence, which enabled me to learn the fundamentals of military intelligence at the battalion level. I found that the principles and techniques were virtually the same as those we employed at the national level, though the level of detail and the relative consequence of the work differed dramatically.

My first task as a military intelligence analyst on Indochina was to develop an order of battle—an understanding of the detailed composition and structure—of both the French Union and Viet Minh military forces in Indochina.* ACSI's responsibilities included providing information on foreign military forces to the Army Department staff in Washington for use in planning for wartime contingencies and for peacetime support of our allies. As a component of the national intelligence community, the ACSI was also responsible for providing information on foreign ground forces for the preparation of National Intelligence Estimates, whose production was coordinated by the Central Intelligence Agency.

---

*French Union forces included all of those regular and paramilitary forces in Indochina fighting under French command, e.g., French armed forces, French colonial forces (Algerian, Moroccan, Senegalese, Tunisian, Indochinese, and Foreign Legion), the armed forces of the "Associated States" (within the French Union) of Cambodia, Laos, and Vietnam, and a wide variety of paramilitary forces (e.g., Garde Montagnarde, Garde Civile, and an assortment of local militias and self-defense groups).

French Union was the term coined by the French after World War II to encompass France and her overseas territories, somewhat after the fashion of the British Commonwealth. After 1951, Cambodia, Laos, and Vietnam were nominally independent states "associated with France" within the French Union. The French government had hoped that most of their pre-World War II colonial possessions would adhere to the French Union concept; few have done so.

The Viet Minh forces included regular (main force and local force) units and irregular formations (guerrilla and militia forces) fighting on behalf of Ho Chi Minh's Democratic Republic of Vietnam. The term *Viet Minh* is a condensed form of the Vietnamese appellation *Viet Nam Doc Lap Dong Minh Hoi*, or League for an Independent Vietnam, which was the national front movement formed in World War II under Ho Chi Minh to fight the Japanese occupation forces.

A great deal of information on Indochina was available, but until 1950 no serious effort had been made to sort it out nor to study in depth the military force structures in the region and assess their relative capabilities. Much of the information was fragmentary, and my initial compilations were necessarily incomplete and tentative. But having established the essential framework and identified the gaps in our knowledge, we were able to begin collecting the additional information we needed. Within months we had a sufficient grasp of the problem to enable us to fulfill ACSI's responsibilities and to gain credence for the authoritative nature of our information on the military forces in Indochina.

The next step was to gain a firm understanding of the political-military strategy of the opposing French and Vietnamese forces. This required studying in detail the available documents and intelligence reports, developing guidance to agencies responsible for collecting such information, and tapping all potential sources of information in Washington and in the field. Within a year we had developed a sufficiently comprehensive understanding of these matters to help keep the National Intelligence Estimate process on the right track with respect to French and Viet Minh military capabilities, strategy, and likely courses of action in Indochina.

Although we had information from a wide variety of sources—some good, some not so good—through 1955 we depended heavily on the French. Many American officials had misgivings about doing this, suspecting the French of duplicity and/or stupidity. Some officers were only too willing to dismiss any information we attributed to French sources. It was true, of course, that most French senior diplomats and military officers, both in Paris and in Indochina, were likely to put the best possible face on their actions and to emphasize those aspects of the situation that redounded to their advantage. At the same time they naturally downplayed, discounted, or ignored those aspects that did not. (The French have no monopoly on these traits.) There were indeed instances in which U.S. officials were deliberately misled or deceived by their French counterparts, as I will show later. (This also is not a trait unique to the French.)

But such instances of ethnocentric bias and cultural disdain on the part of American officials were far less frequent where substantive intelligence matters were involved. In part, the tendency toward "playing it

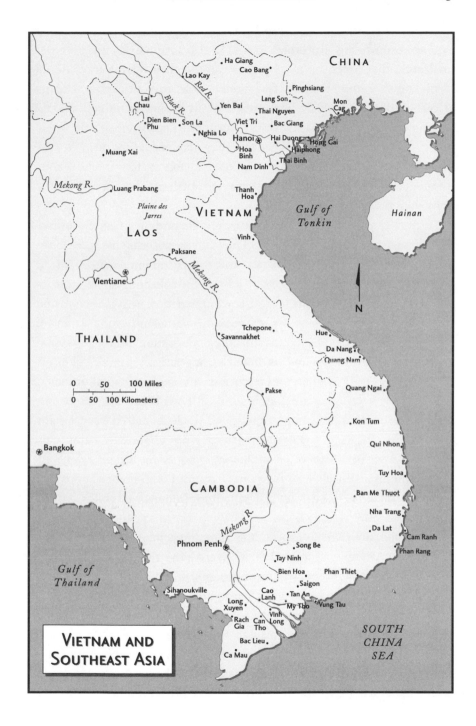

VIETNAM AND
SOUTHEAST ASIA

straight" with intelligence resulted from a sense of rapport that often exists between intelligence professionals. It also resulted from the French realization that American intelligence might very well have access to information that could disprove false French assertions or expose attempts at misinformation about "the enemy." While exaggeration and discreet misrepresentation are not altogether unusual in routine political, diplomatic, and military liaison exchanges, they are far less frequent in relations between interdependent intelligence services, where falsification or duplicity can destroy mutual trust and confidence, thereby denying to both sides the fruits of cooperation.

U.S. military attachés in Indochina were the principal conduit for military information from the French. They functioned effectively as liaison officers with the French commands, and through them we acquired detailed reporting on the nature of the French military effort and on the size, composition, locations, activities, and status of the French Union forces themselves. When we saw gaps in our information and were able to formulate the right kinds of questions, the French were usually responsive at the technical working level, as distinct from the policy level. For example, when Pentagon planners were curious about the national origins of troops in the French Foreign Legion units at Dien Bien Phu, we soon received a detailed compilation from the no doubt bemused French command in Saigon. Such data were sometimes given grudgingly, because the Americans seemed to have an insatiable appetite for details which the French might justifiably have regarded as none of our business, or of such trivial character as to be of no real value to anyone but a French bureaucrat. But in general and on most occasions they were more forthcoming than we had any right to expect, and sometimes more than comparable U.S. military commands might have been under similar circumstances. At the working level our requests for information were usually honored, even when there were "political" difficulties at higher levels.

Some information on the status of French Union forces and on specific units was also obtained through the American Military Assistance Advisory Group (MAAG) in Indochina, which was technically required to make inspections related to the delivery and end-use of military equipment. But there were difficulties in exploiting the MAAG for intelligence purposes (and this problem was not limited to Indochina). Aid recipients—whether French or otherwise—were always suspicious of the intelligence potential of military "advisers," and the MAAG members themselves were reluctant to compromise their "advisory" role by appearing to collect intelligence.

From its beginning in 1950, the Indochina MAAG differed from American military assistance missions in most other countries in that, despite its title, it had virtually no "advisory" role. Its role was essentially limited—at French insistence—to a logistical one, that is, assisting the French in formulating requests for American military equipment and supplies, and supervising the delivery and end-utilization by the French of the materiel after its arrival in Indochina. The MAAG had no training role in the early 1950s, and the French felt they needed no "advice" from the United States on how to conduct a "colonial" war. They wanted no American interference in the conduct of the war, felt they needed no lessons in warfare from the Americans, and later resented the relatively more successful U.S. military effort in Korea. The French military command in Indochina was willing to accept U.S. military equipment and willing to provide enough information about their operations to keep the Americans happy, but Gallic pride made them unwilling to grant any significant access to their planning and policy formulation processes regarding the conduct of the war, the expansion of the military forces of Vietnam, Cambodia, and Laos, and the political relationship of France to those states.

We also depended largely on the French for reliable information on the Viet Minh forces. Here the French were even more forthcoming than with the status of their own forces. They permitted our attachés good access to their intelligence staffs, providing them with increasingly frequent and more detailed briefings as the war progressed. Information on current operations was comprehensive and consistently accurate. Although their intelligence staffs were as prone to errors in judgment as those of any other military command, these were often corrected on their own initiative, and we never caught them in an outright lie or misrepresentation.

The French provided our attachés with a steady flow of information on the Communist forces and their activities, passing on copies of periodic intelligence summaries prepared for the French command. We found no evidence that these documents—which included TRES SECRET studies and reports—were doctored or censored for our benefit. They also furnished us with much of the raw information on which these intelligence studies were based.

In 1954 I asked a senior French intelligence officer in Saigon which sources of information he relied on the most. He promptly said, "Technical means"—that is, information acquired from signal intelligence, photography, and other technical collection systems. I asked why not agents, documents, or prisoners. He replied that agents were not very reliable in the Indochina context, first because of the political character of the insurgency. Many Vietnamese had contacts serving both sides in the war, and one could never be certain of their loyalty. Agents were also subject to "intoxication"—they could always be counted on to provide information telling you just what they thought you wanted to know, and when they sensed great interest in a particular matter, they were more than willing to oblige "for pay." Any expression of intelligence needs would produce dozens of false reports aiming to satisfy this interest. Similarly, the French officer said, prisoners sometimes were so anxious to please their interrogators that their information tended to be unreliable; other prisoners deliberately provided false information under duress. Captured documents could be—and often were—fabricated and planted to deceive the finder.

Thus, while occasionally good information could be derived from any or all of these sources, it was generally out of date before it could be confirmed, or otherwise could not be relied on in the same way as information obtained by "technical" means. The latter permitted one to pinpoint locations of enemy units, he said, and to follow their movements, thereby enabling one to anticipate their actions. They often provided valuable information regarding plans, capabilities, and vulnerabilities.

The United States had unilateral sources of information which supplemented and complemented what we obtained from the French—information from other foreign observers and from CIA sources as well as from Viet Minh publications and radio broadcasts. We also had enough independent access through our own technical means to give us some confidence that the French were not doctoring their reports and studies for our benefit.

By and large, the French had comprehensive information on the Viet Minh movement and its military forces, a product of the investment they had made in collecting and analyzing the requisite information. The French military intelligence services were generally competent and highly professional. Many intelligence positions were staffed by careerists, who alternated twenty-seven-month tours in Indochina with sojourns of a year or so at institutions in France such as the École de Guerre. During these "sabbaticals," these officers often worked in research, producing studies on topics such as the Vietnamese Communist movement and its military forces; on the Chinese Communist military forces; on Communist techniques of subversion, insurgency, and psychological operations; and on geographic, social, economic, and ethnic factors in the Indochina theater of operations. Many of these officers had a keen, professional interest in their jobs and took pride in composing thoughtful and sound intelligence estimates and studies. As a consequence, there were few real "failures" in French intelligence. The Communist forces rarely initiated an unanticipated operation of major consequence or one that demonstrated a significant new capability that had not been anticipated by French intelligence. Most of the alleged French intelligence "failures" were in fact attributable to the failure of the French command to react appropriately to the intelligence it received.

While many junior French officers had a comprehensive grasp of the "people's war" character of the struggle in Indochina, many of their superiors suffered from the tendency—evident later in the American military as well—to be overconfident of the prowess of their own forces, and to discount the military potential of the "primitive, barefoot" Communist forces. Arrogance, narrow-mindedness, and the widespread disdain of the colonial (or Western) power for the native—these were at the root of most French military failures in Indochina, along with a general tendency to discount the potential implications and consequences of what they were being told by their military intelligence services.

The Franco-American intelligence relationship on military matters was enhanced by formal arrangements for an exchange of intelligence related to Southeast Asia between the French, British, Australian, and New Zealand military intelligence services. The agenda for these exchanges included the Chinese Communist forces and activities in South China; Soviet and Chinese military assistance to the Viet Minh; and the composition, capabilities, and activities of the Communist-backed insurgent and terrorist forces in Indochina, Malaya, and the Philippines. This cooperative arrangement was heavily weighted to the advantage of all but the French, who gained at most some useful information on South China; but the quid pro quo operated greatly to the U.S. advantage with respect to Indochina.

These exchange arrangements, and our comprehensive understanding of the nature of the Indochina war, did not exist in 1950 when the United States began its program of military assistance to Indochina. American decisions to support the French military effort were made in relative haste and ignorance. The Marshall Plan, the Truman Doctrine, and the birth of NATO were all manifestations of an emerging cold war policy which formed part of a broad strategy of containing Communist expansion. This strategy had been codified in NSC-68, the now-famous National Security Council memorandum adopted in 1950. Initially aimed at the Soviet Union, the evolving strategy was given a larger scope and new urgency by the Communist victory in China in 1949 and the outbreak of the Korean War the following year.

The flight of the Chinese Nationalist regime to Taiwan in 1949 and the establishment of Mao Tse-tung's People's Republic of China turned American attention toward the problem of checking the extension of Communist influence in Southeast Asia, where a number of Communist-led insurgent movements were active. The Hukbalahap movement in the Philippines, the Communist terrorists in Malaya, a variety of dissident movements in Burma, and the Viet Minh in Indochina all seemed to Washington to have parallel purposes and common origins. Peking's open espousal of these "liberation" movements fed convictions in some quarters that they represented a coordinated and concerted effort to extend China's dominance in the region. In the Truman administration there were natural suspicions that the new Chinese regime would support these insurgent movements, and many leaders feared that the Chinese might openly intervene, though there was little evidence to support this intent.

In the absence of any basis for political or economic cooperation among the states of the region to resist the apparent threat, Washington sought to develop a series of bilateral military aid arrangements, such as those already in place with certain European countries. This would enable the United States to assist these threatened states—most of which were emerging from colonial status—in coping with their internal insurrectionary problems. The British were pursuing their own counterinsurgency effort in Malaya and neither needed nor sought American help. In 1950 the United States developed bilateral military assistance agreements with the government of the Philippines, which had a serious Communist-led insurrection on its hands, and with Thailand, which wanted to be prepared to meet such a contingency.

Indochina, Washington believed, posed the most serious problem. It consisted of Vietnam, Cambodia, and Laos, all of which were in transition to autonomous states within the French Union.* The Viet Minh in early 1950 already constituted the strongest insurgent force in the region. And Indochina's common border with China afforded obvious opportunities for direct support of the Viet Minh by the new Communist government in Peking. These developments led the United States to send two missions to Southeast Asia in March and June 1950 to survey the need for economic and military assistance. The first of these, headed by Robert A. Griffin of the Economic Cooperation Administration, included military officers from the Pentagon. The Griffin mission noted the existence of a military stalemate in Indochina, with the French holding the main population centers and lines of communication. It observed that the conflict was likely to be ended only through a political solution, which necessitated that the French grant full independence in Vietnam in order to attract nationalist elements from support of the Viet Minh.

---

*Vietnam itself consisted of three regions: Tonkin (North Vietnam), Annam (Central Vietnam), and Cochin-China (South Vietnam). These had been governed as separate entities during the French colonial period, when there was no "Vietnam" as such.

The second, more thorough mission, in June, was headed by John F. Melby of the State Department and Major General Graves B. Erskine of the Marine Corps. After three weeks in Vietnam, General Erskine was outspokenly critical of the defensive posture and mind-set of the French command; he believed that a more vigorous military effort could defeat the Communist forces. The mission concluded that the French forces urgently required more supplies and equipment. Its recommendations led to the beginning of U.S. military assistance and the establishment of the U.S. Military Advisory Group (MAAG), Indochina.*

The differing emphases in the findings of these two missions—the one highlighting the political problem and the other holding out hope for a military solution—reflected a divided American outlook that was to characterize our policy decisions throughout the period of our involvement in Indochina. They also illustrated the "can-do" syndrome of the American government at all levels. "Survey missions" sent to determine what might be done seemed always to return with a program for positive action—to propose a solution no matter how intractable the problem might appear to those not participating in the mission. More often than not, such study groups seem to listen selectively, to minimize negative factors, and to find reasons for doing *something*, rather than proposing that *nothing* be done.

The fundamental illogic of both missions' assessments escaped the notice of those in Washington anxious to do something—*anything*—in order to be perceived as acting to block the spread of Communist influence in Southeast Asia. First, it was illogical and irrational to expect France in 1949 or 1950 to move quickly toward complete independence for Vietnam, Cambodia, and Laos. Although an independent Vietnam had become a declared American aim by 1950, Washington overlooked the fact that France's only interest in pursing the war was to preserve a political-economic relationship with Vietnam short of full independence. Ho Chi Minh had proclaimed Vietnamese independence in 1945; the war was a

---

*An excellent account of the early stages of American military involvement in Vietnam is contained in Ronald H. Spector's *Advice and Support: The Early Years* (Washington, D.C., 1983).

consequence of France's refusal to cede its control of Indochina to his revolutionary, intensely nationalist government.

Since World War II, France had been striving to regain a semblance of great-power status, and to most French governments this meant some form of imperial presence in the Far East. London had evolved the concept of the British Commonwealth to preserve the image of global power status; the French were pursuing the concept of the French Union for the same purposes, but with far greater reluctance to permit local autonomy to their former colonies. They had done nothing to prepare the Indochinese peoples for self-government before World War II, and they were reluctant to do so after the war.

The Paris government's failure to work out a mutually acceptable formula with Ho Chi Minh led to hostilities in December 1946. In 1947, French military forces managed to seize most of the major cities and towns in the Red River and Mekong deltas and along the coast, leaving the Viet Minh in control of rural bases and the areas between the coastal enclaves. Modestly reinforced, the French military launched a series of forays into Communist-held strongholds in 1947–1948 but failed to bring the Viet Minh to heel while suffering severe losses themselves. Realizing that military victory would require further reinforcement on a scale that was politically unacceptable, a succession of French governments thereafter became reconciled to a military stalemate. Most French leaders looked toward some sort of political solution centering on the creation of a French-influenced, non-Communist government which might be acceptable to the Vietnamese as an alternative to Ho Chi Minh's Communist-dominated Democratic Republic of Vietnam. But the French never moved seriously to let their Vietnamese allies learn how to govern themselves.

Ho's independent government, established in Hanoi shortly after Japan's surrender in 1945, continued to function from its remote strongholds in North Vietnam, and had forged powerful guerrilla forces which controlled secure bases in many regions of South Vietnam. Paris's optimum objective was to pacify as much of the countryside as possible and lure the populace away from supporting Ho's Viet Minh guerrillas, which would then be left to wither on the vine. But Paris was unwilling to commit the military forces necessary to accomplish pacification on the requisite scale. Most pragmatic observers—including many French politicians—realized that any long-term solution in Vietnam would have to provide a role for Ho Chi Minh and his followers.

Hence by 1950 the French were essentially marking time in Indochina until conditions were "ripe" for a negotiated settlement with Ho's Communist-dominated government. After the outbreak of the Korean War, however, Washington's aim was to defeat Communist expansionism in Indochina by providing a level of military assistance that would enable the French to organize, arm, and equip sufficient military forces in Indochina to achieve victory by destroying Ho's guerrilla forces.

The significance of the fundamental contradiction in American and French political objectives was ignored by American policymakers. They persistently denigrated French reluctance to grant *full* independence to the government of Vietnam, which they had established in Saigon in 1950 under former emperor Bao Dai as a rival to Ho Chi Minh's Democratic Republic of Vietnam. American, British, and other Western diplomats repeatedly urged the French formally to declare Bao Dai's government as truly independent, even though this would clearly contradict the imperial ambitions that underlay Paris's world outlook. France lacked the resources and the determination to wage war in the Far East merely for the sake of containing communism; if there was to be no French Union, there need be no war in Indochina.

A similar incompatibility characterized American and French military objectives. After 1947 the French entertained no hope of military victory. The French government's professions of such a policy in 1953—that is, to win the war—were an unenthusiastic sop to U.S. urgings and a reflection of domestic French political battles rather than a serious commitment. Diehard colonialists in Saigon and Paris had their hopes dashed by Mao's victory in China and Peking's subsequent recognition of Ho's government in February 1950, and by the start of serious Chinese military assistance to the Viet Minh at about the same time. The massive Chinese intervention in Korea in the fall of 1950, coincident with the loss of the French border garrisons in Tonkin to powerful, regularized Viet Minh forces, removed any lingering hope in the minds of responsible French political and military leaders that a successful military effort could be mounted against the Viet Minh. Thereafter the French continued the war only as a holding action pending an opportunity to negotiate an "honorable" settlement. But American officials chose to ignore this and clung to the futile hope that somehow the French might be persuaded to strive for a military victory—a result that was always the aim of American policymakers before, during, and after our own military intervention.

Close students of the Indochina problem—which included intelligence analysts in Washington—understood as early as 1951 the character of the Viet Minh movement. Ample material was available on the origins and history of the movement and on the careers of Ho Chi Minh and others of its leaders. Without question they were Marxist revolutionaries, bent on applying their own blend of Leninist concepts and Maoist strategy to gain control first of Vietnam and ultimately the rest of Indochina. The Viet Minh movement was perceived clearly as controlled by the former leadership of the Indochina Communist party founded by Ho in the 1930s. Although that party had been formally "disbanded" in the 1940s in order to hide its leadership role within the nationalist, anti-Japanese struggle, the dominant position in the Viet Minh movement (the League for an Independent Vietnam) of Ho Chi Minh, Truong Chinh, Pham Van Dong, and Vo Nguyen Giap, left no doubt of its Communist orientation. The announced platform, modus operandi, and leadership of the newly formed Lao Dong (Workers) party in 1951 clearly indicated that it was the successor to the Indochina Communist party. This party assumed the mantle of "vanguard" of the Lien Viet (Fatherland) Front, the new, ostensibly nationalist fig leaf behind which Ho Chi Minh and his Viet Minh cohorts concealed their Marxist-Leninist political orientation.

Specialists on Indochina were familiar with the texts on people's war and the revolutionary struggle written by General Giap and Truong Chinh (the party's secretary general), which spelled out the techniques and strategy by which the Communist leaders intended to gain power in Indochina. Students of Mao Tse-tung's writings readily recognized the origins of the Vietnamese Communist people's war strategy. The key element was to dominate the resistance movement through a tightly disciplined Marxist-Leninist party, which would provide the nucleus of leadership for all elements—government, army, and front organizations—from the national level down through regions, provinces, districts, villages, and hamlets. No organization would be permitted to exist in Viet Minh-controlled areas if it was not controlled or strongly influenced by agents of the Marxist-Leninist party—covertly before 1951, and openly thereafter.

My own attention in the early 1950s was centered on the military manifestation of the Viet Minh—the liberation army—but I studied it in the context of its role as an instrument of the political movement that guided and controlled it. This army was a political force in a way that the non-Communist Vietnamese armies of Emperor Bao Dai and, later, Presidents Diem and Thieu never were. In the Chinese Communist pattern, the commanders of the People's Army of Vietnam (PAVN) at all levels were members of their unit's party cell—frequently the leaders of that cell. Every military unit was energized by party agents. The party wrote the regulations and field manuals, controlled training, planned operations and led critiques of the results, motivated the troops, controlled personnel assignments, and rationalized strategy and tactics. The party apparatus and its political indoctrination activities gave the Vietnamese Communist military forces a generation-long margin of superiority in discipline, will, and moral conviction over its opposition. A not-so-secret weapon, the party was the heart, soul, and brains of the People's Army of Vietnam.

Specialists understood the political character of the Viet Minh forces and its central role in their conduct of the war, but they were never able to persuade nonspecialists of its inherently decisive importance. Most policymakers, diplomats, and military leaders were inclined to "tune out" or strongly discount the political aspects of briefings on Vietnam, their eyes glazing over. They were less interested in the specifics of the situation than in material matters—actions to be taken or equipment provided that would capitalize on the enemy's assumed vulnerabilities or bolster the capabilities of our surrogates. Decision-makers repeatedly ignored or sidestepped the political aspects of the Indochina wars, in part because these seemed complex or potentially intractable, and in part because Americans generally tend to favor mechanical or material solutions—the "quick fix" or the "field expedient."

Intelligence specialists also understood that Vietnamese communism had a strongly national flavor. The record of Ho's efforts to gain American support in the 1940s was well known. By the 1950s, Tito had already demonstrated to the world that international communism was somewhat less than monolithic and that nationalist sentiments could dilute the ideological cohesion of Communist parties. Indochina specialists were also aware of the Sinophobic nature of Vietnamese nationalism, the legacy of millennia of frictions between the Vietnamese people and their northern neighbors. We knew that Vietnam's legendary heroes were those who had led native armies against Chinese invaders. We saw Ho Chi Minh as being nobody's "puppet" but as a pragmatic Marxist revolutionary willing to exploit any potential ally willing to help him achieve his end—the liberation of Vietnam, under his rule. We believed he would jealously protect Vietnam's interests against those of its powerful neighbors. Few of us, however, would have gone so far in the 1950s as to argue that the Vietnamese Communists would some day prove to be a more effective barrier to Chinese hegemony in Southeast Asia than American military power.

The opportunistic nature of Ho's dependence on Peking and Moscow for support in his war against the French, as well as the existence of deep-rooted tensions with the Chinese, were not difficult to discern in the 1950s. But Washington's leaders and decision-makers were immune to intelligence analyses suggesting any potential divergence of interests between Vietnamese Communists and their allies. That possibility would contradict a basic tenet of American cold war doctrine—the monolithic, concerted nature of the international Communist threat. Any evidence detracting from the concept of Communist unity clearly weakened the dynamic of the threat and would have weakened the coherence of Washington's strategy for coping with it.

Policy documents such as NSC-68 illustrate the doctrinal basis underlying the attitudes and concepts of American planners and decision-makers. Any evidence that ran counter to that doctrine tended to be discounted by consumers of intelligence; it failed to match their notions of the problem and its solutions. And, of course, the liturgy of McCarthyism reinforced the idea that it was "politically incorrect" to discount the unity and cohesion of international communism.

The French war in Indochina produced tension between the European and Far Eastern components of the American national security establishment. "Europe first" dogma in World War II persisted in the postwar period. Washington was generally agreed on the paramount importance to America's interests of the Soviet potential for overrunning Europe, but this consensus was troubled by the necessity to counter the actual thrust into Korea, and the vulnerability of Southeast Asia to a similar thrust. With respect to Indochina, the "French desks" in the Washington bureaucracies were driven by concerns for bolstering France's contribution to the political, economic, and military strength of NATO. France's engagement in Indochina detracted from that objective, and the sooner that drain on her resources was ended, the sooner France could be expected to focus its resources on Europe's problems. At the same time the French desks were counseling against the pursuit of American policies in Indochina that would adversely affect France's willingness to collaborate with us in Europe.

The Southeast Asia desks, on the other hand, were the source of American pressure for France to grant independence to Vietnam as a means of reducing the nationalist appeal of Ho Chi Minh's Viet Minh league. They also emphasized the need for a military victory to preclude the loss of Indochina, and raised the specter of the "falling dominoes" if the Communists should win in Indochina.

This variety of bureaucratic interests made it difficult to develop a cohesive, consistent American policy toward the Indochina War and contributed to ambiguity and ambivalence in U.S. strategy.

The origins of the anti-French bias among American officials are unclear, nor can its impact on policy be documented; it probably resulted from a combination of factors. Some Americans viewed with derision the collapse of France in 1940 and the subsequent collaboration of the Vichy

Government with the Nazis. Many American military officers viewed the French as militarily bankrupt, behind the times, obsessed with a "Maginot complex," and afflicted with a defense-oriented military psychology. I heard more than one American general officer assert in the 1950s that one good U.S. division (army or Marine, airborne or infantry, depending on the speaker) could clean up the Viet Minh in six months if the French expeditionary force were removed from the scene so that it could not impede the Americans. One two-star American general heatedly declaimed that he could personally lead a march by one American division from the southern tip of Vietnam to the Chinese border in a month if the French weren't in the way. He refused to withdraw his boast even after I pointed out that he would have to outpace Stonewall Jackson's famous foot cavalry to do so, since no army in history—even a motorized one—had covered a thousand miles in thirty days.

This bias intensified as U.S. leaders grew frustrated with the failure of the French to modify their objectives, policies, strategies, and programs in Indochina to conform more closely to ours. As the scale of our military assistance program mounted, so did the frustration of those directing the program, who chafed at the seeming recalcitrance, foot-dragging, defensive-mindedness, and basic Gallic independence of the French in both Paris and Saigon.

The antipathy was returned, of course, by many French officials, who resented the brash pushiness, evident disdain, cockiness, and self-confidence they perceived in most Americans. Many of the French felt they were owed greater respect for their past glories. Their soldierly pride and Gallic self-esteem was diminished by their seemingly ineffective military showing in Indochina, making it all the more difficult for them to accept American criticism. In their more candid moments, French officers in Indochina expressed resentment at the failure of their government to commit sufficient resources to allow a more aggressive pursuit of the war. In time, leaders of the French army who had served in Indochina would revolt against their government's policies in Algeria, resenting its continued failure to support its armed forces. But the French military in Indochina resented outsiders voicing any such criticism.

The latent anti-French bias that came to dominate American attitudes, coupled with our own frustrations in the Korean War and our growing zeal for containing China, blinded many American officials to the incongruity of our demands for a French victory at a time when we ourselves were negotiating an inconclusive end to our war in Korea. Our policy planners and decision-makers were basically insensitive to French interests. Americans "knew" what was best for Indochina and its people, and we insisted on *our* solutions, regardless of their impact on France. Our frustration with French performance in Indochina led us ultimately to shoulder them aside so that we could at last pursue our objectives in their former colonial holdings without hindrance from Paris.

My aim in emphasizing this issue is not to suggest that justice and truth were on the side of the French. They were, after all, bucking the tide that was running toward the dissolution of the prewar colonial system, and their doing so in Indochina seemed to play into the hands of the Communist-led insurrection. But then, Americans often overlooked the fact that imperialism is, to some extent, in the eye of the beholder. The replacement of French colonialism by an American-backed independent Vietnam did not prevent ultimate victory by the Communists. In the eyes of many Vietnamese, American imperialism replaced French imperialism as the enemy of the Communist "liberation" struggle, and the French "puppets" in Vietnam became the American "puppets."

A Communist victory in Indochina could not have occurred without Mao's victory in China. Before 1950 a prolonged military stalemate in Indochina seemed inevitable. Neither side had a decisive edge in military capabilities, and neither side seemed likely to be able to reinforce its potential without external help. The arrival of Chinese Communist military forces along the northern border of Vietnam inevitably tipped the balance of power in favor of the Viet Minh. China took on the role of the secure rear base for Ho Chi Minh's insurgency—a sanctuary where large numbers of guerrillas could be reorganized, trained, and equipped for more conventional military operations, and where supplies could be amassed to support large-scale offensives.

French military forces proved unable to cope with this change in the nature of the struggle. Because no French government was likely to survive a decision to send French conscripts to fight in Indochina, only colonial forces could be employed there, and these forces were of limited size. The French expeditionary force, which fluctuated between roughly 145,000 and 175,000 men in the early 1950s, included as many as 55,000 French nationals, but these comprised essentially the officer and NCO cadres for Colonial Army units as well as the staffs of headquarters and administrative units. There were no Metropolitan Army units in Indochina; the bulk of the expeditionary force consisted of North African units—Moroccan, Algerian, and Tunisian rifle regiments. Despite its prominence in the literature on the war, the Foreign Legion made up less than a quarter of the force. In addition, there were several thousand Senegalese in infantry units. Up to a third of the force were native Indochinese—Vietnamese, Laotians, Cambodians, and assorted ethnic minority groups—serving in Colonial Army units; these formations were separate and distinct from the national armies of the Associated States which the French began to form in 1948.

All of these colonial troops were volunteers—none was conscripted for duty in Indochina. Their units had been raised for duty elsewhere; they were not formed exclusively for service in Indochina (except, of course, for the units composed of indigenous manpower). These colonial forces could have been expanded to some extent had the French government been willing to commit the necessary resources, though it is questionable whether and how long the authorities in the soon-to-be-independent African dependencies would have been willing to tolerate the drain in manpower necessary to support a force adequate to achieve victory in Indochina.

The French routinely maintained a flow of troops to Indochina, most intended to permit rotation of troops back to North Africa after completion of their twenty-seven-month tours, and others intended to replace combat losses. The Colonial troops (other than Indochinese) served fixed tours in Indochina. But this flow of replacements was "budgeted for," or programmed in advance, and the annual quota for replacements served to set a ceiling on the losses that could be accepted by the Colonial Army. The conduct of operations was thus constrained by the troop ceiling and the rate of flow of replacements. Offensive operations had to be curtailed whenever losses exceeded anticipated arrivals from France and North Africa, otherwise units in Indochina would be reduced below effective manning levels. The personnel pipeline was long in the pre-jumbo-jet era of the 1950s, entailing a month-long sea voyage, thus further inhibiting the operational flexibility of the French command in Indochina. In the mid-fifties this manpower problem was somewhat alleviated by incorporating ethnic Vietnamese into North African and Foreign Legion infantry units, but this "yellowing" of non-Indochinese units was often resented on both sides.

Reliance on Colonial, rather than Metropolitan, army forces inhibited the French military effort in other ways. The Colonial forces were organized, structured, and equipped primarily to suppress local insurrections and to maintain internal security, not to wage modern, conventional combined-arms wars involving substantial forces. As a result they were composed largely of light combat units—infantry regiments, light armored reconnaissance units (armored cavalry), and light artillery. Such units were well suited for operations in the Indochinese environment, but they lacked the heavy firepower that would have given them an edge over the increasingly well-armed Viet Minh.

Although the Legion included some combat engineers, the Colonial Army generally lacked the combat support and logistical units—ordnance, transportation, heavy engineers, repair and maintenance, and depot units—necessary to sustain prolonged combat by large forces in the field. Thus the French forces in Indochina operated on a logistical shoestring—their "logistical tail" was relatively minuscule considering the size of forces and the scope of combat involved. The 175,000-man expeditionary force had a "bayonet strength" of about 90,000 men—that is, just over half its troops were in infantry combat battalions. The "battalion slice" (the total numerical strength of the force divided by the number of combat battalions) amounted to less than 1,500 men.

The relative paucity of the French military support structure contrasted sharply with that of the American forces later deployed to Vietnam, when the comparable American battalion slice exceeded 4,000 men and the bayonet strength of the American force of 500,000 troops was less than 100,000 men. The Americans brought in substantial numbers of supporting troops—transportation units, maintenance units, and engineer construction units as well as large contracting firms—to build and operate new ports, a viable road network, and air bases and supply depots, and to clear "fields of fire" in the jungles surrounding American bases. These were needed to fight an American-style combined-arms war involving mobile mechanized forces employing heavy firepower and intensive air support, in contrast to the "shoestring" operation mounted by the French.

Military forces under French command—in addition to the Colonial Army units described above—also included a wide variety of lightly armed security and paramilitary forces composed of Indochinese natives, such as the Garde Montagnarde, the paramilitary forces of the Cao Dai and Hoa Hao religious sects, and so-called *suppletifs*, or auxiliary units. These were organized and operated under direct control of the French regional and sector commands.

In addition there were the regular and paramilitary forces nominally comprising the armed forces of the Associated States of Vietnam, Cambodia, and Laos. These also were organized and at least partially encadred by the French, and were generally subordinated to the French territorial commands at zone and sector levels. The expansion of these forces was hindered by the very limited output of the schools set up to train officers and NCOs for these armies before an accelerated expansion program in late 1953. Several hundred Indochinese officers—mostly captains and lieutenants—were transferred from the French Colonial Army to the armies of the Associated States in the early fifties. Candidates for the Vietnamese military academy and the regional officer training schools established in 1952 were drawn almost exclusively from the French-educated, urban middle classes; very few were promoted from the ranks. Their cultural background and outlook differed markedly from the enlisted ranks, drawn largely from the peasant and labor classes, whose interests, values, and social concerns the officers seldom comprehended. This cultural distinction was never effectively overcome and constrained the ability of most Vietnamese officers to communicate and identify with the troops under their command—a factor that hindered the development of a truly effective Vietnamese national army throughout the Vietnamese wars.

Because successive French governments were unwilling to accept the economic or political costs involved in substantially reinforcing their own expeditionary force, the only hope of increasing the armed strength of anti-Communist forces was by expanding the armies of the Associated States. But French officials felt constrained from bold action in this regard for a number of what they regarded as cogent reasons. Politically they had no real confidence in the loyalty of the Vietnamese to support a rump colonial government. Unwilling to grant Vietnam full independence, the French felt that the nationalist appeal of the Viet Minh made any force of Vietnamese operating under French control vulnerable to subversion and disaffection. They adamantly rejected repeated American suggestions of a parallel to the situation in Korea, where the United States had successfully organized armed South Korean forces that greatly exceeded the strength of the American forces there, without fear of subversion or disaffection. To the French, the analogy was invalid; the two wars were wholly different. South Korea had been the scene of overt external invasion, and its inhabitants were united against that aggression. The struggle in Vietnam, on the other hand, was far more in the nature of a civil war, a nationwide struggle between rival Vietnamese factions, one that often found family loyalties divided between the two sides.

One of these Vietnamese factions was a centrally directed, dynamic, cohesive, disciplined, and militant force which had proclaimed independence from a colonial power and could count on dedicated adherents in all parts of the country. The other was a flaccid coalition of weak, rival, localized splinter groups patched together by the governing colonial power, France, and lacking any common appeal other than their non-Communist, autonomous stance. Even French observers agreed that, without a grant of full independence, there was little likelihood of undermining the popular, nationalist appeal of Ho Chi Minh's movement. But, as noted earlier, such a grant would have made continuation of the war irrelevant to French interests.

Economically the Associated States lacked the revenues to support armed forces of the size needed to defeat the Viet Minh. The pay and allowances of their forces were comparable to those of the French which, though modest by American standards, greatly exceeded those offered by the Viet Minh. And the French pay scale was not an overwhelmingly attractive inducement for participating in combat against the Viet Minh. The gradual acceptance of the financial costs of the Associated States forces by the United States ultimately invalidated French arguments for not expanding the local forces based on costs alone.

Militarily the French argued that the Vietnamese lacked the skilled and trained officers and NCOs needed to staff a rapidly expanding force and permit a full-scale mobilization of Indochinese manpower. This was true as far as it went, but it begged the possibility of establishing training facilities and programs that could have provided the skilled and trained manpower required. Here America's military leaders felt that our experience in Korea provided a valid model; but the French shrugged this off as irrelevant given the differing political conditions in the two countries; Vietnam was not yet a self-governing entity.

Thus the French effectively painted themselves into a corner. Unwilling to reinforce their expeditionary force, they were also reluctant to push a rapid expansion of local forces as a means of achieving superiority. It is important to bear in mind, however, that they saw no urgency in this regard; they were not seeking victory. They saw no compelling need to develop an overwhelming numerical superiority over the Viet Minh. Because their aim was simply to maintain a military posture from which they could negotiate an "honorable settlement" at a propitious time, they needed only a force sufficient to enable them to avoid defeat. A relative stalemate was thus an acceptable condition over the short term, given the reluctance in Paris to pay the political and economic costs of an attempt to defeat the Viet Minh militarily.

The French never used this argument directly to American officials before 1953, but their acceptance of the stalemate could be inferred from their actions and attitudes as early as 1948–1949. Opposition elements in France called for negotiations as early as 1949, but no government openly embraced that course of action until Pierre Mendes-France came to power in 1954, when international and domestic conditions made it politically and militarily expedient to do so.

The stalemate might have been prolonged indefinitely had not Chinese Communist military aid begun to tip the balance in favor of the Viet Minh. Chinese aid after 1950 permitted a gradual expansion of Ho's military forces, the standardization of their armament and equipment with better and heavier weapons, improved transportation, and the creation of larger and more effective combat formations. A steady and substantial flow of supplies and ammunition from China enabled the Viet Minh to mount and sustain progressively heavier attacks and gradually to wrest the strategic initiative from the French. The Viet Minh could now dictate the tempo and locale of major combat operations, and ultimately defeat the French in open battle.

None of this would have been possible without Chinese aid. Before 1950 Ho's forces were barely able to supply themselves with enough ammunition to mount sporadic guerrilla forays and terrorist acts, and to wage a limited defense against French raids into Communist base areas. They relied primarily on weapons and supplies captured from the French, supplemented by a small, poorly equipped, primitive cottage industry. These sources of supply were adequate to enable them to maintain a standoff against the French through 1949, but their logistical poverty precluded any significant expansion of their military capabilities.

Manpower, on the other hand, was never a restraint for the Communists. Although the French occupied the more densely populated areas, they were unable to prevent the Viet Minh from covertly "proselytizing," even in the major cities and towns. The Communist underground apparatus was ubiquitous, and the nationalist, anti-colonial stance of the Viet Minh was a powerful attraction. Once recruited into the political or paramilitary apparatus, the intensive and effective political indoctrination by Communist cadres tended to ensure the loyal, sometimes fanatical, adherence of recruits to the Viet Minh cause.

Even in the early 1950s, the doctrine of people's war was readily understood by intelligence specialists. Texts of Viet Minh documents outlining Communist doctrine and broad strategic principles, including the basic writings of General Vo Nguyen Giap and party secretary and strategist

Truong Chinh, were available from open sources. Translations of other publications—including those intended for the indoctrination and guidance of their own forces as well as those aimed at Western audiences—contained further valuable information about their aims, purposes, and programs. More than a casual reading was required, of course, to sort the substance from the rhetoric, and even among the initiated there were debates about the correct interpretation of some finer points. But these materials left little doubt in intelligence circles—both French and American—about Viet Minh perceptions of the nature of the struggle, or of their view as to where they stood in the development of their people's war concept.

In critiquing their unsuccessful assaults on French Red River Delta defenses during the first half of 1951, the Viet Minh freely acknowledged that they had shifted prematurely in some areas to the "general counteroffensive" phase. Even their own leaders sometimes failed properly to interpret their strategic doctrine. A senior Viet Minh cadre in the South, who was replaced late in 1951, was castigated for misinterpreting doctrine in a widely circulated document entitled "Why We Lost Confidence in Nguyen Binh." This document was clearly intended to caution others against similar nonconformities.

People's war concepts are adequately treated in some of the literature on Communist revolutionary warfare, so I will not here attempt to summarize them even briefly. It is important to note, however, that although well understood in intelligence circles, these concepts and principles could be oversimplified by American planners and policymakers. Important subtleties and distinctions in the structure, composition, and roles of the regular, regional, and militia/guerrilla forces, for example, were easily—and often—overlooked or dismissed by nonspecialists. Americans generally prefer to focus on pragmatic as opposed to theoretical matters, on material rather than abstract values, on measurable, quantitative distinctions rather than on qualitative factors. When confronted with vague or unfamiliar concepts, they are often prone to force-fit them into familiar, readily understandable molds, thereby distorting their real meaning or value. Doctrinal and theoretical aspects of the Viet Minh war effort therefore were largely the preserve of intelligence specialists; there was no real audience outside the intelligence community for detailed analyses and interpretations of these matters.

Policymakers in Washington in 1950 did not immediately grasp the strategic significance of the loss of the French posts on the Chinese frontier. They concentrated instead on the scale of the tactical reverse and on its immediate impact on the French military effort. Psychologically it was a stunning blow to the French. Never before in Indochina had they encountered regular combat formations with the firepower, cohesion, and determination evident in the autumn 1950 engagements in the Cao Bang–Lang Son area. Never before had seasoned battalions of French forces been overrun in open battle. Forty-seven hundred French were overwhelmed and essentially disappeared, only a few hundred stragglers ultimately made their way back to the French defenses in and around Hanoi.

In French-held Hanoi there were signs of panic. Some civilians fled to the South, and a number of French officers evacuated their dependents. The mood changed, however, with the arrival of Marshal de Lattre de Tassigny, one of the most dramatic moments in the history of the war. Declaring on his arrival that "from this point, soldiers of France, you will be led," he restored French morale, bolstered the confidence of the military units, and formed mobile reserve groups (provisional regimental combat teams). These proved their efficacy in early 1951 by stemming Viet Minh assaults on the French perimeter around the Red River Delta. Seldom in history has a military leader so effectively turned things around; his performance was remarkably comparable to that of General Matthew Ridgway when he took command of a routed and dispirited Eighth Army in Korea at about the same time. The effect in Indochina was, of course, only temporary, and de Lattre's death the following year enabled him to escape involvement in—and responsibility for—the seemingly inevitable defeat of the French three years later.

The real significance of French defeats in 1950, however, was twofold. First, it represented the first test—and a successful one—of the reorganized and reequipped "main force" Viet Minh regiments, the fruit of six months of intensive Chinese Communist assistance. Many of these newly formed regiments had spent months training across the border in China. Their stunning success emboldened them in the October border campaign and led the Viet Minh hierarchy to an overoptimistic assessment of the situation, and to a premature launching of their "general counteroffensive." Second, the loss of French outposts on the border opened up the major roads linking China to the vast Viet Minh-controlled rear area in the mountainous northern provinces of Tonkin, permitting a free flow of Chinese supplies and the establishment of a network of well-stocked logistical depots and operational bases. The resulting steady flow of supplies made possible not only an expansion and conventionalization of Viet Minh "main force" military capabilities with heavier firepower, but also the capacity to sustain major actions at a greater intensity over longer periods of time. It changed the character of the war and broke the stalemate. It meant that any effort by the French—or the United States—to restore the balance of forces by expanding the armies of the Associated States could be offset by a comparable or greater expansion by the enemy. The Vietnamese Communists were now able to reinforce their military potential; escalation would now be a two-way street, not only in their war against the French but later in their war with the United States. All of this was evident to army intelligence in Washington in 1950 and 1951, and was reflected in our analyses.

With the influx of supplies and equipment from Communist China, which amounted to several hundred tons monthly after 1950, the Viet Minh rapidly developed conventionally organized military formations. A "mass of maneuver," comprising five infantry divisions and an artillery division, was formed in Tonkin. A sixth division (the 325th) was formed in Central Vietnam; its components moved to North Vietnam to receive equipment delivered from China; then, after training, returned to its home region where it was based.

The role of these "main force" units was to conduct a war of maneuver against the French, aimed at drawing French mobile forces into combat in areas and under conditions in which French advantages in firepower, motor transport, and air support would be minimized. Rather than continuing their futile assaults against the main French fixed defenses in the Red River Delta, the Viet Minh shifted to attacking isolated French garrisons in outlying areas where the rugged terrain inhibited French mobility. These areas were beyond the reach of French mobile armored columns, and jungle cover tended to mask the direction of the Viet Minh's moves and locations of their units. They also timed their actions to take advantage of weather conditions, such as the *crachin* or misty season in North Vietnam, when cloud cover and low ceilings inhibited French air strikes and aerial resupply efforts. The Viet Minh hoped to force the French to disperse their mobile reserves to isolated garrisons and to wear down French capabilities through attrition. They believed this would gradually swing the balance of military power in their favor, permitting them ultimately to launch the climactic general counteroffensive that would overwhelm the remaining French Union forces. In a nutshell, this was their strategic doctrine. And it worked.

But this strategy did not diminish Communist guerrilla operations or its forces. Giap's early writings, and especially those that criticized the premature shift to the general counteroffensive in 1951, made clear the pragmatic importance of maintaining the "three types" of military forces, and of the necessity of the regional forces (*dia phuong*) and the guerrilla-militia forces (*dan quan* and *dan quan du kich*) to pursue guerrilla activities that would complement the more conventional operations of the main force (*chu luc*) units. All these forces were under complete control of the Lao Dong party apparatus, which ensured that their operations complemented the party's political and subversive activities.

Although the guerrilla-militia forces were at the base of the pyramid of Viet Minh military power, doctrinally they were no less important to the conduct of the people's war than either of the other two categories of forces. They were truly the foundation of the liberation struggle. Without them it would not have been a people's war. Organized at the hamlet and village level, they were the principal means for mobilizing the rural populace and engaging them in activities supporting the Communist cause. Formed into militia units, hamlet youths received rudimentary military training—mixed with a liberal dose of political indoctrination. They stood guard, accompanied guerrilla troops on local patrols, harassed small outposts of the French Union forces, observed and reported on enemy troop movements, prepared local defenses (including planting mines and *punji* stakes, and rigging booby traps), and served as a labor pool to support the operations of other military forces. Militia formations were only partially armed—a hamlet self-defense "platoon" of thirty or fifty citizens might have only a handful of old bolt-action rifles and some homemade grenades, and perhaps a few swords or even spears. But they possessed a modicum of military potential and inflicted many casualties on the French Union forces.

In their cause the Viet Minh sought to engage the entire rural populace. The militia were merely one means to this end. Local party cells also formed "liberation associations" among mothers, peasants, students, youths, the elderly, Catholics, Buddhists—any social group that could be organized, indoctrinated, and manipulated to engage in activities to support the revolution. They could be used in a wide variety of ways— gathering information about the enemy, making uniforms for troops, disseminating propaganda that extolled independence and denounced colonialism, stockpiling food and supplies, digging "piano-key" ditches across roads to inhibit the movement of French forces, staging anti-war demonstrations, and so on. Those recruited into intelligence and covert-action activities collected information, sowed propaganda among French troops and their Vietnamese allies, and recruited agents to undermine French morale or otherwise to act on behalf of the Viet Minh. After involving virtually every social group and age level in their activities, the Viet Minh were able to politicize them through indoctrination to become willing and often enthusiastic supporters of the liberation.

The hamlet militia themselves comprised a manpower pool of partially trained and indoctrinated manpower whose members could be recruited—or impressed—for duty in the other categories of military forces, the normal progression being upward through village guerrilla units to the regional forces—district companies and provincial battalions—and then to main force units. Hamlet militia units worked closely with the village guerrilla forces, the next step up in the pyramid. These were more active units; participation involved a greater degree of commitment to the cause, and they enjoyed an elite status locally. Guerrilla units patrolled the village area and helped train and indoctrinate the militia in the hamlets comprising the village. Being somewhat better armed, they could engage in armed propaganda activities in neighboring hamlets and villages. They were also charged with protecting the village party apparatus and particularly its military political cell, which guided paramilitary activities in the rural areas. They enforced local security, harassed French paramilitary outposts, ambushed unprotected vehicles or small paramilitary patrols, assassinated uncooperative local police and security officials, and otherwise reflected the presence and power of the resistance movement.

The next higher element, the regional forces, nominally comprised a light rifle company in every district (analogous to a county) and a separate light infantry battalion in every province (analogous to a state). In heavily populated areas under firm Communist control, and in rural base areas, there might even be multiple units at these levels. The district companies functioned as local strike forces, backing up the village and hamlet guerrilla-militia forces, and sometimes combining with the provincial battalion in protecting regional command and control and base facilities.

The provincial battalion had similar functions at the province level. It consisted essentially of full-time soldiers, in contrast to the guerrilla-militia forces, most of whom were part-timers. When fully developed, a provincial battalion comprised several rifle companies and a support company equipped with machine guns and light mortars. Although ammunition supplies were not plentiful, these regional units could engage in combat on equal terms with French Union units of comparable size for short periods of time.

All these elements—guerrilla-militia and regional forces—employed irregular tactics—that is, small-scale actions emphasizing stealth in the approach, ambushes, attacks in the form of quick raids, or simply "harassing fire" against fortified enemy outposts. They often set up ambushes to hit unwary forces moving to the assistance of these outposts. They also conducted shows of force or armed terrorist activities. Viet Minh conventional operations on a larger scale sometimes also emphasized these guerrilla characteristics.

The main objectives of the regional and guerrilla-militia forces were to pin down enemy forces, cause them to disperse to protect key facilities, overrun vulnerable outposts, disrupt lines of communication, and thereby help wear down enemy military potential through attrition. When the enemy dispersed his forces into fixed outposts to protect populated areas and lines of communication, his potential to concentrate for offensive action against Viet Minh bases was reduced. At the same time the Viet Minh main forces gained greater freedom of action, which allowed them to select more vulnerable points for their attacks.

This force structure, which characterized both the Viet Minh war against the French and the later struggle against the Americans, was not well understood outside the intelligence community. The lack of understanding led to repeated frustrations among American military planners, who failed to recognize that the movement of a Viet Minh "main force" unit out of an area targeted for a "search and destroy" operation by friendly forces did not mean the area would be clear of enemy units; local forces—regional and guerrilla-militia units—also infested the area and were able to lie low, sometimes hiding in tunnel networks. They could emerge and harass friendly forces or covertly carry out a variety of activities aimed at cowing the populace despite the presence of friendly forces in the area. These irregular forces caused the French to maintain security forces in many areas in order to protect the populace and limit the guerrillas' freedom of movement. American military officers criticized the French—and later the South Vietnamese forces—for their "outpost" mentality. But in an armed insurrection, areas not controlled twenty-four hours a day by pro-government forces become, *ipso facto*, areas subject to insurgent influence, if not dominance. If outlying areas are visited only in daylight by occasional government security patrols, which flag flies over the area at night? Which side really "controls" the area? Which side will receive voluntary support from the populace? Until very late in the game (after the Tet offensive), American military leaders in Vietnam discounted the threat posed by these regional and paramilitary forces, focusing their attention instead on the enemy's main force units.

The French understood the significance of the enemy force structure. The regional and guerrilla-militia forces were reflected in French intelligence studies and were included in their order-of-battle analyses along with the main force units. As resources became available through the

American assistance program, the French Union command sought to de-
sign forces to combat each element of the enemy force structure. The
"light battalion" program, a key element in the Vietnamese army expansion in 1953, was intended to combat the enemy's regional and guerrilla-
militia units and support local pacification. The new units were admirably
suited for that task, but their light armament and reduced manpower levels were no match for the main force units that were successfully targeted
against them when the Viet Minh realized the critical necessity of disrupting this program in order to ensure the survival of their local forces. Lacking the strategic initiative, the French were unable to preempt this Viet
Minh effort, and in 1954 the light battalion program in Tonkin was effectively crushed.

3
A Growing
U.S. Involvement

SECURITY RESTRICTIONS on the distribution of intelligence from sensitive sources inhibited an understanding among American officials of the situation in Indochina. The consequence was a failure to develop effective programs to counter Communist activities, and the pursuit of unattainable ends in Indochina. For example, in the early 1950s the French had detailed information from sensitive sources on the types and quantities of supplies being delivered to the Viet Minh. They provided this information to U.S. officials in "sanitized" form, attributing it simply to "A-1," or very reliable sources. Washington had access to the same data through independent channels, but—having stricter security standards than the French—the dissemination of this information was tightly limited to protect the source. In army intelligence we could use the French data in our secret-level publications, but we could not advise the readers of those publications that we could vouch for its accuracy. Many senior officials whom we briefed orally were not cleared for access to the sensitive information, and could not even be advised of its existence. Thus they could not know that the French information was confirmed.

This situation, which was similar to the compartmentalization of information that had contributed to the "surprise" at Pearl Harbor, sometimes made it difficult for intelligence analysts to gain credibility when memoranda or briefings were based on perfectly valid information provided by the French. We could not disclose what we believed was the probable source of the information; we could merely state that we accepted the French evaluation and brush off any skeptical remarks from the audience.

The potentially serious nature of this problem was illustrated by an episode that occurred in 1952, when General Francis G. Brink, then chief of the Military Assistance Advisory Group in Indochina, was being debriefed in the army intelligence conference room during one of his visits to Washington. When asked for his views on Chinese aid to the Viet Minh, General Brink observed that he had spent a number of years in the Orient, that he "knew the Chinaman just about as well as anybody," and that he had "never known a Chinaman to *give* anybody anything." Thus he doubted that the Chinese were aiding the Viet Minh and hinted that the French were fabricating their data on the flow of supplies.

My own division chief and numerous other army officers in attendance accepted General Brink's remarks at face value; after all, Chinese merchants were renowned for their business acumen and their ability to earn a profit. And General Brink was not only an old Asia hand, having served with General Joseph Stilwell during World War II, but an experienced general officer as well as the responsible U.S. military official on the scene in Indochina. If such a man believed the Chinese would not supply arms and ammunition to their Vietnamese comrades (which they *were* doing under an arrangement which provided for some quid pro quo), and *he* questioned the validity of French intelligence reports on the subject, who in Washington could seriously challenge his authoritative opinion?

General Brink, who was showing signs of infirmity at the time of the briefing and shortly thereafter committed suicide in the Pentagon, was *not* cleared for access to the compartmentalized information on which the French reports were based. Nor were many of those in the briefing room who were quick to accept his views and thus to discredit what we had been reporting about Chinese Communist military assistance to the Viet Minh. My own division chief, who *was* cleared for the sensitive intelligence but was only a colonel, was unwilling to challenge the judgment of a senior officer. Hence the Chinese aid question was soft-pedaled by army intelligence for several months at a time when its significance was becoming increasingly apparent. I was discouraged from preparing new reports on the issue, and passing references to it in our periodic summaries had to be carefully qualified to avoid the impression that we accepted the French reports at face value. The French data on Chinese aid had to be characterized as "alleged" or "unconfirmed." Forthright, matter-of-fact statements on the subject were for a time politically incorrect.

American decisions on Vietnam were also sometimes adversely affected by the inherently conservative views of old-line army officers. For example, sometime in 1952–1953 we were debriefing a team of officers who had just returned from a trip to Indochina, where they had worked out with the French an arms aid package for one of the Vietnamese army (ARVN) expansion programs. One of these officers was an elderly Ordnance Corps colonel who proudly took credit for the decision that the new Vietnamese units would be equipped with the M-1 Garand rifle rather than with the lighter semi-automatic U.S. carbine that had been proposed by some, including the French. When I asked why he favored the M 1, which would seem—because of its greater size and weight—to be more difficult for the diminutive Vietnamese to handle in jungles, swamps, and flooded paddy fields, he replied that the M-1 was "a *man's* rifle," and that with it "a *man*" could readily pick off the enemy with aimed fire at ranges of up to six hundred yards. He scoffed at my suggestion that in Vietnam the enemy would rarely be seen at such a distance, and that the Vietnamese physically were the size of American boys rather than men. Shifting his ground, he insisted that giving the ARVN an automatic carbine would impose an unduly heavy ammunition resupply burden, and cut short my suggestion that the *semi-automatic* carbine I was speaking of would not pose as much of a resupply burden as would the *semi-automatic* M-1 rifle, which used larger cartridges. The colonel adamantly stood by his position that the M-1 rifle was the only proper weapon for the Vietnamese soldier. Ultimately, of course, the ARVN would be reequipped with the lightweight M-16 *automatic rifle*, which had an even more voracious appetite for ammunition.

The divergence of U.S. and French objectives in Vietnam clearly surfaced in April 1953 during the visit to Washington of a French delegation headed by the minister for the Associated States, Jacques Le Tourneau. A bilateral conference in the Pentagon discussed U.S. assistance to Indochina, with senior State, Defense, Joint Chiefs, and armed service representatives on one side of the table, and the French delegation on the other. As a backbench observer, I sat against the wall.

The Americans, anxious to prod the French into a more vigorous French effort to "win the war," offered to provide the additional resources necessary to accelerate the growth of the Vietnamese army during the coming fiscal year (1954) if the French would give us a plan for winning the war. The French replied that for them, "it is not a question of *winning* the war." Their goal, Minister Le Tourneau said, was simply to maintain a position of strength from which an honorable settlement could be negotiated. This, he noted, was exactly what the United States was then doing in Korea. This statement seemed to pass right over the heads of the Americans at the table, who suggested that the French seemed not to understand the American proposal. The American spokesman, an assistant secretary of state, restated the American proposition, emphasizing our willingness to provide the means if the French simply provided us with a viable plan for victory. Le Tourneau, in turn, restated his position, noting that it was "not the policy of his government" to seek a military victory in Indochina, that indeed victory probably was unattainable because of the likelihood that the Chinese would intervene in Indochina to prevent such an outcome, just as they had done in Korea. Therefore, he said, France hoped at some point to engage in talks to arrange an "honorable" settlement in Indochina, such as America was even then seeking in Korea. The senior American officials, evading any acknowledgment of the Korean analogy, continued to press the French for a "victory" plan. The conference broke off without the matter being resolved.

Frustrated at the French government's unwillingness to commit itself to a "victory" plan that would justify our proposed major increase in military assistance, Washington chose to seek such a commitment through the back door. General John "Iron Mike" O'Daniel, then commanding

U.S. Army forces in the Pacific (USARPAC), was sent by Washington to Vietnam to obtain such a plan from General Henri Navarre. A colleague of mine, who held down ACSI's French desk, accompanied O'Daniel's team and served as his interpreter. This officer later described to me the birth of the "Navarre Plan," as he observed it. O'Daniel met with Navarre a number of times, repeatedly pressing him for a plan for winning the war, but Navarre insisted he could not comply. The French general noted that the issue of seeking a military victory was a matter of *national* policy, to be decided in Paris. As a theater commander, Navarre did not *make* policy, he simply executed the mission set out for him by his government. It was for the government in Paris, he insisted, to decide whether it wished to achieve victory in Indochina. His mission was to maintain a position of strength from which negotiations might be undertaken at some appropriate time in the future. In other words, his orders were to maintain the status quo, avoid high-risk operations, and avoid losing territory to enemy control. A plan for "victory" could be drawn up only in Paris.

After fruitless dialogues along these lines over a period of weeks. O'Daniel took his mission to Bangkok, where he asked the members of his team to draw up a concept for winning the war, assuming the American-proposed expansion of the ARVN were to occur. The team's concept provided for only modest reinforcements from France in addition to the projected substantial Vietnamese buildup. It envisaged intensified pacification operations along the southeastern coast beginning in the 1953–1954 campaign season, which would progressively roll up the Communist forces along the coast. This would ultimately free French forces from that region for redeployment to the North. There these reinforcements would permit the buildup of a sizable mobile striking force, which could mount a final offensive in 1955 to destroy the enemy's "*masse de maneuvre*." The expanded Vietnamese forces would occupy and pacify areas formerly held by the Viet Minh as the French mobile forces cleared the way.

Returning to Saigon after his brief sojourn in Bangkok, O'Daniel cornered Navarre (who had been deliberately evading further meetings with the gruff, blunt American general), presented him with the outline plan, and asked for his opinion. Navarre reportedly observed that it was "a plan which, given the appropriate policy decision from Paris, and given the means necessary to implement it, might in time win the war." O'Daniel then returned triumphantly to Washington with the "Navarre Plan" for victory in Indochina, and U.S. policymakers promptly approved some $385 million in additional military assistance to underwrite the requisite expansion of the Vietnamese army.

I should add that a government headed by Joseph Laniel came to power in Paris that summer and endorsed the concept of the Navarre Plan, agreeing to send a few additional battalions of troops from North Africa and to transfer the French battalion from Korea, where it was no longer needed because of the armistice there—to Indochina. The degree of commitment by the Laniel government to "victory" in Indochina was questionable and at best limited. It required no substantial increase in the commitment of French resources to endorse the Navarre Plan, and doing so gave the appearance of Franco-American cooperation. It also put France in position to gain additional U.S. military assistance in Indochina; other benefits beyond the Indochina problem may also have accrued to Paris. Certainly, however, the French bureaucracy and military leadership had no more enthusiasm for, nor faith in, "victory" than before, despite the unenthusiastic implementation by Navarre's command of something approximating the scheme. The Navarre Plan was never vigorously pursued; the basic concept was faulty, and ultimately the Laniel government was replaced by one pledged to achieving a negotiated settlement—an objective more in line with French public opinion than continuation of the "quicksand war" in Indochina.

But American officials in Washington, Honolulu, and Saigon were more enthusiastic and hopeful. Denied victory over the Communists in Korea, it now appeared to American policymakers and senior operating officials that one was feasible in Indochina, and that it was necessary only to keep Navarre's feet to the fire to ensure the defeat of the Viet Minh. Skeptics were dismissed as perennial pessimists.

French plans for the 1953–1954 dry season campaign called essentially for a holding action in the North. The aim was to stabilize the situation in the northwest by evacuating the remaining vulnerable outposts—reestablish-

ing at Dien Bien Phu the base for Thai partisan operations hitherto located at Lai Chau, near the Chinese border, and abandoning the strongpoint at Na San which, though successfully defended earlier in 1953, was
awkwardly sited to resist a prolonged siege. The French hoped to build up
sufficient mobile strength in the Hanoi area to permit an effective response to any major Viet Minh tactical initiative, or—if the opportunity
afforded—to undertake an initiative of their own which might draw the
Viet Minh *masse de maneuvre* into combat near the Red River Delta, where
French advantages in armor, mobility, firepower, and air supremacy could
best be used to inflict severe losses on the enemy. The French had no expectations of a climactic, decisive campaign; their hope was simply to
maintain the status quo in the North while going through the motions of
implementing the Navarre Plan by mounting a sizable new pacification effort along the southern coast, beginning just below Nha Trang. These
coastal provinces had been under Viet Minh control from the beginning of
the war.

The defense of Laos was not the prime consideration in the French
decision to reoccupy Dien Bien Phu in 1953. The main purpose of the
fortified camp built by the French there was to establish a more secure
base for the support of operations by local Thai partisans against Viet
Minh rear areas in the upper Red and Black River valleys. To the French,
the camp seemed to be a low-risk venture. A modest garrison of less than a
dozen battalions, plus White Thai partisans, seemed adequate, and if the
Viet Minh chose to mount any significant counterstrike, the French could
quickly lift sufficient reinforcements by air to mount an effective defense.
Dien Bien Phu was viewed as a diversionary complement to the major
fighting they anticipated closer to their Red River Delta "redoubt."

Some critics suggest that the French were "surprised" when the Viet
Minh chose to move their *mass de maneuvre* to the remote northwest to lay
siege to Dien Bien Phu. Their intelligence had detected many signs that
the Viet Minh were actively preparing major operations against the
French perimeter southwest of Hanoi. As a matter of fact, the Viet Minh
leadership, which had convened in a planning session, abruptly changed
its operational objective for the coming campaign on learning that the
French had seized Dien Bien Phu. Ho Chi Minh, General Giap, and their
colleagues recognized in this French gambit a golden opportunity for a

potentially climactic battle in a remote region where the French military advantages could be neutralized. If there was indeed an intelligence error by the French, it was their failure to recognize that the Communist leadership believed they could mount an operation that far from their own bases on the scale required to overrun a garrison of the size the French could deploy to that isolated area.

In 1952–1953 the Viet Minh had twice attempted large-scale operations in the northwest, failing both at Na San and in the Plaine des Jarres to sustain an active siege at a great distance from their bases. Both of those campaigns were characterized by major Viet Minh buildups in the vicinity of French outposts. The French withdrew their isolated garrisons at the last minute, moving rapidly overland by forced marches (supplied by parachute drops en route) and joining airlifted reinforcements which had prepared strong new defensive complexes several days' march away. In both these instances, the pursuing enemy forces, lacking aerial resupply, rapidly outdistanced the supplies carefully cached in the vicinity of the posts abandoned by the French. Thus the Viet Minh were able to mount only piecemeal attacks, quickly using up the limited quantity of food and the "basic load" of ammunition they could carry on their backs. These limited attacks were readily beaten off by the French, and the Viet Minh troops had to withdraw quickly to their starting point to avoid starvation.

The French command had—with some reason—concluded from these two campaigns that the Viet Minh were unable to sustain active operations more than two or three days' march beyond their forward supply caches. They took comfort also in the fact that the Viet Minh had never overrun a prepared defensive position held by a force larger than a battalion. A well-organized defensive complex, such as those at Na San, in the Plaine des Jarres, and at Dien Bien Phu, manned by a half-dozen or more battalions—isolated but resupplied by air—could surely withstand anything the Viet Minh seemed likely to be able to throw against them.

The French also knew that the Viet Minh artillery, comprising fewer than fifty pack[*] 75mm howitzers and 105mm howitzers (both American

---

[*]"Pack" artillery consists of light, wheeled weapons which can be broken down into animal pack loads for transport over rugged terrain.

made), lacked combat experience and was not even trained in coordinating and shifting massed fire. The French, on the other hand, considered themselves the master artillerists of the world. In the "unlikely" event the Viet Minh managed to deploy their howitzers within range of Dien Bien Phu, they would "surely" be overwhelmed by the superior artillery techniques of the French.

For the Viet Minh, the decision to seek a climactic victory by overrunning a major French defensive complex could not have been an easy one. In the first place, success required that the French garrison at Dien Bien Phu be totally isolated; the potential escape route into Laos had to be denied to them. The French, with their aerial resupply capabilities, might just be able to withdraw overland into Laos. In that event, pursuit by the Viet Minh would be difficult; they would be faced with a repeat of their failures in the two previous campaigns. A 15- or 20-day supply of rice would mean a load of 30 to 40 pounds per soldier. In addition to his other equipment and ammunition this exceeded the optimum load for a Vietnamese soldier on a forced march in rugged terrain. It would allow him a radius of operation of 8 to 10 days—perhaps 100 to 150 miles in the forested terrain of northern Laos. The myth of armies of coolies with supplies trailing behind Viet Minh combat units, created by journalists and fed by Communist propaganda, was just that—a myth. Coolies too must eat, and if a coolie is carrying 60 pounds of rice when he starts off, at the end of 15 days he has only enough left to feed him during his return to his starting point. If he accompanies a combat unit as a porter, at the end of 14 days he can, unless fated to die of starvation, turn over only enough rice—2 pounds—to feed one soldier for one day. An army colleague of mine who had served with pack artillery units in Burma during World War II pointed out to me early in my career the limitations imposed on sustained movement by units operating without motorized resupply. In a pack artillery unit, he said, the point of diminishing returns is soon reached when mules are required to carry fodder for mules, who carry fodder for mules, who carry ammunition for cannon. Each day's additional march increases the requirement for fodder in an almost geometric progression. Military units can live off the country only if it is populated and produces food. If roads and farmers are absent, military units can

move only as far as their ability to carry their own supplies will permit—
unless they have the benefits of an aerial resupply system.

So the Viet Minh logistical problem in mounting an effective assault
on Dien Bien Phu was most difficult. If the French meant to garrison a
division or so at Dien Bien Phu, the entire Viet Minh *corps de battaille*
would be required to mount a successful attack. This meant moving about
40,000 troops (3 infantry divisions and the artillery division) to Dien Bien
Phu, then resupplying that force with at least 40 tons of food per day, plus
at least an equal tonnage of ammunition and other supplies (including the
fuel to move the trucks involved) in order to sustain active operations 150
miles from their principal bases. This could not be accomplished without
extensive reconstruction to restore the long-unused Route 41 for vehicle
traffic and maintain it. It also meant establishing the requisite supply depots and truck maintenance facilities en route, all of this on a scale and
over distances never before attempted by the Viet Minh. Clearly their existing engineer resources were inadequate. Moreover, transporting supplies at the required rate over those distances was beyond the capacity of
their existing 300-vehicle transportation regiment. To support a sustained
campaign would mean establishing fixed facilities, which would be vulnerable to French air attack; this would require anti-aircraft capabilities
beyond the handful of heavy machine guns then available to the Viet
Minh. And some means would have to be found to neutralize the French
airlift; the French could easily deliver a greater tonnage of supplies to the
defenders of Dien Bien Phu than the Viet Minh could supply to the attackers, unless the French airlift capability could be curtailed.

It seems unlikely that the Viet Minh command had devised solutions
to these problems before deciding to mount a response to Dien Bien Phu.
But the potential reward led them to gamble that they would be able to
mobilize the resources—with Chinese aid—to overcome the obstacles.
They decided fairly early in December 1953 to make the attempt, and is-
sued the initial orders to redirect their *masse de maneuvre* to the northwest.
We knew by mid-December that their engineer regiment—augmented by
Chinese technicians and by impressed civilian laborers—had begun re-
pairing and rebuilding the roads, bridges, and fords between the Red and
the Black rivers leading toward Dien Bien Phu. By the end of the month

we knew that the Chinese were furnishing enough new trucks to more than double the number available to the Viet Minh transportation regiment, and that it was establishing a new network of relay stations stretching toward Dien Bien Phu.

In January 1954 we learned that a new anti-aircraft regiment of three or four battalions, equipped with forty-eight to sixty-four 37mm anti-aircraft guns, had entered Tonkin from China, and that thousands of rounds of ammunition for these weapons were en route to Dien Bien Phu. By early February the bulk of three infantry divisions, the artillery division, the anti-aircraft regiment, and other support units were known to have arrived in the area, along with a forward command post of the Viet Minh military general headquarters. We knew they had put in motion supplies of food and ammunition which were beginning to accumulate in the vicinity of Dien Bien Phu on an unprecedented scale for the Viet Minh.

There was little doubt in French and American intelligence circles about the scale and meaning of the Viet Minh buildup. The French command was initially euphoric at the prospects for the long hoped-for "showdown" battle. They were confident that in the relatively open terrain of the valley, their superior artillery proficiency and total supremacy in the air would permit them to destroy the attackers. Tanks (M-24s) had been dismantled and flown to Dien Bien Phu in large transport aircraft (Bristol freighters), reassembled there, and were expected to lead counterattacks through "killing zones" which had been cleared of jungle cover. Tons of barbed wire, cement, pierced steel planking, and other materials for building fortifications were flown in. Fortified positions were established on the small hillocks located adjacent to the two airstrips, within mutually supporting distances. The French command convinced itself that its position was nearly impregnable and gave little thought to the alternative of withdrawing overland once the scale of the Viet Minh buildup became evident. Most visiting American military officers were only somewhat less euphoric. The French defenses and preparations could be seen and inspected at firsthand; Communist preparations were largely hidden by the jungle canopy and could be judged only by reading intelligence reports.

General O'Daniel returned to Indochina in November 1953 with orders to assess French progress in implementing the Navarre Plan, and to encourage them toward a vigorous approach to the war. Toward the end of the month he made his first visit to Dien Bien Phu. Later he presented a favorable report to Washington. I attended his briefing to the Joint Chiefs of Staff, which he opened by stating that he was "encouraged by the prospects for victory in Indochina in the next twelve to fifteen months." This sentence did not appear in his written report, which nonetheless expressed confidence that the French were making progress toward the ultimate defeat of the Viet Minh.

About mid-December, as General O'Daniel was about to leave Washington to return to his post in Hawaii, I was asked to bring him up to date on developments since his visit to Indochina. After relating the details of the initial move of elements of the Viet Minh *corps de bataille* toward Dien Bien Phu, the beginning of the road construction, and the intensive supply activity, I could see that the general was becoming animated. When I concluded, he was filled with wide-eyed enthusiasm. "Brilliant strategy," he exclaimed. "Navarre has them trapped. It's the old hammer-and-anvil tactic. The garrison at Dien Bien Phu is the anvil, and Cogny's forces around Hanoi are the hammer, and he's got the enemy's main force trapped in between. Navarre's a brilliant strategist—he's got the enemy right where he wants him." I vainly attempted to point out that Cogny's armored elements were 150 miles away from Dien Bien Phu; that, as the general himself had seen, the terrain separating Cogny from Dien Bien Phu was some of the most difficult, trackless mountain land in the world; that, given the nature of the opposing forces and the kind of war they were fighting, the Viet Minh divisions were far from "trapped"; that the shoe might well indeed soon be on the other foot unless the French withdrew from Dien Bien Phu. O'Daniel dismissed my caution as nonsense and returned to his post in Hawaii convinced that Navarre was on the road to victory.

Some French officials in Saigon were concerned that the increased Viet Minh anti-aircraft capability warranted an increase in their air-strike capability to suppress the expected hostile fire. Accordingly they requested in about February 1954 that the United States provide an additional group of B-26 bombers under the military assistance program (thirty-two to thirty-six aircraft). The Joint Chiefs asked Brigadier General Thomas Trapnell, who had succeeded General Brink as chief of MAAG in 1952, if he thought the French request was justified. Trapnell hedged; obviously unconvinced, he said he had no independent capability to verify French claims concerning the Viet Minh deployment of a new anti-aircraft regiment in the Dien Bien Phu area. The French advised the American army attaché to notify us in Washington that the presence of the regiment was not only based on "A-1" information (which we in army intelligence already knew) but was also reflected in aerial photographs. Trapnell was shown the photos by the French, but his staff had no trained photo interpreters. The army arranged to fly some in from the U.S. Eighth Army in Korea. Unfortunately, these technicians were accustomed to interpreting photos along the treeless demilitarized zone (DMZ) in Korea, where military units had been in static defensive positions for years, and where many of the rocks lining the pathways linking military facilities had been whitewashed. They were not experienced in analyzing images of activity in a jungle-covered theater of unconventional military operations. They concluded, after studying the French photos, that while there were signs of activity in the area and some positions (open pits in the ground) that could accommodate anti-aircraft weapons, these were unoccupied, and they might be intended for some other type of weapon or even for some other purpose. Although not specifically asked, they added that they saw no evidence to suggest an enemy buildup in the area on the scale claimed by French intelligence.

This report—with its gratuitous final judgment—killed the French bomber request, which was disapproved by the Joint Chiefs. It also temporarily demolished the credibility of army intelligence and of the army attachés in Vietnam. Although the Joint Chiefs themselves were cleared for the sensitive data that enabled us to vouch for the validity of the "A-1" information provided by the French, most of their working-level staff personnel were not so cleared, and we could not convince them that we had valid reasons for accepting the French intelligence judgments. They rejected our protests concerning the probable inexperience of the Eighth

Army's photo interpreters. Trapnell's report on their findings reinforced the Francophobia prevalent in Washington, and we in army intelligence were looked upon as dupes of the French.

After the Viet Minh onslaught began in March 1954, the French renewed their request for additional B-26s, and the Joint Chiefs approved it in April. The aircraft arrived in Indochina in June, a month after the fall of Dien Bien Phu. Their earlier arrival would not have prevented the loss of the French garrison, but it would have increased the price paid by the Viet Minh. It would also have avoided one more burr under the saddle of Franco-American cooperation and understanding.

The key elements in the Communist success at Dien Bien Phu were: (a) their determination to win and their ability to motivate their forces to continue the siege despite horrendous losses; (b) their use of seventeenth-century siege tactics to offset French advantages in firepower and air supremacy; (c) the relative effectiveness of their primitive artillery and anti-aircraft techniques; and (d) their ability to overcome seemingly insurmountable logistical difficulties.

The will to win of the Vietnamese Communists at Dien Bien Phu— and later in the struggle against the Americans—was awesome. Its decisive significance is difficult to convey to those who have not studied their efforts in detail. This was their greatest strength, and their ability to inculcate the will to win in their people spelled the difference between success and failure for their cause. Their sense of purpose, commitment to the cause, determination to succeed, and confidence in the ultimate outcome resulted from a unique compound of xenophobic Vietnamese nationalism and stubbornness, the willingness of the Tonkinese people to struggle and endure hardship, the faith of their leaders in the "scientific correctness" of Marxist socialist doctrine, their Leninist revolutionary zeal, their ideological conviction of the rightness of the Maoist doctrine of peasant revolt, and the firm discipline imposed by a tightly organized cadre party structure with continuity of leadership.

In his *People's War, People's Army*, published in 1961, General Giap extolled the leadership of the party, whose unifying role was the key to victory. This should not be dismissed as mere propaganda; a careful study of such publications is essential to understanding the Communists.

Giap notes that after the second phase of the campaign at Dien Bien Phu, in which the Communists suffered enormous losses for relatively few gains, "negative rightist thoughts cropped up again to the detriment of the carrying out of the task. . . . We opened in the heart of the battlefield an intensive and extensive struggle against rightist passivity, and for the heightening of revolutionary enthusiasm and the spirit of strict discipline. This ideological struggle was very successful. This was one of the greatest achievements in political work in our army's history. It led the Dien Bien Phu campaign to complete victory." At the time of the battle there had been reports that some Viet Minh units, appalled at the gross slaughter, had mutinied and were refusing to continue the siege. Giap's statement tends to confirm those reports but also suggests the power of the Communist apparatus and indoctrination process in overcoming such difficulties, restoring their troops' will to fight under the most trying conditions.

Tactically the reversion to seventeenth-century siege techniques was the key to victory. First, it enabled the Viet Minh to isolate, pinch off, and overrun the French strongpoints one by one. Practicing the dictum that the "best way to accomplish many things is to do them one at a time," the Viet Minh overran a complex manned by many French battalions by overwhelming them individually and sequentially. Starting well back in sheltered ravines, Viet Minh trenches were gradually extended—like the arms of an octopus—down into the valley floor, gradually encircling outlying French strongpoints. The progressive extension of this network of trenches—scores of miles of them—sheltered Viet Minh troops from French artillery and air attack, and enabled them to move right up to the inner barbed wire of the French defenses before having to expose themselves to French fire in nighttime assaults. The French sought to block the progress of this entrenching pattern, but in doing so they found themselves in the role of attacker and suffered losses disproportionate to the results achieved. With greater numbers of troops, the Communists could extend their trenches faster than the French could fill them in.

Communist artillery and anti-aircraft weapons were employed in an unexpectedly primitive fashion, but with unanticipated effectiveness. Artillery pieces were individually emplaced in tunnels dug from the rear slopes of ridges overlooking the French defenses in the valley below. Each piece was manhandled from the roads over trails through jungles, up slopes, and across ravines and streams. Normally truck-towed 105mm howitzers were moved fifteen or twenty miles beyond the nearest road by sheer muscle-power. The French were correct in their judgment that the Viet Minh could not employ modern fire-control methods and indirect fire techniques. They didn't. Their pieces employed direct fire, ranging in individually on their targets by trial and error. Fires were shifted on signals by rockets rather than by radio or telephone. At a given signal, a designated piece of artillery would shift from one specified target to another for that particular operational phase.

When the French massed their fire to attack one of the individually placed Viet Minh artillery pieces, that weapon and its crew would be moved back into its tunnel or cave for protection while all other Viet Minh pieces continued firing. The French artillery commander at Dien Bien Phu committed suicide early in the siege because he was unable to fulfill his vain boast that he would dominate any artillery the Viet Minh managed to bring to bear on Dien Bien Phu. Forty percent of his gunners, firing from open, shallow gun pits, were casualties in the initial phase of the Communist onslaught.

Viet Minh anti-aircraft weapons were also employed in an unorthodox fashion. Many of them were used primarily in an offensive role—that is, to attack the French airlift, rather than in the traditional defensive role of protecting against air attack. Anti-aircraft gun emplacements were prepared in extreme forward positions, as close to the French perimeter as possible, in order to constrict the size of the drop zone into which supplies could be parachuted. As outlying French positions were overrun, the anti-aircraft guns were moved progressively closer to the remaining French positions. After the first few weeks, French airdrops were conducted through a barrage of 37mm gunfire from all sides of the shrinking drop zone. After substantial aircraft losses, French transport pilots soon stayed well above the effective range of the 37mm weapons, dropping supplies from above 6,500 feet. As a consequence, a steadily decreasing proportion fell within French lines, and a steadily increasing proportion was recovered by the Viet Minh. Only the American pilots flying C-119s at night came in at low altitudes. Their accuracy was also considerably less than perfect, though better than that of the French.*

The scale of the Viet Minh logistical effort was unprecedented. Although it was patched together as the situation evolved, it proved capable of delivering a sufficient quantity of supplies to sustain the campaign until victory was achieved. Almost a thousand trucks were employed in moving supplies from the Chinese railhead at Pinghsiang into the Cao Bang area of Tonkin, and then across the "Viet Bac" rear area to Route 41 and on to the vicinity of Dien Bien Phu. Because of French air supremacy, most movement was by night. The French attempted to interdict the flow of supplies, selecting choke points where they sought to disable bridges, block road junctions, or cut segments of roads by bombing. The Communists managed to circumvent this interdiction effort with techniques applied again during the struggle against the United States—using temporary bridges which could be removed during daylight hours; building fords at redundant river crossing points; manhandling supplies around roadblocks or around cuts or through mined areas; and using coolie porters or bicycles to bypass such areas. Supplies were moved systematically from one relay station to another, at a rate averaging close to a hundred tons a day, to depots in the Dien Bien Phu area. From there they were distributed by porters or on bicycles to unit depots in the trench network surrounding the French defensive complex. Tens of thousands of impressed porters and laborers, male and female, supplemented the motor transport units, which were the prime means of moving supplies. The use of these laborers increased the requirement for food supplies, but

---

*A number of writers have referred to the Viet Minh anti-aircraft guns as "radar controlled." In fact no radars were detected or reported in the Dien Bien Phu area by any reliable source. The type of 37mm weapon used there was not designed to be controlled by gun-laying radar; it was aimed by men seated on either side of the mount who turned wheels to point the gun and track the target visually through simple, open gunsights. Their effectiveness derived from their forward emplacement and the funnelling effect of the mountains, which forced the French aircraft to use a single, easily predicted axis in their approach to the drop zone.

the system soon achieved a stabilized level of delivery sufficient to sustain
the siege and to defeat the French.

The performance of the Washington intelligence community in the Dien
Bien Phu crisis was mixed. Because the problem was largely military in
nature, army intelligence played a key role in analyzing the situation and
projecting likely developments. We tracked developments effectively during the buildup phase, though our wings were clipped to some extent by
the credibility gap created by the photo interpretation problem mentioned earlier. French confidence in their ability to cope, combined with
American skepticism toward the reality of the threat reported by the
French, produced an inclination in Washington to discount the seriousness of the situation at Dien Bien Phu. Our assessments of growing Viet
Minh capabilities there did not carry much weight with our audience,
though they proved to be valid.

During this period I regularly briefed the interagency Watch Committee (then chaired by the deputy head of army intelligence), which met
weekly to consider indications of hostile action against U.S. interests
abroad. The week before the battle of Dien Bien Phu began, I presented a
detailed rundown of the Viet Minh buildup and concluded that the Communists seemed to have completed preparations for combat, and that all
indications pointed toward a massive assault during the coming week. It
seemed to me that it would be useful for the Watch Committee on this occasion to fulfill its function and provide explicit warning of an action in-
imical to the interests of the United States. But the chairman impatiently
suggested that my statement was out of order, that it was not the purpose
of the committee to deal with intentions, and that my evidence reflected
capabilities more than intentions. The committee's report that week noted
simply that Viet Minh forces at Dien Bien Phu had attained a high state of
preparedness, but that there was no evidence they intended to exercise
their capability to attack.

Later that week I encountered the chairman in a men's room in the
Pentagon. He asked whether I still believed the Viet Minh would attack
Dien Bien Phu, and I assured him I did. He suggested that my mistaken

belief was based on ignorance of the Communist doctrine of indirect strategy. Dien Bien Phu was a major strategic strongpoint, he explained, and a direct attack on it would violate this Communist doctrine. I pointed out that Communist preparations in the area had reached the stage where they obviously had decided to attack Dien Bien Phu, which suggested to me that they had concluded it was, strategically speaking, a weak point. They might indeed view Dien Bien Phu as the key to Hanoi and Saigon, the indirect route to ultimate victory. He dismissed my argument as that of an inexperienced youth, suggesting that if I applied myself I might over time become wiser in the field of strategic doctrine.

At the opening of my briefing to the Watch Committee the following week, I observed that, "As we attempted to predict last week, the Communists yesterday began a major assault aimed at overwhelming the French garrison at Dien Bien Phu." This was met by a loud and sustained guffaw from the colonel representing the air force, who almost fell out of his chair with glee at the discomfiture and obvious chagrin of the chairman. I saw nothing humorous in the failure of the Watch Committee to provide effective early warning of the likelihood of such an event; my remarks were intended merely to note the irony of the situation.

After the assault began, in army intelligence we moved easily into producing periodic situation reports, based largely on twice-daily reports from army attachés in Saigon and Hanoi, supplemented by other information as available. Our briefing load was substantial—daily briefings for the army chief of staff, General Ridgway, and other key staff officers on an individual basis. Our graphics people soon prepared an attractive terrain model of the Dien Bien Phu valley, on which we mounted a removable transparent overlay showing the locations of the French and Viet Minh positions in some detail. We used this in briefing General Ridgway but unfortunately left it in his office, where it was seen by the Joint Chiefs chairman, Admiral Arthur Radford, who "had to have one." As a result, we had to make a duplicate terrain model overnight so that the chairman would not be trumped by the army chief of staff.

General Ridgway showed a keen interest in the Dien Bien Phu campaign, seeing it as a fascinating strategic and operational problem. He had a good grasp of detail, remembering from day to day how many artillery pieces were remaining to the French. But he was able to retain a strategic perspective as well, never losing sight of the potential consequences of a French defeat. His mind was quick and active, and he often conceived tactical innovations that he thought might be helpful to the French, and had them passed to the French command in Saigon. They were all practical, and those that the French tried proved useful. It seemed to me that Ridgway had a better feel for the Indochina problem than any other army chief of staff whom I served between 1950 and 1961.

The key question, of course, was whether the Communists would succeed. This was not the sort of question which the intelligence community was prepared then—or on most occasions since—to answer with alacrity, precision, or prescience. In effect the answer entailed an assessment of the likely consequences of the interaction of at least three parties—the Viet Minh (and their Chinese allies), the French, and the United States. We could much more readily assess the likely actions of the Communists than those of the French, and we never seriously ventured to guess what actions Washington might take. (We did answer questions about the likely consequences of specified U.S. courses of action, but we never attempted to predict whether those actions would succeed.) We could measure the Viet Minh effort with some precision and were convinced from the outset that they intended to make a serious attempt to defeat the French. We believed the Chinese would provide essential arms, ammunition, supplies, and technicians, but that they would stop short of introducing combat forces unless conditions reached the point where the total defeat of the Viet Minh cause seemed imminent, and this we considered unlikely. We did not believe the Chinese would intervene to ensure a Viet Minh victory at Dien Bien Phu. The series of National Intelligence Estimates produced during the campaign were consistent on this point.

It was much more difficult to assess the French capabilities, in part because we had so much more relevant information. My own judgment—which proved faulty on this matter—was that the French command would not stand by and permit defeat; this view strongly influenced our input to the National Estimates.

The French had a number of options they might have tried in order to relieve the situation. They had the capability to prevent the loss of Dien

Bien Phu, but would they exercise it? We misjudged their intentions. Two of their options seemed quite viable. One was a foray in strength by mobile ground columns from the Hanoi area into the Viet Minh logistical complex adjoining the north bank of the Red River above Hanoi, with a view to disrupting the flow of supplies to Dien Bien Phu and forcing the Viet Minh to divert combat units from Dien Bien Phu to protect their rear areas. A similar thrust had been mounted by the French the year before and had succeeded in diverting the Viet Minh. But the French were uneasy about penetrating too far, though they had the capacity to mass the necessary forces for a major strike.

The other option was an attempt to extract the garrison into Laos by sending ground columns north from the vicinity of Luang Prabang to link up with airborne forces, which could have established an air-supplied corridor down which the forces might be withdrawn to the Laotian capital. This option involved some risk, depending on whether the French garrison or its Viet Minh tormentors were the more exhausted and capable of a forced march over difficult terrain. But it was the option that the French belatedly set in motion. A ground column was within forty-eight hours of a linkup with Dien Bien Phu, where it was to be reinforced by airborne units, when the garrison collapsed in May.

It was inconceivable to me that the French would fail to take some action within their capabilities to preclude a climactic defeat. They made no plans for such action before the battle because of their convictions that Dien Bien Phu could be held. Their confidence was shaken somewhat when the enemy overran several outlying positions in the first onslaught in mid-March, but they still hoped the Viet Minh would lose heart because of their heavy losses, and the French felt no sense of desperation. After the second series of assaults at the end of March, however, the French commands in both Hanoi and Saigon became transfixed by the spectacle unfolding at Dien Bien Phu, and seemed to be paralyzed by the fear of potential defeat.

By the end of the first week in April, when the Viet Minh shifted from the sledgehammer blows that had characterized the first two phases to a more sustained but low-key pressure, it became apparent that the French lacked the will to mount an effective response. The French command re-

gained its composure later in April, but then it was too late to try the option of a foray into the Viet Minh base areas, because enemy supplies had
probably already left those depots and were in the pipeline to Dien Bien
Phu. Only an attempt to extract the garrison offered any hope, and the
margin of risk of that operation was so high that the attempt was implemented sluggishly. It seemed clear that it would amount to too little, and
be too late.

In Washington there was little sense of urgency about Dien Bien Phu
until the end of March. Although army attaché reporting had continued
to reflect skepticism about the Navarre Plan, its impact on operating officials was more than offset by the continuing optimistic reports of visitors
to Vietnam, particularly those of General O'Daniel. On the eve of the battle, "Iron Mike" had again visited Indochina and Dien Bien Phu, and had
confidently advised Washington that the defensive complex could be held,
that the French position elsewhere in Indochina was growing stronger,
and that the French were gaining confidence in the possibility of victory.
Intelligence assessments in Washington, which tended to focus on Communist capabilities and to take French reactions for granted, did little to
impress senior planners with the developing seriousness of the situation
against the background of General O'Daniel's optimism. Hence there was
little serious contingency planning for a substantial French military defeat.

Early in 1954 there had been only three of us in army intelligence assigned to the Indochina desk full-time. We were progressively augmented
as the siege developed, and by the end of the battle more than fifteen people were working on the problem. This included a team of reserve officers
busily preparing handbooks on the Viet Minh forces against the possibility they might be needed by American forces sent to the area.

Part of our responsibility was to contribute to the development of
army staff views on Joint Chiefs actions and position papers on policy
matters. The views of army intelligence were not always decisive; many
considerations other than intelligence affect policy decisions, and the
"terrain, weather, and enemy" (the classic responsibilities of army intelligence) are not in every case viewed as the most critical issues affecting
military decisions. But the army staff system requires the heads of all gen-

eral staff components, including intelligence, to advise the army chief of staff regarding the position he should take on important issues on the agenda of the Joint Chiefs. The recommendations of the assistant chief of staff for intelligence were based largely on the interpretation of his analysts working on the issue or area under consideration.

Thus we were consulted on the Joint Chiefs' decision regarding the initial French request for additional B-26 bombers. We had advised that, contrary to the MAAG's belief, the French request was justified by reliable intelligence on the enemy buildup at Dien Bien Phu, and in view of the likely presence there of 37mm anti-aircraft weapons as reported by the French. Army intelligence had recommended that the army support the French request.

When the question of American intervention began to be seriously considered in late March 1954, Admiral Radford led the majority of the Joint Chiefs in espousing the commitment of American airpower to prevent the loss of Dien Bien Phu. From the outset, General Ridgway disagreed with this view, and we in army intelligence wholeheartedly backed his position. We consistently argued that the employment of U.S. airpower alone could not be decisive under the circumstances prevailing in Indochina. This smacked of parochialism to some, who suggested that we were simply seeking to rationalize an institutional army viewpoint. Our position was, however, a principled one. Our fundamental view was that history had demonstrated that airpower alone could not effectively interdict land lines of communication if the opposing side had the resources and determination to keep supplies moving, as we judged the Viet Minh did. The Italian campaign in World War II and the war in Korea had both demonstrated the inability of airpower to prevent the flow of supplies even when geographic conditions were favorable—that is, when the approaches to the front were constricted by a peninsula. Indochina offered no such constriction. We were also already aware of the ease with which the Viet Minh minimized the impact of French aerial interdiction efforts, and we were convinced that adding additional sorties to the French effort would not decisively affect the ability of the Viet Minh to move supplies. Moreover we believed that tactical aircraft operating from American carriers would be little more effective than those operating from the French carrier in the Gulf of Tonkin. Flight time by propeller-driven aircraft precluded a quick response to tactical demands, and the imminent start of the monsoon season meant that heavy cloud cover and low ceilings would limit visibility and effectiveness. Nor would "saturation bombing" by B-29s or B-50s be effective, given the enemy's entrenchment pattern at Dien Bien Phu and the limited number of strategic aircraft then available in the theater. (The debate between airpower advocates and the intelligence community over the effectiveness of interdiction in this theater would continue for the next twenty years.)

Interdiction of Communist supplies was, of course, only one of the issues to be considered in determining whether it made sense for the United States to intervene. It was clear to us that the gradual upgrading of Viet Minh military capabilities made possible by Chinese aid was offsetting the gains in French Union strength from the expansion of the Vietnamese army. In army intelligence we believed that the advantages of the French Union forces in numbers (a 5:3 ratio in manpower, a 10:1 edge in artillery, and at least 5:1 in motor transport) and technology (absolute supremacy in armor, airpower, and naval forces) were largely neutralized by geographic, political, and psychological factors, and by the largely unconventional character of the war. Without substantial reinforcement of their ground force capabilities—beyond what could be anticipated under the "accelerated" programs for expanding the Vietnamese forces—we believed there was little hope of gaining sufficient resources to support effective pacification programs and at the same time to conduct offensive operations that would enable the French to dictate the tempo and locale of the large-unit war. Army planners at the working level in Washington generally shared this view, believing the French Union side needed more resources to wrest the initiative from the Viet Minh. And doubt lingered that the French had either the will or the military proficiency to make the best use of whatever resources they had.

In late March 1954, General Ridgway pressed the army staff for a detailed study of the problem of employing American ground forces in Indochina. He wanted to know what additional ground forces would be required and how they ought to be employed if the United States were to introduce forces with a view to defeating the Viet Minh. One Saturday morning he called for a meeting of the senior army staff, which began with an intelligence briefing I presented—without prior notice. It soon became evident that what Ridgway wanted was detailed information on the physical environment in Indochina—particularly in North Vietnam—to a depth not readily available in Washington: open and covered storage space in Haiphong, road capacities of newly built roads, the potential for expanding the cargo-handling capacity of Haiphong and lesser ports in North Vietnam. To get this data, a team of staff officers was sent on a quick trip to Indochina. On their return, detailed studies were completed, in which the views of army intelligence were fully reflected.

When President Eisenhower was told of the army's dissent to the Joint Chiefs' recommendation that the United States intervene with air strikes to prevent the loss of Dien Bien Phu, he asked for a briefing on the reasons for the army's negative view. General Ridgway's briefing to the National Security Council was based on these staff studies, which concluded that airpower alone would not affect the outcome at Dien Bien Phu; that only the introduction of a ground force equivalent to a U.S. Army corps of three or four divisions could effectively alter the balance in favor of the French; that a substantial number of army reserve units would have to be called up to furnish the necessary logistical support in the resource-poor environment of North Vietnam; and that ammunition plants would have to be put back into production to meet anticipated needs. All of this would entail the expenditure of at least $3.5 billion for the initial year. What was more, the war might not be decided within a single year, and the suggested force level might not be sufficient to oppose Chinese intervention, which was considered likely if the Viet Minh faced defeat. Ridgway's briefing rationalized Eisenhower's rejection of the Joint Chiefs' recommendation.

I believed at the time—and still do—that the president's decision was correct, that in the broadest geopolitical strategic context there was nothing in our national interest to justify committing resources on the scale that would be required to ensure the defeat of the Viet Minh. At the time, some officials thought General Ridgway's position overstated the requirement for U.S. ground forces. Later events amply demonstrate, I believe, that—if anything—the need was understated.

4
After the Geneva Accords

I FIRST VISITED INDOCHINA after the French defeat at Dien Bien Phu. Arriving in Saigon about July 10, 1954, I spent the next five weeks under the wing of the army attachés, meeting with French intelligence officers and visiting French Union military facilities throughout Vietnam, Cambodia, and Laos. I spent a week in North Vietnam, contriving to have my arrival in Hanoi on July 16 reported to Washington in order to demonstrate to my colleagues there the validity of my earlier insistence (during the preparation of an estimate in late June) that the French could hold Hanoi at least until mid-July. On July 19 or 20, I visited the command post of a French *division de marche* near Bac Ninh, northeast of Hanoi. Over lunch, the commanding general, a man named Bastiani, outlined the difficulty of his situation, expressing doubt that his division could continue effectively for more than ten days. Their task was to protect the northern flank of the Hanoi-Haiphong corridor, keeping Viet Minh main force units from penetrating into the delta to disrupt that vital communications link. The mission was clearly beyond his capabilities, because elements of the Viet Minh 308th Division—redeployed to the delta after the fall of Dien Bien Phu—had already penetrated to the south of his line, and he was having trouble maintaining contact with those elements of his division on the extreme right. When I asked him what form of American assistance would at that point help most, he immediately exclaimed, *"Les bulldozers!"* He explained that every night one or more of the bridges along the main road linking his *groupes mobiles* were destroyed, and whole sections of the road were dug up by enemy forces. As a result, each day it was taking longer for his limited engineer resources to repair or replace the bridges, grade new approaches to the banks of the canals and rivers, and fill in the road cuts. Without more bulldozers he would soon be paralyzed; his units would become immobile and isolated, and they would be vulnerable to being overrun in piecemeal fashion. An armistice, he said, was essential within two weeks at the most to preclude a total collapse of the French military position in North Vietnam.

This was the gloomiest assessment I had encountered thus far in my visit, but I suspected also that it was the most honest. I was wearing my army reserve uniform during the trip so that I could more easily move about in the war zone and among the French military commands, and my documentation clearly indicated my association with army intelligence in Washington. Two days later, when the Geneva Accords* were signed (on July 21), I was in the coastal town of Mon Cay on the Chinese border northeast of Haiphong. When news of the signing came over the radio just before dinner, the French officers showed no elation. Most were relieved that the war was at last ending and that they had survived. But nearly all were dejected at their failure to win, and many were bitter at their "betrayal" by politicians back home. No one celebrated in the officers' mess that night in Mon Cay; each officer drifted off after dinner to reflect privately.

The trip to Indochina gave me an opportunity to exchange thoughts

---

*The agreements reached at Geneva provided for a cessation of hostilities, to be implemented incrementally, region by region, over the next ten days, and for the regrouping of all French forces—and their allies—to the region south of the 17th parallel, and of all Viet Minh forces to the area north of that line. Withdrawal of opposing forces to these regions was to be accomplished in several stages, with the last movements to be completed within three hundred days. These "temporary regroupment zones" were to be reunified into a single Vietnam through elections held in 1956.

with dozens of people there whose views I might otherwise not have heard. This included ambassadors and lesser diplomats; French, American, and Vietnamese military officers; French *colons*; and Vietnamese government officials, merchants, and refugees. I shared a jeep for two days with a Vietnamese driver who was a corporal in the French army, who had nothing but disdain for his fellow countrymen serving in the Vietnamese National Army. I learned much from him about the nature of the war and how one survived frequent travel over a mined highway by driving down the center of the road—well away from the shoulders where mines were usually planted—in a continuous game of "chicken" with traffic coming from the other direction. My driver never yielded. The breakneck speed at which he drove was necessary, he explained, in order to minimize the likelihood of being ambushed or hit by sniper fire from villages along the road.

From him and other Vietnamese I learned much about their regional antipathies—how southerners felt inferior to northerners; how the others attributed inherent dishonesty to central Vietnamese; how the southerners were viewed as lazy but wily intriguers; and how the northerners were regarded as pushy, hard-driving, and industrious busybodies. I also became more aware of the xenophobic pride felt by all Vietnamese, of their fierce ethnic loyalty and unity against foreign intruders and outsiders. But I also learned of the depth of their religious differences, their ambivalence toward communism, their abhorrence of colonialism, their resentment of Westerners, and their great respect for "Uncle" Ho Chi Minh. I made the acquaintance of some Vietnamese army majors whom I would later know as general officers. I encountered Catholic refugee mothers on the sidewalks of Haiphong who beseechingly offered their ten-year-old daughters for my pleasure for enough piastres to buy a couple of loaves of bread so that the family might postpone starvation at least one more day. And I witnessed surprisingly small numbers of people in both Hanoi and Saigon responding glumly and unenthusiastically to pleas from bullhorn-bearing cheerleaders sponsored by the Diem government who called stridently for the people to march in protest against the division of the country under the Geneva Accords.

In mid-August my Washington boss, General Arthur Trudeau, then the army's assistant chief of staff for intelligence, arrived in Saigon during the course of a swing through the Far East. I accompanied the army attachés to the airport to welcome the general and sat in the back of the room as they briefed him on the situation as they saw it. When they finished, Trudeau asked each of them in turn for his views on the prospects for Vietnam. Some were cautiously optimistic, some painted an unduly rosy picture, and a couple were cautiously skeptical. After they all had their say, he asked over his shoulder whether I had anything to say that might justify my seven weeks away from my desk in Washington. Having in my hands an appraisal I had drafted the previous afternoon for cabling to Washington, I followed its general outline in offering a brief overview of the basic factors in the situation—geographic, demographic, psychological, sociological, economic, and military. In the aftermath of Dien Bien Phu and the Geneva Accords, I observed, virtually all of these were favorable to the Communists. It seemed to me highly probable that they would easily win any elections held in the next few years to reunify the country; that if elections did not take place, the Communists would almost certainly rekindle a people's war in South Vietnam; that it would not be possible to develop a cohesive, popular government that would be strong enough to resist such an effort; that no amount of U.S. material assistance was likely to alter the outcome; and that even if we were to commit substantial ground forces, we probably would be unable to defeat the Vietnamese Communists as long as they received military support from their Soviet and Chinese comrades.

This was strong stuff and generally ran counter to the views of the embassy at that time. General Trudeau listened attentively and asked me to send my assessment to Washington through the "privacy" channel, addressed to him for his "eyes only." This was done through the army attaché's office.

This assessment was probably one of the most lucid, comprehensive, succinct, and prescient I ever wrote during my intelligence career. Because this was clearly an important juncture in the history of our postwar policy in the Far East, I called it as I saw it. I believed that events had shown we could not accomplish our aims in Southeast Asia through surrogates who did not share our aims and objectives, and who lacked the will to persevere. I believed we could not kindle the cohesion, the unity, and the will among the people of South Vietnam to resist the strength, the power, and the determination of the Vietnamese Communists.

I have recalled this assessment many times over the years and have sometimes regretted that I failed to preserve a copy of it for posterity. It caused little stir in Washington. Because it was sent for General Trudeau's eyes only, it was not given the routinely wide distribution of messages from the army attaché's office in Saigon. Ultimately, however, it did have an impact on U.S. policy deliberations. Sometime in late September, an air force colonel from the foreign military assistance office of the Department of Defense was conferring with me about the deteriorating situation in Saigon, where the Diem government was clearly floundering. He asked if I had a paper reflecting my gloomy views about the prospects for Vietnam, and I let him read a copy of my cabled assessment from Saigon. He asked if he could borrow it to show to his boss. I agreed but pleaded with him not to make any copies nor to pass it around freely, since it was marked "eyes only" for General Trudeau. A few days later he returned my copy of the cable and told me that it had led his office to push for urgent interagency action to deal with the situation. This action culminated in the decision to send General J. Lawton Collins, the former army chief of staff, to Indochina to develop and implement a "crash" program to arrest the deteriorating situation and ensure the survival of a non-Communist South Vietnam.

Later that fall, a National Intelligence Estimate was produced that generally accorded with my views. Noting the steady deterioration of the situation, it expressed doubt that South Vietnam could develop the strength to prevail against Communist subversion. It suggested that the Communists were likely to embark on a program of subversion and guerrilla activities if elections to unify the country were not held in 1956 as specified by the Geneva Accords. Even this formal assessment failed to dissuade policymakers from trying to circumvent the elections while pledging unswerving American support to the fragile "government" of South Vietnam.

The French defeat at Dien Bien Phu and the agreements at Geneva signaled the failure of America's policy of helping France defeat the Viet Minh. The northern half of Vietnam was, in effect, conceded to Communist control. But in the aftermath of this setback the Eisenhower administration chose to believe we could "hold the line" against further Communist gains in the region. This sanguine view belied the realities of the situation.

The withdrawal of the French military forces from Tonkin meant that the northern part of Vietnam came under the de facto political control of Ho Chi Minh's Democratic Republic of Vietnam. Similarly, Bao Dai's French-sponsored government of Vietnam now found its authority confined to the region south of the 17th parallel. Both governments retained their claim to sovereignty over all of Vietnam, but for a few years each would have its hands full attempting to administer that portion of the truncated country into which its military forces had been regrouped.

These troop withdrawals were completed by the end of the three-hundred-day period specified at Geneva. More than 150,000 troops of the French Colonial Army and of Bao Dai's Vietnamese army and their dependents were successfully moved to the South, mostly on shipping provided by the U.S. Navy. They were accompanied by the hastily organized exodus of some 800,000 civilian refugees—mostly Roman Catholic Tonkinese—who heeded the advice of their bishops to "follow Christ" to the South. Viet Minh troops ceremoniously occupied Hanoi, Haiphong, and the other cities in the North, and Ho Chi Minh's shadow government, which had governed the rural and mountain districts while directing their successful war effort, established effective political and administrative control over all of Tonkin and northern Annam. Meanwhile the Viet Minh moved about 90,000 troops and most of their seasoned administrative cadres and agents to the North aboard Soviet-bloc merchant ships. An international control commission, made up of Polish, Canadian, and Indian military representatives, supervised the regroupment process.

After Dien Bien Phu fell, Bao Dai had named Ngo Dinh Diem to the post of prime minister of the French-backed rump government of Vietnam in Saigon. Diem was a devout Roman Catholic who had once served as an administrator under the imperial government. He held a reputation as an ardent nationalist who had remained aloof from Vietnamese politics since the 1930s. Diem had refused to support Ho Chi Minh's wartime nationalist coalition and had stubbornly refrained from participating in any of Bao Dai's earlier postwar governments. France reluctantly acceded to Diem's appointment as premier under pressure from Washington, which had urged that a man of his nationalist credentials and political independence deserved, finally, his turn at a post in which all before him had failed.

Unwilling to sanction defeat at Geneva, Washington had maintained a relatively detached posture during the conference. While formally announcing that the United States was not bound by the agreements reached between the Viet Minh and the French (which were warmly accepted by all other participants at Geneva except South Vietnam), we also stated that we would not work to thwart their implementation. But ensuing events indicated that this was exactly what the Eisenhower administration had in mind, and some of us were surprised and dismayed by what followed.

Most of my colleagues at the working level believed even then that the dice were heavily loaded against the success of any effort to prevent the unification of Vietnam. The French clearly had no stomach for further military action in Indochina; they had signed the Accords and were bound to oversee their implementation in the areas still occupied by their military forces. The Chinese and the Soviets favored the results at Geneva, as did the British; India and other neutralist countries also approved. For the United States to challenge this broad consensus unilaterally, after we had been unwilling to commit our own military power on the side of the French without support from other allies, seemed to many of us an exercise in futility.

Moreover the Viet Minh had proved themselves a formidable adversary. Through more then a decade of struggle they had achieved an enviable unity and cohesion and had demonstrated the ability to mobilize and harness the energies and will of the populace in support of their "revolution." Giap's military forces had defeated the best units of the French Expeditionary Force and were clearly far more effective than the still nascent forces of the Associated States. In addition, even after the outflow of refugees, the population of the North was still 15 to 20 percent larger than that of the South, and it was tougher, better disciplined, and more inured to hardship. Economically the North was marginally more industrialized and could export as much as a million tons of high-grade anthracite coal annually. But it was a food deficit area, and therefore life had always been harder in the overpopulated North than in the South.

The South was far weaker politically. Non-Communist political groups and religious sects abounded, but they lacked cohesion or a sense of common purpose. Diem's own political base was limited to the Roman Catholic community. Although this comprised little more than 10 percent of the people, it did include a much larger percentage of the educated Vietnamese middle class. Diem's brothers had set out to organize the Catholics into a malleable, active political force by creating a number of front organizations, controlled by a secret cadre party organized along Leninist lines; but this effort was just beginning and had a long way to go. The Diem government was weak and inexperienced and confronted many major problems, including resettling the masses of refugees from the North and assimilating the sizable military forces withdrawn from that area, and reestablishing control over those areas in the South that had been firmly under Viet Minh control for eight years.

The French held powerful political strings which they pulled in a covert attempt to remove Diem. All senior Vietnamese military officers were alumni of the French Colonial Army, and most of these retained close ties to their former mentors. Diem could not initially count on the loyalty of the army; more than six thousand French officers and NCOs had been integrated into the Vietnamese army, and they held many of the key command and staff positions. French banking and commercial interests still dominated much of the economy in the South; the French still controlled the system of higher education, and French colonials held key positions in what was still really a rump colonial administration in the South. The French were thus still in a position to broker political power in the South and could be expected to use their influence to ensure compliance with the Geneva Accords in South Vietnam. They certainly could not be expected to work for the creation of a strong, independent anti-Communist government in the South, nor to support an American policy aimed at circumventing the reunification of Vietnam through elections.

Despite all this, Washington embarked on what amounted to a deliberate policy of thwarting the Geneva Accords by creating and preserving an independent, non-Communist government in South Vietnam. This meant building a viable self-governing state where none had existed for centuries, providing that state with military forces capable of defending its independence against an aggressive North Vietnam, and creating for that state a new, viable, stabilized economy. And since these aims were inconsistent with those of France, it meant shouldering the French aside—displacing them as the basis for South Vietnam's political, economic, and military strength—in effect assuming the de facto mantle of colonial administration in a country not yet capable of self-management in any field. In April 1956 the French withdrew the last of their military forces from Vietnam. After Diem had ousted Bao Dai and gained tenuous control of South Vietnam's army, he suppressed rebellious paramilitary forces backed by the French and declared the creation of a new Republic of Vietnam. But we never attained the degree of influence and control over the Saigon government and its military forces that the French had exercised during the colonial period. Instead, for the next twenty years we relied on friendly advice, persuasion, and occasional clumsy attempts at coercion and sanctions to urge and encourage an inept, corrupt, often uninterested, and sometimes adversarial government to conform to our aims in Vietnam.

Initially Washington's problem stemmed from the character of Diem himself and from the kind of government he and his family were trying to create. His ascendancy to power was the culmination of a well-laid scheme they had worked out in the early 1950s. I recall an intelligence report from Hanoi in late 1952 or early 1953 which outlined the plan of the "brothers Ngo." One of his brothers would concentrate on creating a political base among the Roman Catholic populace; another would work to gain allies, or splinter adversaries, among other political groups in Vietnam; a third would seek to gain support from Catholics in other countries; a fourth (a bishop of the church) would nurture the flock. Diem himself would go to the United States where, with the help of friends, he would lobby for American backing for his cause and then await the "inevitable" summons to form a cabinet in Saigon. His American backers included Francis Cardinal Spellman, Senator Mike Mansfield, and Senator John F. Kennedy.

In army intelligence we were invited later in 1953 to attend a session at which Diem's American backers had arranged to give him "exposure" to the "brass" in the Pentagon. Although still a relatively obscure figure in Vietnamese politics, we knew he was appearing with increasing frequency on lists of potential nationalist leaders, and I was looking forward to hearing him. Unfortunately I got caught up in other business, and one of my military colleagues was sent in my stead to the session with Diem. The major came back from the meeting shaking his head in disbelief and bewilderment. He described Diem as some kind of a mystic "nut" who spoke no English, and when what he said in French was translated for the benefit of the audience, it seemed to make no sense at all. I was not to see Diem myself until three years later when he visited Washington as president of Vietnam and spoke at the National Press Club, where he still had difficulty communicating his ideas coherently.

Ngo Dinh Diem was very much his own man, a chain-smoking monologuist, consistently unwilling to listen to—let alone heed—advice from anyone outside his inner circle. He lacked personal charm, charisma, the social graces, and the "popular touch." His ideology—a vague, mystical doctrine which he labeled "personalism"—seemed deliberately designed to defy Vietnam's need for a leader who could attract widespread support from all sides of the political spectrum in the South. From the beginning, Diem seemed to be politically inept, unable to work effectively with others, unwilling to trust them—and incapable of gaining their trust. Nor did he demonstrate practical managerial or administrative talents. He was a political anachronism, resembling more a mandarin of the seventeenth-century imperial court at Hue than a twentieth-century postcolonial Asian national leader. In any popularity contest with the venerated "Uncle Ho," Diem was certain to lose by a landslide.

Not all of Diem's weaknesses were so clear in mid-1954, but there certainly were strong hints as to his true character, and no visible strengths other than his reputation as a rabid, independent "nationalist." Many of

us at the working level in Washington had our doubts about him and will-
ingly expressed them when asked. The French had reluctantly acceded to
American pressures for the appointment of Diem as prime minister. They
were deeply distrustful of him. The very credentials that gave him stature
in American eyes—essentially his deserved reputation as an uncompro-
mising nationalist—made him an uncertain vehicle for the pursuit of
French policies in Vietnam. Paris saw Washington's backing for Diem as a
threat to the achievement of their aims.

This dichotomy of aims and interests led to an intense political struggle between the French and Americans. The contest began to take shape
during the summer of 1954 and continued for a year, with Washington
seeking to ensure that Diem remained as head of the Saigon government
and the French working to have Bao Dai replace him with someone more
amenable to Paris's interests. Our ultimate success in pushing the French
aside led inexorably to the twenty-year struggle pitting the United States
directly against the Vietnamese Communists. By displacing the French
and thwarting the reunification of Vietnam, we were denying Ho Chi
Minh and his followers the fruits of their hard-earned victory at Dien
Bien Phu.

After the Indochina cease-fire, my own access to the decision-making
process was substantially reduced—military intelligence was no longer a
prime ingredient for policy considerations. My contacts with colleagues
in the intelligence community continued, and we often exchanged views.
Our informal consensus was generally inconsistent with the outlook that
prevailed at higher policymaking levels. Leading members of the administration seemed to be basing their views on a set of assumptions that we
believed were entirely unrealistic.

This set of assumptions included a belief that the Vietnamese Communists were inextricably bound—and subordinate to—a monolithic international movement directed and controlled by a Moscow-Peking axis;
that the South Vietnamese people would embrace any alternative to domination by Ho Chi Minh's Communist-dominated nationalist movement;
that the U.S. government could take on the French role of power broker in
Vietnam without acquiring the taint of colonialism; that the people of a
predominantly Buddhist country would be attracted to support an in-

effectual, flaccid, but autocratic government dominated by a highly parochial and militant Catholic minority; and that a vanquished, uninspired, and inexperienced Vietnamese army could develop the self-confidence, resourcefulness, élan, and combat effectiveness that would enable it to stand up to the Viet Minh's battle-tested "people's army" and become a "modern" Western military force backed by seemingly unlimited U.S. military aid. These assumptions, and others of the sort, were just that—assumptions. They were not based on a careful calculation of the strengths and weaknesses of all the factors in the equation. The intelligence estimates of the period clearly showed that these assumptions were tenuous if not invalid, but they were ignored in favor of schemes and programs designed to turn these assumptions into facts. In effect, these erroneous assumptions led the United States to set and pursue unattainable objectives in Indochina for the next twenty years.

In the contest for power between the United States and France, both sides at the highest levels knew what was at stake and proceeded accordingly. Of course, neither Paris nor Washington was aware of every tactical ploy made by its wards in Saigon, nor did senior French and American officials know every detail of the "secret war" that unfolded between the French and American secret intelligence services and their Vietnamese minions. In this struggle the French seemed to hold most of the cards at the beginning. The nominal chief of state, Bao Dai, whose function was to appoint and replace prime ministers as suggested by the French, was fully responsive to French influence, as were many of the Vietnamese political hacks in Saigon, most of the senior officers of the Vietnamese army—who had served earlier in the French Colonial Army—and the leaders of the religious sects, whose large paramilitary forces were subsidized by the French. Moreover, French influence still predominated in the National Police. Prime Minister Diem had only a narrow political base and enjoyed no significant support outside Catholic circles. But he had the backing of the U.S. government. In successive attempts to oust Diem, the French squandered their assets piecemeal, trying to hide their hand while their General Ely—who was both high commissioner and military commander—appeared to cooperate with General Collins, the U.S. minister. The Americans, on the other hand, worked largely through Colonel Lansdale, head of a "special military mission" in Saigon operating under CIA direction. It supported Diem's secret services, which had broken free from French influence and been placed under his brother Nhu, and which played a major part in the clandestine struggle against the French.

The only apparent signs of this struggle were a series of "terrorist" bombings and minor clashes between armed groups in Saigon. Behind the scenes there were crosscurrents of political maneuvering in Saigon, such as the Vietnamese army chief of staff's almost open defiance of the Diem government. He was ultimately removed for his insubordination, though it seemed for a time that Diem would not be able to bring him to heel. Being "outside the loop," I had to read between the lines of the official reports from Saigon to gauge the flow of this struggle. Although I was able to piece together a fair picture of what the French were up to, I was generally ignorant of U.S. covert actions in support of Diem until some time later.

This clandestine power struggle climaxed in April 1955 when Diem survived the final French attempt to force the collapse of his government. The French had formed a coalition of the Cao Dai and Hoa Hao religious sects—whose large paramilitary forces were directly subsidized by the French—and the Binh Xuyen group, a mafialike criminal amalgamation which controlled gambling and other vice-related rackets in the Saigon-Cholon area. Some years before, the French had entrusted direction of the National Police to this venal group. This unlikely collection of bedfellows publicly threatened armed revolt unless Diem resigned his post as premier. Through a series of adroit covert maneuvers, engineered at least in part by Colonel Lansdale's group, one major faction of the Cao Dai sect was split off from the others, allowing Diem to deal with the remainder of the erstwhile coalition in piecemeal fashion. Army units, under the leadership of General Duong Van "Big" Minh, drove the Binh Xuyen out of Saigon, destroying their power in a month-long military campaign; this also brought the National Police under the control of Diem's government. Elements of the Cao Dai and Hoa Hao paramilitary forces were then brought into line successively, largely knuckling under to demonstrations of force by Vietnamese army units loyal to the government. By the summer of 1955, Diem was in uncontested control of the country's military and police forces, and French influence was no longer the dominant factor in South Vietnam.

The April 1955 crisis illustrates the weaknesses of the strict compartmentalization that existed in the intelligence and policy communities. At the height of this historically critical episode, the intelligence community was asked to prepare a special estimate on the prospects for Diem's survival in the face of the seemingly united opposition from the sects. In army intelligence we had no knowledge of Colonel Lansdale's operations nor of the nature and scope of the secret intelligence activities on Diem's behalf. In our ignorance of these matters, we believed Diem was unlikely to survive the major French effort to oust him. This placed us—and similarly "uncleared" elements of the intelligence community—in a position contrary to the CIA's view that Diem would prevail. At the final meeting at which the estimate was approved by the U.S. Intelligence Board, a CIA colleague took me aside to urge that army intelligence drop its dissent to the estimate, arguing that we should take his word for it that the anti-Diem coalition would not hold together. But he could cite no evidence to support this contention. I later learned that he was not authorized to disclose to us in army intelligence that the Cao Dai sect had already been covertly splintered through Lansdale's efforts. Unconvinced because of the lack of evidence, I advised the head of army intelligence to stand by his dissent; the State Department's intelligence chief, also apparently uninformed, joined us in the minority position. Had they been told the facts of the matter, these intelligence chiefs might have been spared the embarrassment of having "erroneously" misread the situation in this formal National Estimate.

Several aspects of this episode strike me as reflecting potentially significant weaknesses in the U.S. national security decision-making process. First, excessive compartmentalization of "sensitive" information can unduly narrow the consensus behind important policy moves and thus limit a thorough analysis of alternatives and consequences. Yes, sometimes this is essential in order to protect the secrecy of covert actions. In this case, our ignorance did not critically affect the tactical outcome, since the majority view reflected in the estimate encouraged the planners in their attempts to ensure the survival of the Diem government. But if the majority had embraced our view, the CIA would have had to disclose enough about their covert operations to bring us around to their position on the estimate. As a matter of principle, I believe that at least the heads of our intelligence services should be apprised of U.S. covert actions that affect situations in which their advice is sought by the National Security Council.

Another potential weakness in our system lies in the tendency of decision-makers to focus narrowly on what *we* are doing—on individual tactical initiatives—at the expense of broader strategic implications. This is especially true when our actions involve "sexy" covert actions such as a Bay of Pigs landing or support of a coup d'état. In this instance—breaking the power of the coalition against Diem—Washington seems to have given scant consideration to future consequences. If our action were to deprive the French of their position in guiding the future of South Vietnam, were they not likely to withdraw their military forces? Without their presence, the Vietnamese army would lack the capability to defend against North Vietnamese aggression. The French Expeditionary Force was also the largest Western military force in the region; no others were in a position to come quickly to the aid of the South Vietnamese. Without the assurance of such backing, could the South Vietnamese military forces gain the self-assurance and confidence necessary to stand up to the North Vietnamese? Secretary of State John Foster Dulles was thinking in terms of forming a South East Asia Treaty Organization (SEATO) to provide a defensive "umbrella" over Vietnam, but the withdrawal of the French army would diminish SEATO's military strength by some 150,000 troops. What would fill the strategic military vacuum created by their withdrawal?

The chief policymakers presumably would have urged that we take one step at a time, that the first step was to ensure the survival of a pro-American, non-Communist government in Saigon. Francophobes would have added that if this meant the elimination of French influence and power from the region, so much the better. It would simplify matters and rid us of a major nuisance and hindrance. The policies favored by the French would not, after all, preclude the absorption of South Vietnam by Ho's government in Hanoi. Washington believed that the successful implementation of our policies, on the other hand, would ensure the survival of a non-Communist government in the South. Little thought was given to the long-term consequences of our short-term success. Nothing in the historical record indicates that Dulles or any other responsible official at the time was concerned about the likelihood that displacing the French from Indochina would lead to the ultimate commitment of a half-million American troops in pursuit of our aim of preventing the unification of Vietnam.

With the ouster of the French, the South Vietnamese—not the United States—became the dominant voice in Vietnamese politics. Contrary to some assertions, Washington never exercised anything near the degree of influence or control over the Vietnamese government under Diem—or any of his successors—that the French did before 1955. Washington had neither the inclination nor the knowhow to exercise leverage skillfully and effectively. In November 1960 we intervened when Vietnamese army airborne troops under Colonel Thi attacked Diem's palace in an attempt to overthrow the government; the American MAAG chief engineered a ceasefire between the rebels and the Presidential Guard, enabling Diem to summon enough loyal troops from nearby provinces to suppress the coup. In the early fall of 1963, we sought—unsuccessfully—to dissuade the Diem government from its forceful suppression of the Buddhists by cutting off funds used to support his special forces, which had raided a number of Buddhist temples. The Kennedy administration "leveraged" Vietnam's unstable political future by indicating to the Vietnamese generals that we would not disassociate ourselves from any non-Communist successor government to Diem, thereby encouraging them to mount their coup in November 1963. Our December 1972 bombing of Hanoi was a form of leverage aimed more at encouraging a reluctant Saigon to accept a virtually suicidal cease-fire agreement than at bringing Hanoi back to the negotiating table. But on other occasions we temporized, exhorted, or pleaded, yet otherwise refrained from applying leverage commensurate with our escalating investment in the destiny of South Vietnam. We consistently failed to employ our leverage to coerce Diem into instituting the political reforms necessary to attract more popular support to his government. On many occasions our self-righteous refusal to intervene in internal Vietnamese political matters dictated a course of events against our interests.

My point here is to emphasize that, having eliminated French influence and military power from Vietnam, Washington created a strategic geopolitical vacuum in Indochina which fatally handicapped our ability to achieve our long-term goals. Many voices within the U.S. government at the time suggested that Diem's one-dimensional government would prove inadequate to the task over the long run, as indeed it did. I remember discussing these matters in late 1954 or early 1955 with Paul Kattenberg, then the State Department intelligence bureau's Indochina desk officer, and agreeing with him that the most profitable American course of action over the long term would be an offer to Hanoi of $500 million in grant aid for the reconstruction of war damage. We saw such an offer as one that Ho Chi Minh would not refuse, since it would afford a means for maintaining independence from Soviet and Chinese domination. It would certainly have been less costly than the alternative we chose.

After 1955 it became popular in Washington to speak of Diem's "miracle" in South Vietnam. This miracle went beyond the fact of his mere survival, though his admirers in Washington were quick to nudge intelligence analysts who had predicted he would not succeed. Diem did manage to gain control over the army and police, and over the refugee problem, gradually resettling hundreds of thousands in new, Catholic ghettos in the South Vietnamese countryside. He had also managed to make a start toward economic development and agrarian reform. At least on the surface, South Vietnam enjoyed a substantial measure of peace and stability. I began to feel that perhaps my earlier pessimism had been unjustified.

But this was merely a lull before the storm. The Communists were not actively and seriously contesting the Diem government in the South; they were preoccupied with consolidating their position in the North, just as Diem was consolidating his in the South. Although almost a million northerners—mostly Catholics—had fled to the South, the Hanoi regime had to establish an effective government over the more than twenty million people remaining in the North. Ho's Democratic Republic had governed the outlying regions, but with the French withdrawal they had to establish administrative functions throughout the densely populated Red River Delta and in a number of major cities (Hanoi, Haiphong, Nam Dinh). They had to take control of the economy of a rice-deficit region and reshape it along "socialist lines," ruthlessly implementing a thoroughgoing Communist-style land-reform program which sparked substantial popular resistance and provoked a major uprising in at least one region (Nghe An Province). They strove to modernize their army and to assimilate into their regular forces the ninety thousand troops and political cadre withdrawn from the South.

Hanoi's policy toward the South was for the moment one of "legal struggle." Some ten thousand hard-core Communist covert agents—a clandestine network—remained behind in the South to organize and lead legal opposition groups in a peaceful struggle against the Diem government. They formed "committees for the strict application of the Geneva Accords" and "struggle groups for the defense of the people against reactionary oppression," and so forth. Their main aim was to make it difficult for the Diem government to consolidate its position, and to develop a broad-based political demand in the South for the reunification elections called for in the Geneva Accords. The Diem government in 1955 refused to enter discussions with Hanoi about such elections. Hanoi denounced Saigon's refusal, but at that time it was not in a position to do much about it.

In the spring of 1956 we began receiving reports in Washington of a Communist military buildup north of the DMZ, the demilitarized zone between North and South Vietnam called for in the Geneva Accords. There began to be some uneasiness over the likelihood of military action by Hanoi to unify the country by force. As the deadline for the elections grew near, reports of the buildup increased. Most of them were from agents (untested ones) who claimed to have access to the panhandle of North Vietnam. Because there were no confirmations from other sources, we suspected that these reports were a product of "agent intoxication."

When we briefed the Watch Committee on the situation in late June, we noted that a massive buildup was being reported, but we had no hard evidence to support the claims of the agents. We were not anxious to issue a serious warning of possible hostilities on the basis of the flimsy information available, but at the same time we could not categorically reject the notion that a buildup was underway; the absence of other indicators might be part of a deception plan or a reflection of airtight security measures north of the DMZ. We suggested an aerial reconnaissance mission to check on the reported buildup. At that time U.S. aircraft were not permitted to overfly Communist territory (the U-2 was just coming into use). But a week or so later I saw reports from an international control commission team reporting that they had seen contrails from high-flying jets over the DMZ, and I assumed that the mission had been flown. I had been requested to identify potential targets which would permit us to verify whether a buildup was in progress. A few days later, a friend in the army intelligence collection staff advised me that my needs had been "taken care of" and that the results would soon be available. Weeks went by, however, with no further word, while agent reports continued to indicate an ongoing buildup. Finally, about two days before the ostensible invasion date (July 22, the second anniversary of the Geneva Accords), I pressed the issue, raising substantial hell and pointing out that if a reconnaissance mission had indeed been flown, someone ought to make the information obtained available to those responsible for analyzing the situation. So I was ushered into a small room in a specially secured area, where I was allowed to view some overlays prepared by photo interpreters, sketching a dozen or so military installations in the panhandle area northward from the DMZ to the city of Vinh. I had nothing in the way of previous sketches or photos with which to compare these overlays, and it took some hours of study before I was able to conclude that the kinds and sizes of military facilities shown on these overlays were compatible with what we knew from A-1 sources to be the normal deployment pattern of the North Vietnamese army in the region. Thus photos taken by the U.S. carrier-borne jet fighters that conducted the reconnaissance mission emphatically disproved the reported massive buildup north of the DMZ.

Reports from the mission had been delayed because a new, restricted compartment had been created to handle the results of "sensitive" reconnaissance programs, especially the U-2 program. I was not cleared for this

Demilitarized Zone

Dong Ha
Quang Tri
Cam Lo
Khe Sanh
Tchepone
LAOS
Hue
Phu Bai
THAILAND
An Hoa
Da Nang
REPUBLIC OF VIETNAM
Tam Ky
Chu Lai
My Lai
Route 14
Dak To
Kon Tum
Route 19
Pleiku
An Khé
Qui Nhon
0   25   50 Miles
0   50 Kilometers
Route 7B
Tuy Hoa
Ban Me
Thuot
Route 21
CAMBODIA
Gia Nghia
Nha Trang
N
Da Lat
Cam Ranh
Phnom Penh
Song Be
Bao Loc
Phan Rang
Nui Ba Den
Tay Ninh
Lai Khe
Route 1
Ben Suc
Bien
Hoa
Phan Thiet
Saigon
Ha Tien
My Tho
Long Binh
Vung Tau
Vinh Long
Rach Gia
SOUTH
CHINA
SEA
Bac Lieu
Gulf of
Thailand
Ca Mau
Peninsula

new compartment and did not even know of its existence; clearances were handled on a very limited "need to know" basis. My situation created a dilemma for the system, however, since I had requested the photo mission, had listed the targets, and was one of the few people in Washington who could have made sense of the results. Photo interpreters unfamiliar with the area could make sketches of trenches and barracks and identify military facilities and anti-aircraft positions, but they knew nothing of the structure of the North Vietnamese army nor of its normal deployment patterns. Thus the new system almost defeated itself—the person who most needed to know was not cleared for access. (Shades of Pearl Harbor!) As it was, common sense prevailed, the information was made available at the last minute, and we were able to advise all interested parties that information "from a reliable source" clearly refuted the likelihood of an imminent invasion.

One of the major post–Geneva issues confronting Washington concerned the optimum size of the Vietnamese military force structure that the United States was willing to support. From 1954 through 1958 the issue came up repeatedly. The Vietnamese army was in considerable disarray after the Geneva armistice. Many northern soldiers simply disappeared rather than move to the South, and others in the South simply wished to go home, whether or not demobilization was permitted. The regroupment to the South caused considerable confusion and disruption, since more units had to be accommodated than could be handled by military facilities in the South. Equipment and supplies hastily evacuated from the North were scattered about in almost haphazard fashion. No one knew how much there was or where it might be located. The need to occupy regions in the South that had long been under Communist control taxed the operational planning apparatus, and much of the army was busy for prolonged periods in operations against the dissident sects. When these extraordinary problems had finally been resolved, the question remained of what kind and size of military force would be required in the South. There were serious concerns that Washington avoid trying to maintain a bloated military force far beyond the limited ability of the Vietnamese economy to support. Sometime in the autumn of 1954, as I recall it, the State Department asked the Joint Chiefs of Staff to recommend a force level adequate to defend South Vietnam. In army intelligence we spelled out the nature of the threat, and the joint staff—after some interservice pulling and shoving—arrived at the judgment that a force level of about 300,000, including naval and air components, could defend the country. This did not include the necessary paramilitary forces to maintain internal security. The secretary of state rejected this Joint Chiefs judgment and asked for another look at the problem with a view to determining the *minimum* force required. The joint staff restudied the problem, shaved a few thousand here and there, revised a few assumptions, and submitted a new figure still above 275,000. This too was rejected by State, with a demand for a figure that reflected an *absolute minimum force* for a limited defense of the South. After a third look, the joint staff sent back the second figure virtually unchanged, declaring that from a professional military standpoint, an effective defense could not be ensured by a smaller force. When told that the costs for a force of that size were well above what State believed was appropriate for the United States to support, the joint staff inquired what costs would be considered appropriate. State then provided a cost figure and asked what force level could be supported by that amount. The joint staff studied the problem and came up with a considerably smaller force structure, on the order of about 150,000, noting that the smaller force level could not provide an effective defense of South Vietnam. Nevertheless the smaller force level was adopted as the one the U.S. would support. American aid programs—and the Vietnamese military forces—were revamped accordingly, bringing a considerable reduction in the standing military forces of South Vietnam.

The considered judgment of the Joint Chiefs of Staff was rejected as the basis for U.S. policy decisions for fiscal and political reasons. The recommended larger force would have cost twice as much as the smaller force that was approved, and it would ultimately have saddled Vietnam with a burden it could never have assumed on its own. But the large figure would have inflated the budget and made it vulnerable to congressional objection. The fundamental incongruity of pursuing a course of action that would almost certainly invite a strong Communist reaction, while at the same time deliberately refusing to establish the military capabilities required to cope with that reaction, escaped the decision-makers but was apparent to some of us then and over the next few years.

By 1956 we had concluded that the principal threat from the North was not an open invasion but rather a resumption of the people's war in the South, supported by infiltration from the North. We expected the Communists to embark on this course in the absence of progress toward unification within the Geneva framework. We were convinced they would not long accept a divided Vietnam; that they had agreed to the armistice at Geneva reluctantly and only with what they believed to be assurances of ultimate unification; and that they would renew the armed struggle at the earliest opportunity if denied the fruits of their defeat of the French.

The likelihood of a renewed insurgency was not seriously accepted outside the intelligence community. Diem's miracle was given greater credence than it merited, because it was the kind of good news that policy-makers welcome; it confirmed the correctness of their earlier policies and programs, and allowed planners to focus on other, more immediately pressing matters. Our intelligence judgments tended to be dismissed as typically Cassandra-like, and some officials even suggested we were shifting our ground (to emphasize the potential insurgent threat) merely so that we could cover all bets. Our continued expressions of concern were also thought to be "sour grapes" for having been "wrong" in predicting that Diem would not succeed.

In army intelligence we agreed with the CIA that the Communists seemed likely to turn toward large-scale guerrilla activity after 1957 as the only means of achieving their objective. We also calculated in 1956 that the current South Vietnamese forces could delay the seizure of Saigon by the North Vietnamese in a direct invasion by no more than two months—just about the time it would take to walk briskly there from the DMZ. But we repeated our view that the more likely threat was a major guerrilla effort supported by infiltration. We noted that despite security improvements in the South, the Communists remained capable of developing a level of guerrilla activity that could deprive the Saigon government of effective control over wide areas.

One of the primary tasks of the joint staff is to develop plans for the defense of American interests against potential threats. Such plans include an intelligence annex, which outlines the threat that the plan is designed to counter, lists the enemy forces that can be brought to bear, analyzes courses of action open to the enemy, and assesses the relative likelihood of their adoption and the enemy's capabilities in each instance. This annex also assesses terrain and weather factors, limitations imposed by lines of communication, and political and economic factors affecting the conduct of military operations in the area. Intelligence staffs are responsible for preparing these annexes; in army intelligence we usually worked closely with the intelligence section (J-2) of the joint staff in developing their contributions to Joint Chiefs' operations plans.

Working within the framework of the situation illuminated by the intelligence annex, the planners first develop a concept of operations, then a detailed plan for implementing the concept. Such concepts usually involve a statement of the friendly forces required, an outline plan for their deployment to the area, and a concept for their employment after arrival, including locations of major support facilities and lines of communication. The detailed plans deal with ways of implementing the concept— that is, moving the troops and their supplies: numbers of airlift sorties and surface transport and cargo ship voyages; tonnages of fuel, ammunition, food and other supplies required; and where, when, and how these would be moved. It is never assumed that these plans will be pulled off the shelf and implemented as originally written, but their existence and periodic refinement give staffs a degree of familiarity with the potential theaters of operations. They serve as useful guides to the problems that would affect the use of military forces there, and indicate what would be required to move an American force of a given size to that region and to sustain it there in active operations.

The plan for the defense of Southeast Asia came up for revision in 1956, at a time when the Eisenhower administration was pushing the "massive retaliation" concept and redesigning American forces to take advantage of our nuclear supremacy. Earlier versions of the Southeast Asia plan had called for eight to twelve U.S. Army divisions as the minimum

ground force required to assist the Vietnamese in defending against an
overt North Vietnamese invasion—the only enemy course of action that
the Joint Chiefs wished seriously to address. In 1956 the belief grew in
some circles that the United States could not—and should not—consider
using a force that large; our Korean experience had shown the disadvan-
tages of engaging in a land war against the population masses of Asia.
Hence there was considerable pressure for the joint staff to devise a much
more conservative plan, one that would not entail the commitment of
large numbers of ground troops but would take advantage of our nuclear
capabilities. The army staff was adamantly opposed to any significant reduction in the proposed army force level in the operation plan, for both
professional and parochial reasons. Professionally, the application of army
doctrine to the geographic and military conditions that would exist made
the larger force requisite to success. Parochially, acceptance of a lower
force level would tend to reduce the need to maintain larger army forces.
At one point the army did consider falling back to a U.S. ground force of
five or six divisions as the minimum reinforcement to avoid defeat of the
South Vietnamese under certain assumptions regarding the availability of
nuclear weapons to the American commander. This was still considered
too large a force by the nuclear warfare proponents, whereupon Admiral
Radford, chairman of the Joint Chiefs and the leading advocate of "massive retaliation" among the senior military officers, directed one of his
personal aides to develop a concept for the use of tactical nuclear weapons
with minimal ground forces to check a formal North Vietnamese invasion.
This officer tested the concept on me before submitting it upward for approval. I told him it was totally infeasible, unworkable, and based on
wholly fallacious assumptions. It provided for two forces, each comprising
a nuclear-equipped Honest John rocket battalion backed by an infantry
regimental combat team to secure a beachhead perimeter to be put ashore,
one at Da Nang and the other at Nha Trang. The concept assumed that
the North Vietnamese would mount a formal, direct invasion (contrary to
intelligence estimates), that they would advance along the coastal road
(where they would be vulnerable to interdiction), and that their advance
could be effectively blocked by the nuclear rockets in the northern beachhead. The southern force was actually superfluous if the northern force

did its job; it was added primarily because no one would believe that a single U.S. regiment could block the advance of the entire North Vietnamese army.

Admiral Radford quickly embraced this concept, which became known as the Radford Plan, and he rammed it through the Joint Chiefs, which passed it on as simply a concept worth noting. The army dissented strongly. The admiral briefed President Eisenhower on the concept. Ike is reputed to have observed that he would be "interested" in seeing such a concept developed further. (I'm not convinced that he actually believed it was feasible). In any event, Radford sent the concept to the commander-in-chief of the Pacific Theater (CINCPAC), and asked him to develop a detailed implementation plan. The Radford Plan continued to be kicked around at CINCPAC until about 1960, despite its blatant unworkability.

General Maxwell Taylor, who succeeded Ridgway as the army's chief of staff, was disturbed at the relative inflexibility of the nuclear-first strategy of the times. Shortly after he took office, he asked the army staff to prepare a study of how nuclear weapons might have been employed at Dien Bien Phu to prevent a French defeat. Our understanding was that he intended to discuss the subject with President Eisenhower over lunch, with a view to illustrating his argument for a "graduated response" to foreign aggression, rather than the immediate use of nuclear weapons. I worked through the night with a team of operations planners and nuclear effects experts to put the study together, using my knowledge of how the opposing forces had been deployed during the Dien Bien Phu siege two years earlier—the enemy's entrenchment pattern, his supply system, and so forth. The nuclear-effects officers, after studying my reconstruction of the battlefield conditions, devised a concept of placing fifteen or sixteen nominal-yield (twenty-kiloton) weapons in a circular pattern around the French defensive complex, detonating them as close to the French defenses as possible (without subjecting them to blast damage) in order to "take out" the maximum number of enemy forces in forward positions. Our calculations showed that the roughly doughnut-shaped area of maximum effect would have inflicted about ten thousand casualties on the enemy, less than a third of his forces in the Dien Bien Phu area. The study noted, of course, that the presence of winds from any direction in the target area would have covered the French defenses with lethal radioactive debris; the plan would thus have been feasible only in the unlikely event that the air was absolutely still. Beyond the human casualties, a nuclear strike of that sort would have had, of course, a traumatic psychological effect on the surviving Viet Minh troops. But there was some question whether the French—even without an "illwind"—would have been in any better shape to continue the battle than the Viet Minh forces. In any event, the study apparently suited General Taylor's purposes.

Parenthetically, my work on this study did produce an incident that discouraged my attitude over the years and was among a number of similar incidents that contributed to my ultimate decision to leave the Pentagon's sometimes overwhelming bureaucratic parochialism. Early the next morning, after the staff study had been completed, I was to brief the general then heading army intelligence on its outcome. Introducing the purpose of the briefing, my division chief noted that I had spent the entire night at the office, getting home only briefly to shave and put on a fresh shirt before coming back for this briefing. The general glared at me and asked, "What do you want me to do, weep?" I responded, "No sir. It wasn't the first time I've done so, and I imagine it won't be the last." The general's remark stung me deeply and erased the satisfaction I had gleaned from a job I thought was well done.

Shortly thereafter I briefed General Taylor at length on Laos. It was not a formal presentation—he simply wanted to talk to someone who knew about conditions in Laos at a time when we were seeing fresh signs that the North Vietnamese were not complying fully with the Geneva Accords there. My new division chief, who had accompanied me to the general's office, was clearly petrified lest I embarrass him by failing to perform satisfactorily in the presence of the "almighty." He sat stiffly at attention, grasping the armrests of his chair in the manner of a white-knuckled airline passenger, throughout the session. General Taylor, meanwhile, was quite relaxed, coming round to the front of his desk and leaning back against it while studying the map I had placed on an easel. He had many questions about terrain, lines of communication, and the positions of the opposing forces, and was obviously seeking an education about a strange new part of his world. In this regard he was much easier to brief than his immediate predecessors, Generals Collins and Ridgway. I respected "Lightning Joe" Collins, but he seemed to have difficulty bridging quickly from one set of facts to another. During the Korean War, my briefings on the situation in Indochina were always preceded by a presentation on Korea at the weekly Army Policy Council meetings. My In dochina map had the same dimensions as the one used for Korea—about six feet by six feet—but because Indochina was twice the size of Korea, my Indochina map was only half the scale of the other. General Collins, among others present, had trouble retaining this differentiation. He repeatedly asked why the French did not establish a line across the "narrow" waist of Indochina similar to that in Korea—overlooking the fact that such a front would extend over 250 miles in Indochina in contrast to the 125-mile front in Korea. I repeatedly explained the difference in scale of the maps, pointing out that to defend a line of that length would require a force much larger than that available to the French in Indochina.

Similarly, Collins more than once asked in frustration why the French did not simply withdraw southward down the coast from Tonkin to establish a more readily defensible line across Indochina. Each time I had to explain that this would not simply involve a "withdrawal" but would require the French to mount an offensive campaign and fight their way through three hundred miles of enemy-occupied territory to reach the proposed new defensive line. I didn't feel that Collins—or most of the other officers present—fully grasped the difference between the kind of war we were fighting in Korea and the one the French were fighting in Indochina. When he was U.S. minister in Saigon in 1954–1955, moreover, he sometimes displayed political naiveté in his unwonted trust of General Ely during our struggle to oust the French from Vietnam.

General Ridgway never demonstrated naiveté in my presence; he correctly recognized the significance of almost any set of facts without requiring a full-scale explanation. He was, I believe, the most brilliant of the early postwar army chiefs of staff. Although he may have lacked some of the suave social graces and intellectual breadth displayed by General Taylor, Ridgway seemed to me to be equally sharp, far more decisive and self-confident, and more consistently on the mark in his grasp of complex situations than either Generals Taylor or Collins.

I was less at ease in Ridgway's presence. His bearing seemed always erect and formal; he listened attentively to all that was said to him. His cold grey eyes bore in intensely on those of the speaker, and his demeanor exuded such seriousness that it never seemed appropriate—at least to me—to inject a humorous note into the discussion as a means of relaxing the tension. But he was an admirable soldier, and I would sooner have served under General Ridgway than under any other military officer I have known. He had a way of instilling confidence in the people with whom he worked. I believe he is the most underrated senior U.S. military officer of the immediate postwar generation, superior in most respects to his contemporaries—Mark Clark, Joe Collins, Omar Bradley, Maxwell Taylor, Arthur Radford, Arleigh Burke, the lot.

The Geneva Accords bound both sides—the French Union and the Viet Minh—not to increase the size of their military forces in Indochina above that existing on the date the armistice was signed. State Department lawyers were of the opinion that the U.S. military advisers then in Vietnam could be construed as being included on the French Union side, and therefore they interpreted the agreement to mean that our Military Assistance Advisory Group in Indochina could not exceed 342 officers and men, the number present on July 21, 1954. Frantic efforts were made to move some of these MAAG personnel to both Cambodia and Laos before the cease-fire took effect, to establish our right to have military missions in those states as well as in Vietnam.

This self-imposed ceiling on the strength of MAAG was an irritant to U.S. policymaking over the next eight years or so. Initially Washington strictly observed the limit, but late in 1954 the Eisenhower administration felt it necessary to augment our military mission to help bring order out of chaos in the French logistical situation following the relatively hasty withdrawal of their forces from Tonkin. A Temporary Equipment Recovery Mission (TERM) was established for this purpose. Its creation was cleared with the international control commission responsible for supervising the Geneva Accords, which sanctioned a temporary increase of some three hundred in the number of American military men in Vietnam. Members of this increment were to wear civilian clothes rather than military uniforms while in Indochina, in order to avoid any visible impression of an augmented U.S. military presence. The subterfuge that we were staying within the Geneva "ceiling" was maintained until about 1961, when we began an open reinforcement of our military mission. But as late as 1960 we continued to hamstring the effectiveness of our military activities by adhering to the fiction of the augmented ceiling, and the control commission meticulously kept count of the arrivals and departures of American military personnel at the Saigon airport. The U.S. mission took intricate steps to shift some of its members temporarily out of the country to cool their heels in Bangkok, Hong Kong, or Manila, so that special teams on temporary duty from the States could enter Indochina and carry out their assignments without our exceeding the ceiling.

This restriction inhibited the determination of our military to take over from the departing French full responsibility for training the Vietnamese military forces. MAAG had been anxious to become involved in such training as early as 1951, and had been particularly frustrated during the accelerated expansion of the Vietnamese forces in 1953, when the French dragged their feet in applying modern training methods and techniques. But the French resisted our entry into the training field in Vietnam because it would have represented an inroad in their special standing as the metropolitan state in the French Union; they were reluctant to give up any more of their status as the colonizing power than they had to. Our army was proud of its achievement in creating a large Republic of Korea (ROK) army in the midst of an active war, and believed that our experience there applied to Indochina as well. The French visited our training facilities in Korea at MAAG's request but remained unmoved and insisted on adhering to their "less effective" techniques. They refused to acknowledge that our mass-production training methods in Korea were in any way relevant to their needs in Indochina.

By the spring of 1955, however, they apparently saw the handwriting on the wall, and agreed, after protracted negotiations, to incorporate American military personnel in a joint training mission, which the Americans dubbed TRIM (Training Relations and Instruction Mission). No new ceiling was authorized to accommodate this additional MAAG function;

TRIM had to be fitted under the ceiling of 642 that had been set for MAAG and TERM combined. The "equipment recovery" function of TERM had largely been completed, and it could be phased out in large part, though there was a continuing need for advisers in the logistical field above the number that had been present before the cease-fire. Some historians have speculated that TERM and TRIM were used largely to cover the introduction of CIA personnel into Indochina. While some army Special Forces teams detailed to work with CIA in Vietnam may have been brought in under one or the other of these programs, this was by no means the major premise for either; our military rigorously guarded the limited number of "slots" available for the essential tasks of those missions—to bring the chaotic arms inventory under control, and to train Vietnam's conventional military forces.

TRIM continued as a joint mission with the French for some time after the departure of the last of the French expeditionary force units in April 1956. The French briefly maintained a military mission in Vietnam, most of it comprising their contribution to TRIM. But this mission was soon reduced to only a fraction of its pre-cease-fire size when more than six thousand French officers and NCOs had been assigned to the Vietnamese army. Many of them served in Vietnamese combat units down to the company and platoon level; others occupied many of the key positions in training facilities and staffs above battalion level.

Our MAAG had mixed reactions to the rapid reduction in the size of the French mission after the cease-fire. They were glad to see the French go, because this gave the Vietnamese the opportunity to "mature" by gaining experience in more senior positions in their force structure, and it held promise for greater American military influence. On the other hand, it was increasingly clear that the Vietnamese were ill-prepared to assume full responsibility at the higher command and staff levels and in technical areas. Moreover, the ceiling on the size of MAAG precluded it from establishing itself in the intimate relationship with the Vietnamese that the French had enjoyed, and as we ourselves had practiced in Korea. There were simply not enough MAAG personnel to replace all of the six thousand French "advisers" who were leaving Vietnam; MAAG could not provide advisers below the regimental level.

Nonetheless, for twenty years after 1956 the U.S. military had exclusive training and advisory responsibilities with the Vietnamese military forces. MAAG, and later MACV (Military Assistance Command Vietnam), shaped ARVN's (Army of the Republic of Vietnam) combat units after U.S. models and concepts; we molded its training facilities in the image of our own institutions; we inculcated in ARVN our doctrine and practices; and we supervised the operations and activities of those forces in peace and war. We brought thousands of Vietnamese officers and men to the United States to attend our own military schools and for on-the-job training—six thousand of them by 1961. One of the great mysteries of the American involvement in the Indochina wars is why the Vietnamese army failed to develop into a first-rate military force, as did the ROK army. Why did our efforts not "take" on the Vietnamese as they had on the Koreans? Why were our training methods and techniques effective in one case and not in the other? A chronic complaint of our advisers in Vietnam from the 1950s to the 1970s was inadequate leadership in the Vietnamese army—inadequate both in numbers and in quality. Yet for twenty years we supervised the organization and training of that army and advised in its administration and operation.

While the personnel ceiling did limit our involvement to some extent in the 1950s, we overcame that by bringing Vietnamese to our own schools for training. After 1961 there was no limit on the number of advisers we could maintain. I am unaware of any studies of the reasons for our lack of success in this regard, by the Pentagon or by any of our staff colleges. But I believe this phenomenon was one of the most important factors contributing to the failure of our Vietnam policy, and I should think it is important that we understand the reasons for it.

5
The View
from
Pearl
Harbor

AFTER EIGHT YEARS in the Pentagon, focused exclusively on the Indochina problem, I accepted an opportunity in the summer of 1957 to transfer to the intelligence staff at the army's headquarters for the Pacific Theater in Hawaii. In this new assignment my duties were somewhat broader; our area of interest ranged from the Soviet Far East down through China and Southeast Asia. My initial duties were as deputy chief of the branch responsible for intelligence analysis of all types. Soon I was given the task of planning for the integration of the intelligence analysis components of the army portion of the Far East Command in Tokyo, which was several times the size of our staff in Honolulu. To accommodate most of these additional people without inflating the size of our headquarters complement, we decided to create a separate intelligence support center operating under the staff supervision of the intelligence section. To plan for the staffing of this center, we prepared an intelligence production program aimed directly at supporting the various war plans for the expanded Pacific Theater, and I visited Washington to coordinate this program with army intelligence in the Pentagon and with the CIA.

We created a four-man team to perform the detailed research necessary for data on the Vietnamese Communist military forces. We proposed, and ASCI Washington agreed, that we assume full responsibility for this order-of-battle problem on behalf of the U.S. intelligence community. Never before had the work of army intelligence elements in a theater headquarters been so neatly dovetailed with that of the army staff in Washington. Unfortunately the arrangement did not pan out at all. USARPAC kept up the effort for some time after my departure late in 1960, but it gradually lost impetus. Perhaps the reasons for its having been undertaken were forgotten over time, or perhaps those responsible for the work assumed that the intelligence staff in Saigon, which mushroomed after 1962, had become responsible. When the Defense Intelligence Agency was established in 1961 in Washington, it absorbed the analytical component of the army intelligence staff. Thus by 1962 there was no institutional memory in Washington about where the responsibility for the North Vietnamese order of battle had been assigned.

In any event, by the mid-1960s no intelligence staff at any level was doing the basic intelligence research job that ought to have been done on Vietnam. As a result, there was a general absence of competent research on the role of the North Vietnamese army in supporting the insurgency in the South, and how that mission had affected the people's army in the North.

Success in working out an intelligence production plan led to my being asked to revamp the army intelligence support structure for the Far East–Pacific region. Here the objective was not to save manpower but to make the best use of the limited resources available. Our solution led to some reduction of the theater military intelligence group then based in Tokyo, an augmentation of the Eighth Army headquarters in Korea with specialized intelligence elements, creation of a new detachment to support the IX Corps headquarters in Okinawa and also to function as a modest theater intelligence reserve, and realignment of the detachments in Hawaii belonging to the 25th Division and to our own headquarters.

This project helped equip me with skills and understanding that would come in handy in the not too distant future.

While engaged in these broader planning tasks, I worked closely with our current intelligence staff in order to improve the quality of its work. We wanted it to move beyond traditional current reporting, which produced routinized, cautious, bland, and not very helpful information without much interpretation. We wanted to place events in a broader context and to project the likely implications and consequences of current developments. We wanted our analysis to be more "apperceptive," never assuming that the consumer knew everything the analyst knew and was able to read between the lines. The general also wanted me to work closely with our estimates officers, to urge them to undertake more perceptive analyses of enemy capabilities and probable courses of action, to spell out more clearly how our potential adversaries might react under differing circumstances, and to highlight those factors that would most critically influence their decisions.

Our people did good work on the Vietnam estimates, ultimately convincing our colleagues in the other services and at CINCPAC of "massive infiltration" as North Vietnam's most likely course of action in the South. But we could not seem to persuade them of what the consequences of that course of action would be. Improving the quality of our current intelligence also proved to be difficult.

My own duties broadened progressively during my three and a half years at USARPAC, shifting from direct management of intelligence analysis to longer-range planning for the employment of army intelligence resources throughout the theater. The intelligence chief, however, wanted me to keep a close eye on our current intelligence and estimative work, even after I was moved up to become his special assistant. Hence I continued to follow closely the evolving situation in Indochina as well as to maintain an overview of the rest of the theater. I was also able during three years to visit at least once nearly all the countries in the Far East, and to become familiar with their military intelligence services. USARPAC assisted in training intelligence personnel from many of these Asian states, and we also worked closely with the Australians and New Zealanders. All these activities contributed substantially to my professional education.

My visit to Malaysia in 1958 was particularly instructive. It began with a formal conference in Singapore with British, Australian, New Zealand, and American military intelligence specialists; I was one of several U.S. Army representatives attending from Honolulu and Tokyo. At the conclusion of this meeting, where we exchanged information on Far East developments and arranged for future discussions among us, I traveled by night train to Kuala Lumpur, where I was the weekend guest of an old friend with whom I had worked in Washington. He was a British colonel, who at the time was commanding the Malay Federation's armored car regiment. This unit's discipline and esprit, which I observed in training and in garrison, surpassed those of any Vietnamese army unit I saw before or later.

While I was there, the colonel found it necessary to sack one of the British squadron commanders for failing to execute an order properly, and replaced him with a Malay—the first Malaysian officer to command an armored unit. The new squadron commander was, of course, jubilant, and the entire unit rejoiced at this fresh sign of the evolving Malay nation's progress toward ultimate autonomy. It was evident that the officers and men both loved and respected their leader, and would rather have been in the Federation armored car regiment than anywhere else in the world.

After this weekend sojourn I rejoined some of my fellow American conferees for a week-long tour from Kuala Lumpur back to Singapore. En route we visited a wide variety of British and Malaysian military, security, and civil administrative posts and training facilities. We visited a British army division command post, lunched with a British army battalion in its jungle barracks, visited Federation police headquarters, were briefed at sector and regional operational centers, and toured the Royal Army's jungle warfare training center. Our main interest was in the intelligence and security setup employed in the British campaign against the Communist terrorist movement in Malaysia, which was in its last successful stage. We visited the combined intelligence and security facilities at every territorial command level as well as those of the major military units. We were

briefed as well on the major pacification concepts and operational techniques employed against the terrorists, including population- and food-
control measures, search operations, jungle tactics and patrols, and
specialized intelligence operations such as "defector inducement," which
played an important role in the British success. They were proud of their
achievement, though neither arrogant nor boastful, and were quick to
point out the special character of the insurgency problem in Malaysia in
contrast to those in the Philippines, Vietnam, and Burma. In this connection, the most important factors, they thought, were the proximity of a reliable supply source for the Viet Minh in China—as opposed to the
relative isolation of Malaysia—and the fact that the terrorist movement in
Malaysia was based primarily on only one element of the population, the
"overseas" Chinese.

There were many other reasons behind the successful counterinsurgency operations of the British in Malaysia, but perhaps the most important was the effective integration of intelligence and operational activities.
This was feasible largely because of the complete unity of command on
the British side, which was from the top down to the lowest level. The
British high commissioner was responsible for overall direction of both
civil and military activities, British and Malaysian. Military forces and
civil government institutions operated under his direction. There was little doubt at any level about who had overall authority for directing counterinsurgency activities. A combined intelligence center was established at
every echelon, through which the intelligence activities of the British and
Federation military units and police and security forces were meshed and
directed. A senior intelligence officer was designated at each center; all
intelligence, counterintelligence, and security services were represented
there, and all activities of those services were conducted under his supervision. The British believed that intelligence was the key to success in
eliminating the terrorists, and devoted the resources necessary to accomplish the task efficiently.

Each intelligence center maintained detailed order-of-battle data files
on the terrorist forces within its jurisdiction, and insured that all intelligence services and operational elements had access to all the information
they needed to perform their roles. The center ensured effective exploita-

tion of prisoners and defectors for the benefit of all intelligence services. It prepared intelligence reports and studies to support operational planning by civil agencies and military units in the area. It maintained close liaison with the combined intelligence centers in adjacent districts and ensured an effective flow of intelligence vertically as well as laterally. By 1958, at the time of our visit, the British intelligence and security system was functioning smoothly and with precision. Although austerely manned—like all British military organizations we visited—its degree of professionalism and efficiency and the success of its counterinsurgency effort attested to its effectiveness.

On display in each intelligence center was a schematic diagram of the Communist structure in that particular district, including photos of key members of the organization. The extent of the information was phenomenal, often including even the type of weapon carried by an individual terrorist, sometimes the number of rounds of ammunition which he had available to him, and occasionally even the serial number of his weapon. This reflected painstaking care in the collection and collation of information, meticulous debriefing of defectors and interrogation of prisoners, and methodical interviews with relatives and acquaintances of known terrorists. Such detail was possible in part because of the relatively limited size of the terrorist organization—never more than ten thousand in the Malayan People's Liberation Army at any one time—and organized civilian support of similarly manageable size. By May 1958, at the time of my visit, fewer than fifteen hundred active terrorists remained, and large areas of the country had been totally cleared of armed insurgents. Nevertheless our group, traveling in unmarked sedans, was trailed throughout our journey by an armored car, with its machine-gunner at the ready to deal with any possible ambush.

Another impressive aspect of the tour was the brightness and "keenness" of the Malaysian officials—civil and military—whom we encountered. Always smartly turned out in freshly laundered and pressed khakis, they were obviously well trained and answered all questions quickly and with an air of self-assurance (and plausibility) seldom encountered in Vietnam. Nowhere in evidence were the hordes of bewildered clerks, bookkeepers, and scribes one usually encountered in Vietnamese army headquarters, command posts, and administrative bureaus, who always seemed to be at a loss to find the one document that would answer the question of the moment (they never seemed to know the answer offhand), and who could only shuffle through stacks of folios, moving them from one pile to another, with an air of helpless futility and impatience overlaying their chagrin. While the language barrier in Vietnam undoubtedly contributed to the unresponsiveness of the Vietnamese, it does not explain the wholly different atmosphere of structure, order, sense of purpose, discipline, efficiency, and élan that permeated the military and civil apparatus observed in Malaysia.

Part of this difference was due to the effectiveness of British military training and the relative austerity of their traditional approach to colonial administration (except perhaps in India), which contrasted sharply with the labor-intensive bureaucratic approach of the French. The French military setup in Indochina in 1954 had been characterized by an atmosphere of seediness, decay, bureaucratic confusion, and marginal competence which stood in marked contrast to that of the British in Malaysia in 1958. Americans in Vietnam never succeeded in erasing the unfortunate legacy of inefficient colonial administrative methods and work attitudes instilled by the French.

Our tour of Malaysia concluded with the opportunity to observe a Gurkha battalion in a field exercise that marked the conclusion of its "retraining" for conducting conventional infantry tactics. British battalions in Malaysia normally engaged only in small-unit patrol activity in the jungle. They rarely performed even at the company level; even then, the company would normally operate under a local territorial command, without contact with its battalion headquarters. Hence every two years or so, or when the battalion was scheduled for deployment to another theater, its troops would be pulled out of their jungle bases and moved to a training area. There the entire battalion would go through a training cycle to "relearn" conventional infantry tactics. This retraining program was climaxed by an exercise in which the full battalion would conduct an assault on a simulated enemy force entrenched on a high, wooded ridge. Live artillery fire and tactical air strikes were employed to add realism. The exercise was not put on for our benefit—our presence was coincidental to this "final exam" intended to demonstrate how well the battalion had re-learned its basic functions.

The Gurkhas put on a remarkable show, displaying even under exer-cise conditions the esprit and determination that have marked the exploits of these legendary Nepalese formations in British service since the nine-teenth century. Observers were spared the arduous climb to the crest of the ridge that the Gurkhas assaulted. Arriving at the objective by heli-copter shortly after they had seized the ridge, we found the Gurkhas—undaunted by their charge up the steep, jungle-covered heights at midday—busily digging in to "consolidate" their newly won position on the ridge. And they were not simply going through the motions. They were rapidly moving great quantities of earth as they burrowed eagerly, digging foxholes and weapons emplacements. Each soldier was quite evi-dently trying to outdo his neighbor and thus to earn merit and respect in the eyes of his superiors. There was no undue prodding, bullying, or shouting by the junior officers and NCOs of the unit, all of whom were Gurkhas; the troops worked enthusiastically without goading. The com-pany commanders and battalion staff officers supervising the effort, who were British, occasionally offered quiet suggestions for shifting the posi-tion of an automatic weapon or straightening out a tangled field telephone line.

The Gurkhas continued their energetic work until the senior British training officers, satisfied with the unit's performance, gave the signal for "recall." At this point a Gurkha bugler—in the best "Gunga Din" tradi-tion—mounted a commanding boulder and, silhouetted against the after-noon sky, sent the call echoing off the surrounding hills. Only then did the soldiers collect their gear, form into columns, and, chattering gaily like squirrels on a playful romp, march off—in step and at regulation inter-vals—down the ridge to a column of trucks waiting for them on the road far below.

I never saw a Vietnamese army unit, in training or in operations, display such enthusiasm, élan, and obvious professional dedication, com-petence, and enjoyment in training. Some Vietnamese paratroop and ranger battalions might have compared favorably with that Gurkha battal-ion. But most were much more matter-of-fact—if not complacent and lethargic—in their attitude. Perhaps some of the difference resulted from the seemingly unending nature of the Vietnam War, which made it seem that today's activity really didn't matter, or would not significantly alter the ultimate outcome. Another factor was the Gurkha tradition of superior performance, which provided a model that every unit was expected to emulate. Perhaps it was due to a basic difference in the ethnic character of the Gurkha and the Vietnamese; the Gurkhas may by nature be more willing to subordinate themselves to a common goal for the common good than were the perhaps more independent-minded Vietnamese. Perhaps a major factor was the leadership of the Gurkha unit—British officers and NCOs held the key positions. They were in command, not advisers. They were able to instill in the Gurkhas a respect for the best traditions of the British army, and the Gurkhas were all volunteers—soldiering was their chosen profession and the means by which their families could achieve a good life in their homeland after decades of loyal service.

I came away from the Malaysian trip with the feeling that the British performance could be looked to profitably by anyone concerned with combating a Communist-led insurgency. The Malay terrorist threat, of course, never reached the scale of that movement which the French—and later the Americans—encountered in Vietnam. But many of the British concepts and techniques reflected principles that were broadly applicable.

Perhaps the most important factor in the success of the British in Malaysia was the unity of command over all aspects—political, military, and economic—of the counterinsurgency effort. During the Americanized war in Vietnam, there was no semblance of the requisite unity of command. General William Westmoreland commanded only those American military forces actually deployed in South Vietnam. He had no command authority over Seventh Air Force and Seventh Fleet units supporting his operations in the South or against North Vietnam. Nor did he command the native forces, as had the UN command in Korea. Broad cooperation was achieved through joint planning in Saigon and through the influence of the American advisers with Vietnamese units. But "cooperation" and "coordination" are not the same as command; the Vietnamese government and military jealously guarded their separateness.

Second, and directly related to unity of command, was the British emphasis on the central importance of intelligence, on integrating civil and military intelligence activities at all levels, giving it constant attention, and putting the highest priority on its demand for resources. In Vietnam there was no effective collaboration between all the military and civil intelligence agencies until the late 1960s. Before then there was little effective cooperation among the seven separate Vietnamese military intelligence services themselves, nor between them and the National Police. Similarly, MACV and CIA intelligence activities tended to go their separate ways in the first eight years of MACV's existence.

Third, the British aimed to develop competent indigenous military and security forces, operating ultimately under indigenous authority, to suppress the insurgency. With the "Americanization" of the Vietnam War in 1965, MACV's primary focus was on directing its own "main force" war rather than on improving the effectiveness of the ARVN. Nixon's "Vietnamization" program beginning in 1970 turned the attention back to developing the ARVN to assume ultimate responsibility for defeating the Communist forces—but only at the eleventh hour.

The British in Malaysia won the support of the populace by making it absolutely clear at all times that progress was being made toward establishing an independent, viable Malaysia, governed by Malaysians. They worked diligently to develop Malaysian civil and political institutions that would clearly reflect the interests of the local peoples and form an effective bridge between the local cultures and Western democratic concepts. These aims were approached deliberately, rationally, and in close cooperation with native leaders, whom the British schooled and groomed for the task. In this fashion, and drawing upon their colonial experience, the British forged a stable political base and administrative structure to undergird the military and security operations needed to defeat the insurgents. Without a viable political base, the counterinsurgency effort would have failed. With that base, defeat of the insurgents was ensured. Malaysia has enjoyed forty years of peace, disturbed only by a short-lived outbreak of jungle terrorism in Borneo supported by Indonesia.

Obviously I was impressed by what I had seen in Malaysia and I was determined to spread the gospel of these principles in so far as my position permitted. Unfortunately the Malaysian model was not embraced by Americans until very late in the game, long after the scale of the Communist effort in South Vietnam exceeded that of the Malaysian terrorist movement.

In 1958 I was asked to escort a group of Vietnamese army generals on a day of official visits to the American commands in Hawaii. They were en route home after attending a special weapons course at Fort Bliss and were to be briefed on the mission and activities of our Pacific area commands. Three of these officers later achieved some prominence in Vietnam. Brigadier General Tran Van Minh ("Little Minh") later commanded the Vietnamese Command and General Staff College and in 1963 was a member of the group of generals that overthrew Diem; afterward he was appointed ambassador to Tunisia. Major General Duong Van Minh ("Big Minh") headed the group of generals that overthrew Diem but was himself then shoved aside. Thereafter he played a forlorn, peripheral role. Brigadier General Hoang received little subsequent attention. Colonel Nguyen Van Thieu, the junior member of the group, was charged with looking after the luggage of the generals. As the ultimate "survivor," Thieu later became president of Vietnam and oversaw its demise in 1975.

After leading the group around to various appointments, I was authorized to treat them to dinner at Waikiki, during the course of which I discovered they were to be stranded with nothing to do the following day, a Saturday. They spoke little English—we communicated mostly in French—and they seemed downcast at the thought of spending an idle day. They eagerly accepted my offer to take them sightseeing on my own. We had a delightful, leisurely day-long tour of Oahu, which they enjoyed immensely. "Big Minh" was particularly pleased since, on learning of his avid interest in orchids, I took him to visit several of the largest orchid nurseries on the island. We all talked long and earnestly of the situation in Vietnam, and I gained new insights in addition to developing contacts that would later prove helpful.

In Hawaii we were able to follow developments in South Vietnam fairly well, receiving virtually all the intelligence information available to Washington. We were aware in 1959 of the gradual increase in armed terrorist activity in the countryside, which seemed to begin in response to growing pressures by the Vietnamese security services on the Communist apparatus in the late 1950s. Many of the "legal" political agents who were leading agitation against the Diem government were rolled up by his security forces, as were members of many disgruntled non-Communist groups. All opponents of the regime were under continual harassment by the National Police. There were reports of contacts between the clandestine Communist agents in the South and the Hanoi regime, and of liaison visits between representatives of the two via Cambodia and Laos. And there were indications that the stay-behind Viet Minh agents were attempting to coopt the non-Communist dissident groups.

The frequency and scale of armed dissident activity were mounting steadily, and the pattern of these actions suggested that the Communists were carving out secure bases in areas where they had been strong during the war against the French. When a guerrilla force estimated at several hundred men overran a Vietnamese army regimental headquarters in Tay Ninh Province in January 1960, it was evident that South Vietnam was on the verge of another people's war. Some of us believed we were at a critical period which called for concerted military and political efforts to nip the insurgency in the bud, including an intelligence effort following the principles that had led to the British success in Malaysia. We knew the situation, if unchecked, would only snowball, and—with the aid of inevitable infiltration from the North—it would be only a matter of time before South Vietnamese forces were confronted with well-equipped main force military operations such as the Viet Minh had developed in the war against the French.

Reporting from Saigon was, as usual, hopeful. Neither the embassy nor the MAAG reflected any sense of urgency, and it was clear that nothing effective was being done to cope with the deteriorating situation. General "Hanging Sam" Williams, who had assumed command of the MAAG, was single-mindedly pursuing his program of training a conventionally structured Vietnamese army to defend the South against a direct invasion down the coastal route from the North. He steadfastly opposed the diversion of ARVN units from that purpose in order to deal with the growing armed dissidence in the countryside. He insisted that the insurgents were not the Vietnamese army's problem. Like his predecessors, he saw them as an internal security problem and therefore the responsibility of South Vietnam's civil guard and self-defense forces.

Unfortunately these internal security forces were not up to the task. They were poorly armed, indifferently trained, and clearly unable to deal with the dissident forces. The U.S. economic aid mission was responsible for supporting these forces, and General Williams refused to divert any of his precious military advisers to assist in their training.

Meanwhile it was evident to us at USARPAC that the situation was growing serious and would become more so, and that the Vietnamese army clearly needed more intelligence resources to cope with the growing dissidence. Our collection operations specialists decided early in 1960 that the answer was to try once more to get approval for bilateral clandestine intelligence operations with the Vietnamese army. The CIA had over the years successfully headed off repeated army attempts to do this. The CIA station chief in Saigon, as elsewhere, was responsible for coordinating all American clandestine intelligence activities in the country, and he had repeatedly opposed the army's efforts to get its intelligence people involved in South Vietnam. The CIA believed this could jeopardize its own operations and complicate those of the Vietnamese intelligence services. The army's peacetime reputation in the clandestine area was one of ineptness and unprofessionalism, and the CIA didn't want the army stumbling around on its turf.

I suggested an indirect approach, staking out ground that the CIA could not deny us: we should make our proposal within the context of the military assistance program, which was designed to prepare the Vietnamese army for war. Since any army would obviously need intelligence to fight a war, it was in our purview to provide the ARVN with the intelligence tools it would need in combat. This included a capability for collecting intelligence by clandestine means. Such a capability was provided in U.S.

Army military intelligence detachments, and we should have long since been helping the ARVN to form similar support elements.

The general was delighted with my approach and had me draw up a modest plan for such units for the Vietnamese army. He then sent me— rather than the colonel responsible for collection activities—to Saigon to help the ARVN get such a plan developed and approved by MAAG. We could proceed with the project provided the CIA station in Saigon had no objection. I departed for Saigon via Tokyo, where I picked up an experienced army specialist in clandestine operations, one who had worked with an OSS team that trained Viet Minh guerrillas in 1944–1945. We stopped en route to check in with the army's intelligence school at Okinawa, where foreign military officers were trained in a variety of intelligence specialties. If we were successful in Saigon, this school would soon be asked to train a significant number of Vietnamese intelligence officers.

In Saigon my reception was initially mixed. My first contact was with a colonel who was the senior intelligence "adviser" of the MAAG, who assured me that he was not an intelligence officer, hoped never to become one, and intended that his current assignment would never be reflected in his official record. He had been assigned to this job as punishment, having been the senior advisor to the ARVN regiment whose command post had been overrun by guerrillas in January. The colonel said he had no desire to know my business in Saigon and wished to be left out of it. He told me to deal with his deputy, who handled liaison with Vietnamese army intelligence. I did not see him again during my visit. It could have been worse: his total lack of interest could have led him to block my efforts rather than to ignore them.

His deputy, on the other hand, was more hospitable. He had previous intelligence experience, sympathized with the purpose of my visit, and arranged an early meeting with the Vietnamese intelligence chief. We agreed that our best chance for success would be to make this an ARVN project; we would help them develop a plan that was acceptable to them, that they could staff through their high command and then formally request MAAG's assistance in implementing it. Colonel Phuoc, the Vietnamese military intelligence chief, received me with open arms; he saw me as someone who could do something to help him, therefore I was his instant friend. Phuoc listened eagerly to the concept I outlined for creating a set of military intelligence support detachments, including particularly the one for clandestine collection, and he designated a pair of young captains to work with me.

Colonel Phuoc decided I could help him in other areas as well during my visit. He was working on a plan for ten-man special intelligence teams which would be assigned to work with newly formed "commando" companies. These units were to be assigned to work in specific districts and provinces against local insurgent forces. They would conduct reconnaissance and collect intelligence in their assigned localities in order to target operations by the "commando" units.

The colonel then showed me storage rooms filled with dozens of wooden boxes containing dossiers on several hundred thousand Vietnamese citizens, North and South. These files had once belonged to the French Sûreté but had been lying idle for five years. He wanted to know how they could be put back into active use to support counterintelligence operations. I arranged through MAAG channels a requisition for an adequate number of filing cabinets for Colonel Phuoc's use.

He also wanted me to work with his analysts, to critique their intelligence studies and estimates so that they could improve their analytical techniques. I was the first American professional military intelligence specialist he had met who had any familiarity with the situation in Indochina, and he wanted to make maximum use of my brief visit to Vietnam. None of his MAAG "advisers," he said, was broadly expert in intelligence matters, and none knew very much about Vietnam or about guerrilla warfare.

I told him I would do my best to help him during my visit and would try to arrange for continuing help after my departure—and there was one thing he could do for me: have his people bring me up to date on the situation in detail, region by region. I wanted to be briefed on the enemy situation, the status of the Communist organizational development, both political and military, the nature of their logistical setup and capabilities, their order of battle, and especially the extent of their support from the North. If his people would give me detailed assessments of the situation, I would be glad to critique them. Colonel Phuoc eagerly agreed, and

I embarked on an extremely busy—and mutually profitable—working arrangement.

We quickly worked out a proposed military intelligence support structure, including a clandestine collection detachment, which he approved. I met with General Williams and received his quick assent when I explained how these units would significantly enhance the ARVN's intelligence capability and thereby minimize the time necessary for operations against the insurgents.

My deepest concern on this mission was how the CIA station would react to the project. The station chief was clearly upset, but he grudgingly acknowledged the legitimacy of my proposal to conduct training for "wartime" contingencies. He merely warned that he would burn my ass if the army went operational with these Vietnamese clandestine assets. He was convinced that was what we had in mind. His deputy, William Colby, whom I first met during this visit, was less demonstrative and seemed to accept the inevitability of what we were up to.

With the CIA's reluctant concurrence, we asked the Vietnamese to select their officers for the initial training program, and I radioed our theater intelligence school to expect an initial increment of trainees. Two days later I touched base again at the Okinawa school en route home so that I could reassure my boss upon my return to Hawaii that everything was on track. That evening, as I prepared to board my flight at midnight to continue on to Hawaii, thirty-five bewildered Vietnamese officers descended from the plane. Recognizing their leaders as the staff officers who had worked with me on the program in Saigon, I quickly took the group in tow. The school had not received confirmation of their departure, and the Vietnamese had moved more swiftly in this instance than one would have expected. I was able to call the school and arrange for a bus to pick up their new clandestine trainees before boarding my flight for Hawaii. It had been a hectic two weeks, but I had accomplished my primary mission, and then some.

Other aspects of that May 1960 trip were less satisfying. Colonel Phuoc's concept for intelligence teams to work with the projected commando companies didn't pan out. I had arranged for a pair of army intelligence training specialists to come to Saigon to help put together an appropriate training program for Colonel Phuoc's teams, but the effort was for naught. MAAG had reengineered the ARVN concept. In place of commando companies to be employed in local counterguerrilla operations in their home territory, MAAG called for ranger battalions to operate in a mobile general reserve "strike force" role. MAAG eliminated the intelligence teams as superfluous to units to be employed in such a role. I debated this issue with the bright young MAAG lieutenant colonel ramrodding the ranger concept. He had been a ranger himself, and he insisted that these battalions would need every rifleman that could be made available so that they could close with the enemy and destroy him. He insisted that the rifleman with the bayonet was the decisive element in infantry combat, and that was what fighting insurgents was all about. He totally rejected my suggestion that substituting an intelligence specialist for one rifleman might ensure that the battalion would find an enemy to close with, and that without knowledge of where the enemy was, the rangers would be blind. He made it clear that he found my remarks not even worthy of further comment, and that as a civilian, I would never understand military science.

Colonel Phuoc's initiative had reflected the Vietnamese belief in the importance of a territorial approach to regional security—the creation of regular military formations to carry the war to the Viet Cong's local forces, which represented a serious threat to government control in heavily populated rural areas. Each team's ten-man intelligence component would have represented a major step toward creating effective military intelligence targeted against the Viet Cong's military structure within each of the country's 244 districts. The MAAG took this concept and forced it into an American mold, and by the summer of 1960 the Vietnamese army's ranger battalion program was born. Under the U.S. army's guidance, these units provided Vietnamese corps commanders with conventional, mobile "strike" forces operating under their direct control anywhere within the corps boundaries. Among others, Colonel Phuoc was bitterly disappointed that the prospects for creating badly needed new intelligence resources at the grassroots level had been so abruptly eliminated.

My own understanding of the situation in Vietnam, on the other hand, had been considerably enhanced by the series of briefings that Colonel Phuoc had arranged for me. Most striking to me was the clear evidence that the enemy was rapidly forming new military units throughout South Vietnam—a half-dozen or more new local force platoons and companies every week. It was clear that the former Viet Minh elements were developing a force structure replicating what they had in confronting the French during the earlier war. ARVN intelligence had positively identified elements of the same three kinds of forces as before—main force, local force, and guerrilla-militia. They had established secure bases in many areas and had begun to extend their influence and control outward from these bases into the neighboring countryside. The government's access to parts of the rural areas was gradually being curtailed, and enemy forces had already shown they could mass the equivalent of two battalions in a single attack.

There were gaps in this information—Colonel Phuoc lacked some of the "technical means" that had served the French so well, and his analysts were not capable of performing uniformly sophisticated work. I did manage to critique some of their studies and estimates, but the language barrier made this difficult: few Vietnamese could yet speak English well, and I spoke no Vietnamese (though I knew the meaning of a number of military terms). Their growing chauvinism made many of the younger Vietnamese reluctant to speak in French, though it was then still the primary language in the system of higher education, and many officers seemed more comfortable speaking French than Vietnamese.

During the trip I had met twice with General "Little Minh," who struck me as one of the more thoughtful senior Vietnamese officers I encountered. He was now the commandant of ARVN's command and general staff college, where we had a lengthy visit one morning. The following Sunday afternoon I accompanied him on a drive through the countryside northeast of Saigon. Minh was unhappy with the trend of events in his country. As we drove over a major bridge at Bien Hoa, he noted that it was guarded by regular army troops rather than by Civil Guardsmen. I asked how he could tell, and he pointed out they were wearing helmets and were equipped with M-1 rifles; the Civil Guard was not so equipped. When I asked why the paramilitary Civil Guard was not being used to protect the bridge, General Minh answered that the military commanders had no confidence in them, that they could no longer be relied upon to protect key facilities but would melt away at the first sign of a direct guerrilla threat. The Civil Guard itself lacked self-confidence in the face of the growing Vietnamese Communist (now called Viet Cong) guerrilla forces, some of whom were better armed than the Civil Guardsmen. The Civil Guard had become worthless, Minh said. Unless local military commanders assigned regular army troops to protect the bridges, they would be destroyed by the guerrillas.

When I remarked that this was contrary to General Williams's view that the army should be training to combat an open invasion and not employed in local security against insurgents, "Little Minh" vented his wrath with our "shortsighted" MAAG policies. He berated MAAG's "conventionalization" of the ARVN's commando company concept. MAAG, he said, tended to conventionalize everything. The Americans were creating the wrong kind of Vietnamese army and training it to fight the wrong kind of war. For the Americans to make a light artillery battalion organic to a Vietnamese infantry division was to make the ARVN immobile. We were teaching Vietnamese officers our American army doctrine regarding artillery support, and this meant that Vietnamese regimental and divisional staff officers would never allow a battalion to go more than ten thousand yards from the nearest road, because that was the limit of the range of the 105mm howitzer that the United States insisted be made part of the division. General Minh believed it would be better to omit artillery from the division altogether, and have the infantry depend on mortars which could be carried by the troops. Then the infantry would be mobile, their thinking would not be inhibited by considerations of firepower, and the Vietnamese army could effectively engage in the coming war of maneuver with the Viet Cong's developing main-force capabilities. But with American advice, the ARVN would stay close to the roads, and the enemy would march in circles around the ARVN road-heads, immune beyond the range of the ARVN's 105s, and carry the war to the ARVN's rear.

"Little Minh" obviously had thought deeply about these matters. As the commandant of the Vietnamese staff college, he felt responsible for what was being taught to ARVN officers, but his American advisers—none of whom had ever fought an enemy like the Viet Minh—thought they knew more about what the ARVN needed than did officers like himself, who were older, had more experience in both command and staff jobs, and had spent more time in combat.

Apparently on a sudden impulse, the general headed off the main highway onto progressively less developed side roads, in a direction that made me uneasy. I knew we were heading in the general direction of the infamous Viet Minh War Zone D. After a time, as we drove slowly over narrow dirt roads through unkempt, poor-looking rural villages, he urged that I observe closely. This, he said, was a Communist war zone; some of the people we saw moving along the streets were, most likely, Communist troops or administrative cadre. The people would not bother us; they knew whose car it was and were not anxious to draw attention to themselves—or bring army or security forces crashing through this base area—by creating an incident. If we had a company of troops with us, the general said, we would have difficulty fighting our way in, but since we posed no direct threat and were traveling alone, there was no reason for the Communists to attack us. But, he said, observe closely, because we might be the last non-Communists to move through the area unmolested. The curtain would soon fall around this area, and roadblocks might preclude access next week or next month. These people, and those like them, were denying access to more and more of the countryside. Unless his government shifted the focus of the Vietnamese army to deal with the growing Communist guerrilla strength, unless something were done to improve the confidence and capabilities of the Civil Guard, and unless the ARVN began preparing for the right kind of war and began fighting it, South Vietnam would be lost.

We returned safely from that ride, and I cannot vouch for our actually driving within an enemy base area. But we had been close to it, and I had been apprehensive because with my special intelligence clearances I was not supposed to expose myself to potential capture by leaving the relative security of Saigon. Many times over the years I was to recall that conversation with "Little Minh."

Another conversation during my visit left me equally uneasy about the future of Vietnam. One evening I dined with the two ARVN captains, members of Colonel Phuoc's intelligence staff, with whom I had been working for more than a week. During dinner I learned that they had both served with infantry units in combat during the French war, one of them in the Catholic provinces in Tonkin. Both were from the professions; before they had been mobilized in 1952 "for the duration of the emergency," one had been a lawyer, the other a pharmacist. The emergency seemed destined to last forever (it continued for another fifteen years), and they were resigned to indefinite military service.

I asked whether they enjoyed the military life. They said the work was not overly taxing, either physically or intellectually, the pay was not bad, and there was the possibility—if one survived—of being promoted to a rank where one could acquire both influence and affluence. I asked whether they preferred their present staff assignments to duty with troop units. Having been professionals, they naturally preferred staff jobs; moreover they were safer and had a better chance of survival. On the other hand, they observed, their pay was less than when they served with troops. When I expressed surprise that the ARVN had a bonus arrangement for "troop duty," they quickly explained that the basic rate of pay was the same, but the take-home pay in a staff job was less because they had to give Colonel Phuoc about 10 percent of their monthly pay for the privilege of remaining on assignment to his staff. When I asked whether all the officers on the colonel's staff had to comply with this arrangement they said, "Of course, and all the NCOs as well." They believed this was common practice throughout the army.

I later learned that this sort of arrangement permeated Vietnamese government and commercial life. Influence, privilege, and favors—even in routine transactions—cost money, and the higher one moved up the hierarchy in the government, the military, or commercial life, the greater the opportunity to gain affluence through the sale of these commodities. This was in part why there was such a chronic shortage of company-grade officers in Vietnamese rifle companies; those who should have been assigned there had paid someone for the privilege of being assigned or detailed elsewhere. In future years I came to understand why there were often dozens of idle ARVN lieutenants lolling among the jeeps parked behind Vietnamese army corps headquarters. These young officers, who should have been in the field with tactical units, had paid for the privilege of being detailed as drivers for staff officers in the headquarters. After the Diem coup in 1963, when there was a rapid succession of coups, it became evident that a major reason for the housecleaning at all levels of the national government was not so much to ensure loyalty to the new government leaders. Rather, it represented the wholesale peddling of positions at almost every level by each successive government. A new corps commander could appoint a dozen province chiefs, each for a fee that the province chief might then recover two or three times over by selling appointments to a half-dozen or more district chiefs. Corps, division, province, and district staffs all offered opportunities for the sale of positions to people willing to pay the price.

Many Vietnamese military officials made fortunes in 1964 when the government changed hands at least five times, even though they may have been in office only a few months. Usually the officers themselves avoided soiling their own hands, turning over to their wives the responsibility for negotiating the arrangements with the wives of the subordinates. This form of corruption was a fundamental characteristic of Vietnamese society, and was accepted as a way of life. Not everyone saw it as morally justified; it was simply the way things were done, and it was easily rationalized by the players in the game. Those who never had a chance to benefit were probably alienated by the system, as were most Americans who were aware of it. And the system created still another popular grievance which received due attention from Communist propagandists.

On my return to Hawaii I was eager to brief the army and CINCPAC staffs on what I had learned about the situation in Vietnam. I had concluded that the insurgency was progressing far more rapidly than either the embassy or MAAG believed, and that a more vigorous, concerted effort was required to prevent an accelerating deterioration of the situation. I was not optimistic even if we were to intensify our efforts, but I was convinced we would fail otherwise. I was also concerned with what I had seen of the repressive methods of the Diem government and their effect on popular attitudes. Police corruption and repression were blatant on the streets of Saigon, and the population was being alienated by it; I was concerned that unless Diem's government took steps to gain the sympathy and backing of the people, it had no chance of surviving over the long term. None of the Vietnamese army officers I had spoken with was a zealous supporter of the Diem regime. Their criticism was directed primarily at its inflexibility in responding to the insurgency, and to the inadequacy of its military and security policies; few had expressed dissatisfaction on ideological or religious grounds.

The USARPAC intelligence chief accepted my analysis and arranged for me to brief the army commander, General I. D. White, and the full staff as a prelude to a repeat session with the CINCPAC staff. I gave a relatively brief presentation, starkly outlining the facts relating to the buildup of Communist strength, and concluding that the situation was worse than was evident from field reporting, and that if present trends continued (with anticipated support from the North), the Diem government would inevitably be defeated. When I finished, General White said that I could not be more wrong; that my briefing reflected the typical "gloom and doom" pessimism of intelligence people. He had spoken to General Williams the night before at the local army hospital, where he had just reported in for a checkup, and "Hanging Sam" had assured him that the Communist insurgents posed no serious threat to the Vietnamese government. I replied that, unfortunately, it was General Williams who was wrong; he was uninformed, had no intelligence staff, and was ignorant of the kinds of facts I had gleaned from the Vietnamese intelligence staff. Although the intelligence resources of the Vietnamese were limited and needed development, I said, we had no basis for refuting what they had told me; indeed their information coincided with what we knew from technical sources and was consistent with the pattern followed by the Viet Minh against the French.

General White asserted that the French experience was irrelevant; they had been beaten, and we were now in charge. I was exaggerating the threat, as intelligence officers habitually did; he would rather take the word of the responsible American commander on the spot. We had spent enough time that afternoon on the subject and should get on with the next item on the agenda.

My briefing of the CINCPAC staff was dropped, and my cable report to army intelligence in Washington was revised to delete any reference to a deteriorating situation. This unwillingness of U.S. officials to confront reality in Vietnam was not necessarily decisive in our ultimate defeat; at USARPAC in 1960 we would have been only a few months ahead of the remainder of the U.S. government in recognizing the seriousness of the developing Communist guerrilla threat. But it was the period in the Vietnam insurgency when the British methods and techniques applied in Malaysia might have been useful. When Washington did get around to addressing the question a year later, the time had passed when a Malaysian program could have been effectively applied.

It seemed to me that it was time to begin thinking about a return to Washington, since there was no market in Hawaii for realistic intelligence assessments. If policy decisions were to be made, the place to be was where the decisions were made.

While working out arrangements for a reassignment to Washington, I was deeply involved with the psychological warfare section of the USARPAC staff on an issue raised by General White. He had expressed frustration over the apparent consistency with which the Communists seemed to be able to inspire their clients throughout Asia more effectively than we could motivate ours. The most recent example had been an action in Laos, where a superior government force had been completely routed by a smaller number of Pathet Lao troops. General White asked the staff to look into the problem and see what could be done about it by our own command or by the U.S. government in general.

Many factors, of course, contributed to the Communist successes. But we concluded that a common denominator existed in the superior will to fight of Chinese, Vietnamese, and Laotian Communist forces in most situations. In each instance their military forces were conceived by their masters as political instruments, were permeated by a unified and centralized political party structure that controlled every aspect of their activities, and were subjected to a consistent and intensive political indoctrination that rationalized and gave direction to the daily lives and activities of their troops within the framework of broad but clearly articulated objectives.

The non-Communist forces in these countries, with rare exceptions, lacked an effective political base and had no consistent motivational force or ideological system to rationalize or guide their military efforts. The Chinese Nationalists were the principal exception; their military forces were controlled by the Kuomintang party. It operated in a fashion similar to that of the Communist parties, but its political content was apparently "stale" and uninspiring, and had proved ineffective in the struggle for control of mainland China in the late 1940s.

The psychological warriors on the Pacific army staff devised a concept for enhancing the political effectiveness of non-Communist forces in the Far East, utilizing a system similar to that employed by the Communists but based on a democratic ideology. The approach would use Western democratic ideals and concepts to provide indoctrination themes in a framework that emphasized freedom of expression. It amounted to a system of benevolent but systematic thought control and psychological motivation. Although idealistically appealing in some respects, the solution was inherently impractical because it required the reshaping of the political institutions and ideologies of our client states into a common framework based on American ideals. It would not work unless backed by these governments, and many of them were based on institutions and practices that were inconsistent with the proposed ideology. Moreover, any attempt on our part to impose such a framework on these countries would be vulnerable to the same charges of imperialism we were trying to combat, and would be just as unacceptable to Asians as communism. So the concept was dropped. I later learned that the Joint Chiefs had addressed the same problem and had arrived at a similar solution, complete with an ideological platform based on a suggested doctrine of "Militant Liberty." I could see the hand of Colonel Lansdale in this concept. But that proposal too was dropped, for the same reasons, presumably, as was our concept in Hawaii. This issue of motivating our non-Communist clients and allies continued to vex us throughout our war in Vietnam, and remains a dilemma today.

6
At the
Center of
Policymaking

I RETURNED TO washington in January 1961, the day before President Kennedy's inauguration, encouraged by the prospect that a change of administrations would lead to more effective and dynamic policies in the Far East and in Southeast Asia. I reported back to army intelligence as a senior analyst-consultant on Southeast Asia, eager to participate in research on the nature of the reviving insurgency threat in Indochina as a means of illuminating the path toward realistic national objectives and policies in the region. I did not pretend to have the answers, but I believed I knew what questions should be asked, and I wanted to contribute to rational solutions. This was difficult to accomplish in the transitional atmosphere of 1961, particularly because of the fast-moving developments in Southeast Asia and because of the new administration's ad hoc method of dealing with the situation, in contrast to the previous administration's usually systematic but often cumbersome approach.

The intelligence community had maintained a healthy skepticism about the Indochina situation. In 1959 a National Estimate had criticized the Diem government's capacity to deal soundly and effectively with growing domestic opposition. In 1960 another estimate noted the deteriorating political and security situation in the South, and warned that if trends continued, the Diem government was doomed to defeat. The community had also warned of the significance of the Lao Dong (Communist) party's third national congress in the fall of 1960, which ratified an earlier Politburo decision to transform North Vietnam into a "firm base" for the reunification struggle, and set the "immediate task" of intensifying the revolutionary struggle to overthrow the Diem government as the essential step toward the reunification goal. These intelligence assessments were fully consistent with my own perceptions. It was good to be back in "friendly" territory.

In early 1961 the administration's focus was on Laos, where the non-Communist position was particularly weak. Initially confined by the Geneva Accords to two northeastern provinces adjoining North Vietnam, the Communist Pathet Lao, grouped by the North Vietnamese into tactical units and bolstered by covertly introduced North Vietnamese combat and support units, gradually had overrun most of the northern part of Laos, except for parts of the *Plaine des Jarres* region, and had gained effective control over eastern portions adjoining Vietnam down to the Cambodian border. This was accomplished against incompetent government forces who found themselves confined essentially to the Mekong Valley, except for armed outposts held by Meo tribesmen in the area around the *Plaine des Jarres*. These Meo elements, being supported covertly by the United States through the CIA, had been a thorn in the side of the Communists since the early 1950s, when they were first organized and equipped by the French. In 1953 they had played a significant role in French operations in northeastern Laos. The following year I had flown in a C-47 piloted by the French, which parachuted ammunition and other supplies and free-dropped sacks of rice to four Meo outposts in the vicinity of Sam Neua; at least three of these were still holding out against the Communists throughout the 1960s, and one of them into the early 1970s. Contrary to some popular mythology, the CIA did not create the Meo problem; it simply inherited "leftovers" from the French War and kept the Meos going for another twenty years.

The Communists' principal aim in Laos was to develop a secure corridor for the movement of supplies from North Vietnam to support the insurgency in the South. The DMZ in Vietnam was too narrow and too easily policed to permit effective infiltration; a route through Laos offered greater security and flexibility and was less susceptible to interdiction. The Communists had developed routes through the area during their war against the French, and these had acquired notoriety as the Ho Chi Minh Trail. This was not a single trail but a maze of tracks with organized way stations, guard posts, and rest points along the way, and was used extensively as a liaison and supply route linking North and South Vietnam and bypassing the French-held coastal strip between Quang Tri and Da Nang. Until 1953 the French had held the town of Tchepone and posts at the major passes from North Vietnam into Laos, but these were overrun by the Communists that year. The Ho Chi Minh Trail was not used to transport large quantities of supplies on a sustained basis during the French war, but porters did move from time to time carrying a limited quantity of weapons and special equipment to Communist forces in the central highlands of South Vietnam.

The Viet Minh had never developed in the South powerful, well-equipped units of the sort that operated in North Vietnam, and the insurgency there seldom involved actions by units larger than a battalion in size. In 1953 and 1954 the Communists launched a major campaign into central and southern Laos, cutting Route 9 which linked the French forces on the coast to Savannakhet in the Mekong Valley. Some elements of that campaign penetrated down either side of the Bolovens plateau into northeastern Cambodia, effectively reconnoitering terrain and movement conditions in the region. These units returned to the North after the armistice, but they had demonstrated the feasibility of movement from North Vietnam through Laos into eastern Cambodia. (Motor roads were built along this corridor in the 1960s and 1970s.) The operation in 1960 seemed to be aimed clearly at following up on this earlier thrust.

Army intelligence was not a major player in the interagency task force on counterinsurgency formed by the Kennedy administration to deal with the deteriorating situation in Vietnam and Laos. We were aware of its creation and of its mission to develop a program of political, economic, psychological, and covert actions to strengthen the Diem government, which had been shaken by the aborted military coup of November 1960, and to counter the Communist threat to the South. We were aware of broad policy decisions, such as authorized increases in the size of the Vietnamese military forces structure, which the United States would support, but we were not represented on the task force. I was involved in a few actions in support of the Joint Chiefs and Department of Defense planners, and dealt with (now) General Lansdale on a few minor points of detail, but I was not consulted on broad policy or strategy questions.

We did participate in the preparation of several National Estimates in 1961, which echoed earlier conclusions that a direct invasion from the North was unlikely. The estimates suggested that the Communists would continue to focus on a people's war strategy in the South, reinforced by infiltration from the North; that the South Vietnamese army could not effectively seal the border with Laos to prevent such infiltration; and that a prolonged and difficult struggle was likely in the South. We also provided inputs to the State Department's 1961 White Paper on North Vietnamese aid to the South.

One episode that involved me concerned an alleged massive buildup of North Vietnamese forces at Dien Bien Phu in April 1961, at the height of the flurry of interest in Laos. The problem stemmed from a U-2 reconnaissance mission, the first over Dien Bien Phu, whose photography showed large barracks areas—apparently new—along with substantial construction activity. Information from U-2 missions was still carefully compartmented to limit its access to the fewest number of people possible. As a result, the people reporting the results of the mission sometimes did so in ignorance of what was known through other sources, and without consulting with specialists on the region in question. Thus planners and operating officials in Washington had been startled by briefings presented by special compartment briefing officers who suggested that a massive new military buildup had been discovered at Dien Bien Phu. The briefers also hinted darkly at the ominous import of such a buildup on the deteriorating situation in Laos. The specialists on the region had been saying that North Vietnam would not intervene openly on a large scale in Laos but would continue to pursue its objectives there through covertly introduced battalion-sized units, operating in conjunction with—and in the guise of—Pathet Lao units. This new, alleged buildup suggested that the specialists were in error. The fact that the Communists were winning in

Laos without massive, direct intervention was overlooked in the face of the dramatic "new" evidence of a buildup.

My own clearances were hastily restored, and I was asked to assess the scale and meaning of the buildup. It was evident that the facilities, including those under construction, were sufficient to house an infantry division, which was the size of the North Vietnamese force that had been stationed there since the 1954 battle. We had firm information from other sources that the division there—the 316th—had been building permanent barracks, storage, and training facilities at Dien Bien Phu for its own use, in phased increments for the past several years. The facilities observed to be under construction fit what we knew of the final increment, scheduled for completion in 1961. Thus there was nothing new or dramatic in what was happening at Dien Bien Phu; there was no buildup of additional forces there; there was no greater threat to Laos than had existed for the past seven years. The photo interpreters had simply reported the difference between what was evident in 1961 and what they had seen when Dien Bien Phu had last been photographed in 1954, and the briefers had been off and running without checking to see what might be known from other sources about events at Dien Bien Phu during the intervening years.

Unfortunately the damage had already been done—the planners had reacted to the "buildup," and the president had appeared on national television to demonstrate our concern over this new "crisis," of which the alleged buildup at Dien Bien Phu was a prime ingredient. (The "crisis" over the Soviet brigade in Cuba in 1979–1980 was reminiscent in many respects of the April 1961 concern over the North Vietnamese buildup at Dien Bien Phu. What it basically illustrates is the danger of excessive compartmentalization of information, which should have been one of the lessons learned from the Pearl Harbor intelligence failure.)

My own duties changed in June 1961 when I was assigned to coordinate the army's current intelligence program, becoming in effect, the managing editor of its daily and weekly intelligence summaries distributed throughout the army staff and elsewhere in Washington, and the

producer-director of its weekly briefing program for the army's senior
staff. My interests were thus extended to worldwide coverage, and Vietnam became just one of many critical issues I had to be aware of. I maintained a special interest in the area for the next few years and was directly
involved intermittently, but I was not an active participant in the policy
formation process on a continuing basis.

In October 1961 the Defense Intelligence Agency was created, and the
army's current intelligence function was integrated into DIA's Current Intelligence and Indications Center. I became a "consultant" to the chief of
the center, with vaguely defined functions, no specific duties, no authority, and no responsibilities. I tried to make myself useful and contribute to
the mission of the center, and over the next couple of years I managed to
find things to do. But it was a difficult role. The air force dominated DIA at
the time; all three of the hierarchical levels above me were headed by air
force officers: the head of the center, the head of intelligence production,
and the director himself. In effect, the air force's current intelligence fa-
cility had absorbed its army and navy counterparts. The air force intelligence philosophy differed from the army's. The air force was concerned
primarily with strategic matters—that is, the Soviet nuclear strike threat
to the United States. They were interested primarily in things that flew—
heavy bombers, ICBMs and other missiles, sortie rates, and so forth—and
on the nuclear weapons they carried. The air force had a peripheral interest in some political developments because officials seemed to find coups
and other changes of government exciting and worthy of note. But there
was little concern or sustained interest about developments that did not
directly threaten American military bases or forces, and particularly little
interest in—or understanding of—guerrilla warfare. For two years I tried
to broaden this narrow outlook, but I left the DIA without having had
much impact and with a sense of regret that it was not evolving more
rapidly and effectively into a mature, balanced military intelligence operation. (It began such an evolution in the later sixties and by the mid-
seventies had reached maturity.)

Because my duties in DIA were ill-defined, I had some leeway in pursuing things that interested me, and I was able to keep abreast of developments in Vietnam. My efforts to improve the agency's understanding and

interpretation of the situation there were hindered by the three-way split in DIA between the current reporting, estimative, and basic research functions (which had been done essentially by the same analysts in the army intelligence setup). In DIA the functions were scattered about in various facilities in northern Virginia, precluding effective integration and coordination. Thus my influence on DIA's work on Vietnam did not extend beyond the current intelligence function—and even there was limited.

When the mission of Maxwell Taylor and Walt Rostow to Vietnam was scheduled in October 1961, I consulted with the DIA officer who was to accompany the team, helping him prepare for the assignment. I also debriefed him on his return, advised him on the formulation of his recommendations concerning intelligence matters, and had an opportunity to peruse the final report. I was moderately cheered by the emphasis on the need for political reform but was later disappointed that we failed to predicate our increased military involvement on the implementation of such reform. I had urged my colleague to "fall on his sword" if necessary in supporting anyone on the mission who favored making our aid conditional on political reforms, because I still believed that military measures alone were not sufficient, and that even with political reforms there was no guarantee we could prevent a Communist victory. Without a broader political base and increased popular support for the Diem government, there was no hope at all.

Fortunately I was still in step with the National Estimates, which saw Diem's support declining, with prospects for a successful coup by disgruntled elements, especially within the military. The estimators also concluded that our new military programs would not provoke new Communist initiatives. I shared their view that the Communists would probably calculate that with only a modest increase in infiltration they could keep pace with the expansion of our advisory and limited combat support activities. I also agreed with the estimate that any bombing of the North would probably lead to the emergence of a North Vietnamese air force and a substantial increase in air defense capabilities through assistance from the Soviet Union and China. Almost everyone agreed that the Chinese would not intervene directly with their own forces unless North Vietnam's survival were threatened by direct American action. It was also recognized that North Vietnam had substantial autonomy within the Communist camp and would pursue those aims it regarded as in its best interests, rather than blindly following the lead of Moscow or Peking.

In February 1962 the new U.S. military headquarters in Saigon—the Military Assistance Command, Vietnam (MACV)—asked DIA to make me available to help establish a new Joint Evaluation Center there. The new center, recommended by General Taylor, was to be jointly staffed by the military command, the CIA station, and the embassy staff. It was to have access to information from all sources, and, reporting directly to the ambassador, was to analyze the situation and provide him—and Washington—with accurate, objective assessments independent of institutional or service biases.

My task was to help MACV set up the center, establish its work procedures, and train the military people who would be assigned there. En route to Saigon, I stopped briefly in Honolulu to see the intelligence staffs at both CINCPAC and USARPAC to update myself on their interests and needs and on their ability to assist our effort in Saigon. While there I learned that my mission might be altered. One of the periodic conferences involving Secretary of Defense Robert McNamara, the Joint Chiefs, CINCPAC, and the American embassy and command in Saigon had just concluded in Honolulu. The newly appointed intelligence chief in Saigon had been unable to answer McNamara's questions about the size of the enemy's forces, and McNamara wanted MACV to formulate a definitive answer before their next conference. Thus the Viet Cong order of battle had become the top intelligence priority for the military command in Saigon.

On my arrival in Saigon, I was taken to meet the new MACV intelligence officer, air force Colonel James Winterbottom, whose intelligence career had centered on SAC reconnaissance programs. He had quarreled constantly with his army deputy, Colonel Robert Delaney, whom I had known in the Pentagon, and whose generally sound advice Winterbottom usually rejected out of hand. He knew the U-2 and SR-71, and how to assess poststrike damage in a nuclear environment. Unfortunately this expertise did not equip him to lead an intelligence effort in support of a counterinsurgency program. When his army deputy and I arrived at his room, Colonel Winterbottom was heatedly reprimanding an army major who was responsible for handling special intelligence communications and other sensitive channel messages. Using highly abusive language, the colonel was demanding that the major show him first any messages coming through his channel, even those marked for the private attention of the commanding general, before delivering them to the addressee. The unfortunate major tried to explain why he could not comply with Colonel W's request, and the colonel was insisting that he would damned well obey the colonel's instructions. He then turned to me and told me in no uncertain terms that though I might have been a "hotshot," big-time, powerful blankety-blank GS-15 back in Washington, in Saigon I was no better than the lowest-ranked private, that I would enjoy no special privileges, that I should remember for whom I was working, that I was not DIA's employee but his, and that if I tried to communicate with my home office without clearing the message with him, he would fix my wagon (to put it politely). When he finished this tirade, I introduced myself, said that I hoped to be helpful to him and to the military command during my stay in Saigon, and left his presence as soon as I could.

I will omit any further details of Colonel Winterbottom's behavior, which was consistently vulgar and notorious. His alcoholism (acute and blatant), his paranoia (which caused him to view all subordinates and peers as potential threats to his position), his boorishness (which would have caused a more junior officer to have been sent home in disgrace), and his professional incompetence (which was a serious detriment to the effectiveness of the command) all combined to make him wholly unsuitable for his critically important role. His task was to create and manage an intelligence staff that could accurately assess the enemy threat and identify his vulnerabilities so that the most cost-effective programs for dealing with that threat could be developed and executed. Neither Colonel Winterbottom nor his immediate successor, another air force colonel who was an expert on Soviet strategic weapons systems, was equipped for that task. His successor, who realized he was not up to the challenge, had the grace to have a nervous breakdown just a few months after his arrival, and he was followed by a Marine brigadier general who at least knew what a ground war was all about. But for more than a year and a half, MACV's intelligence effort barely limped along, well below marginally effective.

The news in Honolulu had been correct: I was assigned to a new mission on my arrival in Saigon. Although lip service was paid to the Joint Evaluation Center concept for about ten weeks, those of us assigned there worked exclusively for two months on the Viet Cong order-of-battle project. Neither the embassy nor the CIA station contributed people to the center, and by May it had been relocated from the embassy to the MACV headquarters building, where it became merely another adjunct of the MACV intelligence staff. The concept of a Joint Evaluation Center reporting directly to the ambassador—the chief of mission—was never seriously tested in Vietnam. It has since become standard practice to establish a Joint Intelligence Center, with CIA participation, in major overseas commands.

The order-of-battle project team operated initially in a secure "vault" in the embassy building. The army sent an officer and NCO from Washington and another pair from Hawaii to work on the project, and MACV assigned several additional people. In our secure area we mounted large-scale maps on sliding panels and installed the necessary working files. The small room would not accommodate all of us at once, so we worked in two shifts, collating and plotting data from all sources, going through all reports on the Viet Cong forces and their activities over the previous two years, tracing the evolution of every unit and territorial component of the enemy force structure.

I accompanied Colonel Winterbottom and Colonel Delaney on a visit to the Vietnamese intelligence chief to work out arrangements for obtaining raw data from the Vietnamese army, and to establish procedures for coordinating the results of our research with their order-of-battle holdings. The plan was for our American team to work independently to develop a unilateral understanding of the enemy's force structure, untainted by official Vietnamese rationalizations, and then compare notes with the Vietnamese, who were believed to have inflated their holdings to exaggerate the size of the enemy forces.

When we were ushered into the Vietnamese intelligence chief's office (it was the first visit there by either Colonel W or his army deputy), we were greeted by my old friend Colonel Phuoc, who still headed the Vietnamese military intelligence effort and who was overjoyed at seeing me again. He was delighted to learn that I would be heading the American research team, welcoming the opportunity, he said, to work again with the only American he knew who understood the situation in Vietnam. His glee, and the effusiveness and deference he showed me, greatly annoyed Colonel Winterbottom and did nothing to help my standing with him. Colonel Phuoc agreed to our proposed procedures and begged Colonel Winterbottom to let me serve also as a tutor to the Vietnamese analysts to enhance their professional capabilities during my projected stay in Saigon. Colonel Winterbottom was noncommittal while we were in Colonel Phuoc's presence, but in the car he was quick to warn me that I had better damned well remember my place and not get any inflated ideas about my importance. My job, he said, was to break my butt for Colonel Winterbottom, and he would see that I had no time for anything else.

The order-of-battle project was hard, slogging work, involving painstaking checking and rechecking, collation, evaluation, cross-filing, and careful map-plotting. We each worked on a designated region, but I also coordinated the work of the others, advising them and trying to ensure that we were following common methodologies and criteria, and doing the work systematically and thoroughly.

At the end of six weeks we began the laborious process of comparing notes with the Vietnamese, who listed almost 50 percent more enemy units than we could rationalize. We found that most of their additions were in fact duplicate designations for units otherwise accounted for in our holdings; others did not meet the fairly strict criteria we had established for "accepted" status—at least two reports from reliable sources, accompanied by evidence of activity in the area that would account for a unit of the reported size. In two weeks we finished this comparison and published MACV's first enemy order of battle. We qualified the result as a minimum assessment of the enemy's main force and local force strength, based on confirmed identification of individual tactical units, with an assessed strength for each unit based on the most current specific data at hand. We came up with a total of about 20,000 regular troops in these types of units, omitting any estimate for territorial headquarters or support elements. We stated that there were probably at least 100,000 of the guerrilla-militia elements (this was based on year-old information from a very reliable source), and it was my hope that the MACV intelligence staff would continue research on these irregular elements. Colonel Winterbottom, after consulting with General Harkins, had rejected our proposal to include the strength of additional units that the evidence supported as "probable" and "possible"—units whose existence had been reliably reported but not yet fully confirmed.* Nevertheless I felt we had established a credible base line, and that as new enemy units were formed and met the criteria for acceptance, they would be added to the order-of-battle holdings.

Order-of-battle work is a dynamic process—or at least it should be—with assessments of the enemy's strength changing as he expands his forces, or alters their structure, or suffers losses. Unfortunately, under Colonel Winterbottom's stewardship, MACV's intelligence staff attempted to stand with our initial assessment for the next two years. The failure of the MACV intelligence staff to continue a dynamic and professional approach in analyzing and assessing Communist military strength in the South deprived the military command in Saigon—and the policy planners in Washington—of an accurate understanding of the enemy's military potential. It thus contributed substantially to the failure of our policies in Vietnam. It also led to differences within the intelligence community over the composition and potential of Communist forces in the South, and over trends in their numerical strength.

*John Newman, in his *JFK and Vietnam* (New York, 1992), pp. 173–240, presents a slightly distorted and politically slanted version of Colonel Winterbottom's machinations and the work of our team in Saigon.

7
Politics in the Countryside

DURING MY 1962 VISIT to Vietnam, I flew to Ban Me Thuot in the highlands to visit the intelligence advisory staffs of the ARVN commands in that area. Our itinerary included a visit to the "model" Montagnarde camp at Buon Enao, where the CIA and army Special Forces teams were conducting a paramilitary program to create Civilian Irregular Defense Groups (CIDG). These groups were designed to enable the mountain people to defend themselves against incursions into their isolated mountain villages by armed Viet Cong elements. Men from the villages were being recruited, formed into local paramilitary units, given arms and training, and then returned to defend their home villages. Since 1961 the CIA had been arming and training similar self-defense units in other parts of Vietnam in response to requests by local officials and community leaders, and in cooperation with the Diem government.

The Montagnardes, as the French called them, were not ethnic Vietnamese but members of a variety of relatively primitive tribal groups inhabiting the jungle-covered mountain regions. Some of their strain preceded the Polynesians, who had passed through the region millennia before. The Annamites (central Vietnamese) had been traditionally reluctant to penetrate into the highlands and generally settled along the coastal plain. Thus these mountain people still lived under neolithic conditions, hunting with primitive crossbows and blowguns; they had never been assimilated into the Vietnamese culture. Because of ethnic animosities (the Vietnamese referred to Montagnardes as savages), the French had grouped the highland provinces into an autonomous "protectorate," administered separately from the three regions comprising Vietnam. With the departure of the French and the ouster of Bao Dai, these provinces had lost their autonomy and were now subject to the authority of the Diem Government, which coveted the sparsely populated, undeveloped area. Tens of thousands of northern Catholic refugees had been settled in newly created agricultural complexes in these provinces.

The briefings that Colonel Delaney and I received at Buon Enao were impressive, recounting palpable progress in civic-action activities as well as the paramilitary training at the heart of the self-defense program. The concept seemed sound, and the entire CIDG program seemed to be progressing nicely in consonance with the Special Forces "textbook" for such activities—with one major exception: the portions of the outline on the briefing charts marked "political action" were left blank.

When I asked why there was a gap in that portion of the program at the Buon Enao camp, we were told to tread lightly on that subject. The Diem government was suspicious of American intentions with the Montagnardes. The relationship between Montagnardes and the Vietnamese was somewhat comparable to that between Native Americans and the early white colonists in our own country. The Diem government had no well-defined policy for assimilating the mountain peoples, either politically or culturally, so the CIA and the Special Forces had no basis for spelling out a political-action segment for the CIDG program.

This absence of a viable political rationale to undergird the Saigon government's counterinsurgency effort plagued American efforts throughout the war. It left the CIDG forces bereft of any important motivation other than "self-defense." Saigon's tendency to neglect the Montagnardes fed their continuing disaffection and increased their vulnerability to penetration by the Viet Cong, whose propaganda stressed autonomous rule for all minorities. Indeed, some of the tribal groups—including units trained under the CIDG program—rose up in a violent mutiny in 1964, proclaiming a united front for the liberation of all their people. Naturally the Vietnamese government blamed the United States, and specifically the CIA, for having stimulated rebellion among the mountain tribes. The rebellion was unfortunate, but although Montagnarde dissidence was never fully squelched, it made little difference in the outcome of the war. Few of these groups allied themselves with the Viet Cong, which were led, after all, by Vietnamese.

The American approach to pacification throughout the war emphasized techniques, methods, and tactics but was handicapped by its inability to provide a political context for these actions. The CIA made many innovative contributions to the pacification program. Most were based on concepts developed by innovative ARVN officers serving as province chiefs (and simultaneously as sector commanders) or key members of their staffs. CIA officers worked with these local leaders to develop the more practical concepts, test them in selected areas, and support their implementation in the province of origin. If the program was successful and suited the situation in other provinces, it might be replicated there. Those programs that contributed significantly to rural security would soon be adopted by ARVN regional commanders and ultimately might be used nationwide.

CIA officers worked with appropriate Vietnamese officials at all administrative levels in a number of such programs, which included the training and arming of local self-defense and security elements. The main objective was to restore and extend the Saigon government's administrative authority throughout the countryside, and to protect the people from harassment by the Viet Cong. Other key elements of these programs, designed to improve the standard of living in rural areas, included self-help projects aimed at improving rural sanitation, medical assistance, and the introduction of modern rice cultivation and livestock farming techniques. Other programs aimed to enhance the Saigon government's administrative authority in the countryside through public information programs, local elections, the building and staffing of schools, and the restoration of local police and security activities in areas formerly under Viet Cong control. The pacification program also included a number of activities aimed at improving the government's ability to collect information on Viet Cong forces operating in these areas, and to enhance the capabilities of local government authorities to deal with them. In supporting these programs, the CIA and other U.S. agencies—the economic aid mission (USOM), the U.S. Information Service, and MACV—sought to help the Saigon government and the South Vietnamese people to prevail in their struggle against the Communist-led, Hanoi-directed "Liberation War."

All these projects contributed materially to improved public administration, security, and economic conditions, and tended to raise the quality of life in "pacified" areas. But they had little political impact in attracting the loyalty of the people—"winning their hearts and minds"—because they were conducted in a political vacuum. Neither the Diem government nor any of its successors was keen on developing an ideological base to support its efforts to combat the Communist insurrection. Diem's mystical doctrine of "personalism" was too abstract and amorphous to be understood and embraced by the non-Catholic rural peasantry. The Viet Cong espoused something that had a fundamentally popular appeal to the deeply xenophobic Vietnamese: "liberation"—freedom from domination by the foreign, neocolonialist Americans and their "puppet" government in Saigon. From 1962 on, the American military presence in South Vietnam was increasingly visible to the peasants—helicopter formations, and fighter-bombers raining rockets and napalm against Viet Cong units in rural areas. American advisers were becoming more and more evident among ARVN units in vehicles that crashed through the paddy fields and attacked "enemy-occupied" hamlets. The peasants could witness with their own eyes the validity of the Viet Cong's basic propaganda appeal.

This enemy propaganda could not be effectively countered simply by pointing to the politically sterile "civic action" projects that were obviously spawned by the American "colonialists." The situation called for a government-sponsored, broad-based political action program, with a well-articulated political platform to offset the anti-colonial "liberation" theme of the Viet Cong. By ignoring this political dimension of the war, the U.S. and the Saigon government effectively abandoned the ideological and psychological initiative to the enemy. In my view, this fundamental weakness was at the root of the failure of American policy in Vietnam.

Demilitarized Zone

Quang Tri

Hue
Phu Bai
Da Nang
Quang Nam

THAILAND

LAOS

I Corps

TACTICAL ZONES
IN VIETNAM

Dak To

Kon Tum

Pleiku   Qui Nhon

0   25   50 Miles
0   50 Kilometers

Tuy Hoa

CAMBODIA

II Corps

N

Nha Trang

Cam Ranh
*Cam
Ranh
Bay*

Phnom Penh ⊛

Song Be

Tay Ninh
Lai Khe

III Corps   Xuan Loc

Cu Chi   Saigon

Kien Hou

Can Tho

IV Corps

*Gulf of
Thailand*

Bac Lieu

SOUTH
CHINA
SEA

In the spring of 1962, Secretary McNamara visited Saigon for one of his periodic conferences on the war, together with the chairman of the Joint Chiefs, General Lyman Lemnitzer, and the Pacific commander, Admiral Harry Felt. To help the MACV staff prepare for the conference, our team had put together a map showing the areas of the country under varying degrees of control by either side. The government controlled all of the province capitals and district towns, but its authority weakened progressively as one moved from these seats of power into the rural areas. We developed a systematic approach to evaluating Viet Cong influence in—and Vietnamese government access to —each village in the countryside.

On the even of the conference, when we displayed the map to General Harkins during a rehearsal of his briefing, he and other MACV officers expressed great dismay. There was altogether too much red (signifying Viet Cong control), they said, and not enough blue, and the map incorrectly portrayed the situation as more dismal than it really was. Thereupon Colonel Winterbottom began stripping off areas of the red acetate overlay, converting "Viet Cong control" to "status unknown." He also insisted that large areas shown on the map in yellow and green (tenuous government control) be changed to blue (complete government control) for better balance.

Thus altered, the map was presented by General Harkins to the conference the next day. He introduced it as his "horrors" map, explaining that he thought it was overly generous to the enemy and understated the extend of government control—this after his intelligence chief had already drastically "improved" the security situation by several sweeps of his hands the day before. With another day of editing, Colonel W might have achieved a victorious end of the insurgency throughout the rural areas.

Seated backstage during the initial presentations to the conference, I observed that General Harkins displayed an air of confidence that reflected the basic policy of his command. Before leaving Washington, Harkins had been told that one of his most important objectives would be to encourage the Vietnamese, raise their spirits, and heighten their confidence in our ability and intent to see the war through to victory. This was the policy of the Kennedy administration, and, by God, he made it also the policy of his command. Unfortunately this emphasis on "accentuating the positive" was carried to bizarre lengths by Harkins and his staff. It was turned back into his reporting to the Pentagon, making it seem as though his purpose was to bolster Washington's spirit as well. Harkins's optimism was relentless and effusive; he seemed to exude confidence in every meeting, interview, briefing, and report.

MACV labeled its weekly situation report the Headway Report. Harkins's operations chief was put in charge of its content and carefully edited the intelligence input so as not to convey any lack of "headway" in the war effort. Enemy developments or activities that might reflect adversely on U.S.-Vietnamese progress in the war were carefully reworded, discounted, or simply omitted. Because statistics on Viet Cong activity tended to reflect the enemy's steadily growing capabilities (more frequent and larger-scale military attacks), these data were reformatted to mask their significance where possible, and ultimately relegated to an annex so that the data would not taint the impression of "headway" reflected in the narrative.

These cabled Headway Reports were the most important periodic accounts from the field on military developments in the war. Thus Washington was consistently fed a somewhat distorted view of the situation. For example, data provided to MACV by the Vietnamese government on the strategic hamlet program could reflect nothing but progress, since it was no more than a recital of Vietnamese government data reporting the number of hamlets achieving "completed" status each week—miles of new barbed wire fencing added, number of sheets of corrugated roofing and bags of bulgar rice distributed, number of medical dispensaries established, number of public information booths set up, and so on. In so far as the data were not exaggerated or otherwise distorted by the Vietnamese, these data essentially measured what was going *into* the strategic hamlet program. But they reflected nothing about the viability of the program, nor the impact of Viet Cong countermeasures. There was no reporting on the number of hamlets being harassed, raided, overrun, or razed by enemy action, and which therefore might no longer meet the criteria established for "strategic hamlets." The number of newly "completed"

strategic hamlets was simply added to the previous total each week, offering an impression of unhindered success. A more realistic view of the program could be discerned only by a careful reading between the lines of the
data on Viet Cong weekly activity, which provided figures for the number
of "strategic hamlets entered," and of "armed propaganda incidents,"
"harrassing fire," or "terrorist attacks" against unspecified targets, which
may have been paramilitary outposts, strategic hamlets, or police posts.

Other data of doubtful meaning were also part of these reports. For
example, data on the number of "battalion days" in action, or of "offensive patrols" by friendly forces, were dutifully recorded each week. These
numbers were intended to demonstrate the relative intensity—and aggressiveness—of friendly tactical operations. But they were also, of
course, simply measures of input to the war effort. They reflected nothing
in terms of their impact on the situation. How many led to contact with
the enemy? What were the results of such contacts? Enemy losses?
Friendly losses? The Vietnamese military forces were not alone in their
ability to rack up "offensive patrols" deliberately designed to inflate the
numbers without risking contact with the enemy.

The most grim of the data reported by MACV were the figures given
for the enemy "body count," which presumably resulted from an actual
count of the bodies of enemy troops found on the battlefield after an encounter. In many instances, this might actually have been the case, but
very often it was not. The natural inclination of the commanders at all
levels was to maximize the body count in order to demonstrate a greater
degree of success; there certainly was no motivation to minimize the
number. As a result, the figure was often "adjusted" upward.

Since many of the local Viet Cong guerrilla and military troops wore
no uniforms, it was next to impossible to establish their status as enemy
"troops." And since killing friendly civilians who may have been caught in
the line of fire was politically incorrect, the tendency was to count any
corpse not identifiable as friendly among the count of enemy dead. Another common adjustment was to add a figure for the number of enemy
dead who "must have been" carried off the field by withdrawing enemy
troops. This was readily rationalized when there were far fewer bodies

found than might have been expected from the intensity of a given fire-fight.

I observed one instance of this kind of adjustment while accompanying Colonel Winterbottom on a helicopter tour of a number of provinces in the delta area southwest of Saigon. The purpose of this day-long trip was for Colonel Winterbottom to meet the U.S. intelligence advisers at the regional and sector commands; he wanted to welcome them aboard his "intelligence team" and assure them of his support. In one location, the ARVN division commander was in the field overseeing a tactical sweep through a Viet Cong–held area, so we had to "drop in" on his command post in order to visit his American intelligence adviser. The ARVN advance had been slowed by contact with a "platoon" of enemy troops, who had been observed withdrawing into a tree-lined area just a few hundred yards to our front; thus we had excellent seats from which to observe a low-level strike by B-26 light bombers, which saturated the tree line with napalm bombs. When the ARVN troops reached the target area, they reported no sign of the enemy troops—no bodies, no weapons, nothing. On the helicopter on our way back to Saigon, Colonel Winterbottom asked me how many troops there were in a Viet Cong platoon. I replied that the number might vary between twenty-five and thirty-five. When I read the MACV report on that operation the next day, it listed a body count of thirty-five. I asked Colonel Winterbottom if he had any idea where that number came from, and he replied that I had given it to him when I said that a Viet Cong platoon had thirty-five men; he had himself advised the MACV operations center of the results of the encounter. When I objected that the ARVN troops had said they could find no bodies, he angrily explained that the "goddamned bombers had plastered the frigging tree line, and if a frigging VC platoon had sought shelter there, they sure as hell had been cremated or blown to frigging smithereens, so there would have been no frigging bodies to count." It was, of course, at least as likely that the enemy had moved to safety laterally along the tree line, which was on a dike, or found shelter in undiscovered tunnels dug into the dike—a common Viet Cong practice. So much for the accuracy of MACV body counts as a measure of progress in the war.

The conferences with McNamara were brisk affairs. MACV, embassy, and economic assistance officers would present briefings to the conferees, who would fire back questions. New programs would be suggested, staffed out orally around the table, and often approved on the spot as the defense secretary sought to generate momentum in the American counterinsurgency effort. McNamara wanted to break bureaucratic deadlocks, speed the decision-making process, encourage innovation, and get everyone to move ahead vigorously. His dynamic outlook was perhaps best reflected in his statement during the course of this spring conference that he did not want it to be said later that the war was lost because America was reluctant to furnish material assistance or resources in any form or quantity it was capable of providing. He made this declaration in reaction to expressions of caution, indecision, or inflexibility among some of those at the table. McNamara repeatedly urged boldness, creativity, and open-mindedness among the conferees in devising answers to the challenges confronting us in Vietnam.

One of the major new programs approved at this meeting was the so-called "hamlet radio" project. One attendee remarked on the apparent inability of regular military and security forces to "ride to the rescue" of hamlets under attack because their defenders lacked a means of communicating with nearby friendly garrisons. This piqued McNamara's interest, and under his prodding the meeting evolved the idea of placing a radio transceiver in each hamlet. A suitable civilian—rather than military—model was selected in order to reduce costs, accelerate production, and ensure early delivery. Someone estimated a probable unit cost, and McNamara authorized—on the spot—the purchase of ten thousand of these devices, one for each hamlet under government control in South Vietnam.

Someone then noted that these transceivers had power limitations, and that geographic and administrative factors argued in favor of organizing nets that would connect all hamlets by radio to their respective village center. This gave rise to an expressed need for each village to be able to relay the call for help to its district headquarters. This would require a more powerful radio set than those just approved for the hamlets, so the entire decision-making process was repeated, with McNamara instantly approving the purchase of two thousand civilian-model sets to be placed in every village. It seemed to me that all the deliberations on this matter took no more than fifteen minutes—and this was not atypical of the way the agenda was handled throughout the day.

As the conference drew to a close, the room was emptied of all those not cleared for discussion of the final item on the agenda, which involved sensitive intelligence information. Only three backbenchers stayed in the room—Colonel Winterbottom, Colonel Delaney, and me. When the door shut behind the last of those departing, McNamara waved aside our agenda item, saying the matter could wait. He wanted instead to use the remaining time to discuss the "critical" situation in Laos, which he had visited the day before. Government forces there had just been dramatically routed (again) by the Communists, and there were no government forces in position to block an enemy advance to the Mekong River and the Thai border. Assuming the Communists continued their offensive, the secretary asked, what should the U.S. response be? I started to rise to say that the assumption was invalid, that the enemy had probably intended only to check the Laotian army's timid approach into Communist-held territory; the Communist forces almost certainly did not intend to advance to the Mekong. But the colonels, one on either side of me, hooked my elbows with theirs, holding me in my seat, and sternly hushed me. McNamara asked each of the principals in turn for his views on U.S. options at this juncture in Laos.

Admiral Felt was the first of those at the table to speak. He said we should respond with air strikes; his command had carriers now deployed off the coast of Vietnam that could attack any target in Laos. They could wipe the town of Tchepone (near the Vietnam border and recently occupied by enemy troops) off the face of the earth within forty-eight hours.

Secretary McNamara seemed to wince slightly but turned quickly to the chairman of the Joint Chiefs, General Lemnitzer, who, though flustered, suggested that air strikes alone would not do the job, that we ought to implement SEATO Plan Five, which meant deploying U.S. forces through Thailand into Laos and seizing all the major cities along the Mekong. In his turn, General Harkins offered no specific measures but said something to the effect that our response should be strong enough to halt the Communist advance and to show them we meant business—but at the same time we should avoid overextending ourselves, and our action should be consistent with our capabilities and the resources available. Ambassador Frederick Nolting emphasized the strategic importance of Laos, observing that Vietnam and Thailand were the twin pillars of our policy in Southeast Asia and Laos the keystone—and we could not permit Laos to fall.

Although looking somewhat crestfallen by these responses, Secretary McNamara referred to each of these offerings in turn, raising questions with respect to each proposal, emphasizing that he was deliberately playing the devil's advocate. He asked Admiral Felt whether he believed air strikes alone would halt the Communist advance, how the destruction of Tchepone would affect the advance to the Mekong, what effect our air action would have on the North Vietnamese, whether the Hanoi government might use our air strikes as a pretext for deploying into North Vietnam the MiG units of their nascent air force then undergoing training in Yunnan Province, and what impact that would have on the freedom of movement of Admiral Felt's carriers. Turning to Lemnitzer, McNamara asked what the chairman proposed as rules of engagement for our ground forces after they occupied Luang Prabang, Vientiane, Paksane, Savannakhet, and Pakse along the Mekong (he was the only man in the room besides myself who could cite those cities in descending order from north to south without reference to a map), whether we would merely stand and defend, or counterattack to drive the enemy back, how far we should pursue them if they withdrew, and how rapidly the North Vietnamese would be able to deploy reinforcements strong enough to jeopardize the limited forces that would be deployed under the SEATO plan. The secretary found similarly thoughtful questions to ask about the less specific profferrings of General Harkins and Ambassador Nolting. During this (to me) amazing tour de force, it seemed one could almost hear the whirring as his computerlike mind probed and identified the critical issues raised by each of his "expert" advisers.

When he had finished his challenging questions, McNamara confidently leaned back in his chair as though anticipating a brisk debate. But his remarks drew nothing but silence from the others at the table. They apparently had exhausted their knowledge of the existing options and plans; their briefing books contained no background information on this "non-agenda" item, and there were no staff officers or aides present to pass them notes relevant to the subject. After what seemed an agonizingly long pause, McNamara shrugged, leaned earnestly forward, and suggested that it might be best to meditate on these issues. Then, stabbing at the table with his finger for emphasis, he said there was one thing that ought not to be overlooked. The other side had not begun its aggression in Vietnam and Laos with the intention of throwing in the towel at the first sign of opposition. He was sure they intended to win, and he hoped that somebody, somewhere, was sitting down to figure out what it was the enemy was likely to do in response to the actions that had been approved at this meeting throughout the day. He then rose, and the conference broke up.

I had mixed feelings as we left the conference room. McNamara's performance during the day had been awesome. His ability to keep the overall pattern of the mosaic in view while shaping and fitting each piece into place was impressive. His energy, capacity for detail, grasp of the significance of issues, and willingness—nay, eagerness—to make decisions clearly dominated the meeting. He was the catalyst, the driving force for action, striving to get things moving, to develop effective programs aimed at bolstering the Vietnamese government and checking the tide of the Communist insurgency. He seemed convinced that America could, should, and would meet that challenge if we put our minds and energies to the task of evolving effective solutions. Clearly he saw his task as one of prodding, guiding, and orchestrating that effort.

The secretary did not believe, however, that America should assume full responsibility for the war. During this conference he explicitly declared that our role was to help the Vietnamese do the job, not to supersede or displace them. He asked those present when they thought the Vietnamese would be able to defend themselves. General Harkins's reply indicated that MACV had scarcely thought about the matter; they were still busily expanding their staff structure and struggling to phase in the American tactical and logistical support elements. They had not yet considered the question of how and when all these forces would complete their job and could be withdrawn. MACV had no idea at this point how long it would be before the ARVN could stand on its own feet.

When McNamara recognized this, he asked General Harkins to work up a phased plan for turning back full responsibility to the Vietnamese and for the systematic withdrawal of our military forces. He suggested that 1965—three years hence—might be a suitable target date and requested that MACV present a plan for this at the next conference.

It seemed to me that the secretary was prepared to consider any date that Harkins or his staff might propose, that he was not implying that our forces should be withdrawn at any particular time. At the next conference a few months later, MACV did present a rather generalized plan for finishing its task by the end of 1965, and said that it might even be possible to begin withdrawing some elements in late 1962. McNamara then publicly announced that the United States planned to phase out its military presence in 1965. Frankly I doubted that MACV's "plan" reflected a deep study of the problem or a real commitment to finishing the job in 1965. Nevertheless MACV did go through the motions of a token withdrawal of a military police contingent late in 1962, touting it as a sign that we were approaching a turning point in our military buildup in Vietnam.

McNamara's expressed hope that someone would study the enemy's likely reaction to our continuing escalation of the war momentarily buoyed me. I was encouraged that the secretary of defense was consciously concerned with the importance of such intelligence, and delighted that he had seen fit to urge his top advisers and subordinates to pay attention to it. As we rose to leave, I remarked to Colonel Winterbottom how fortunate he was that McNamara had provided a clear focus for the colonel's long-overdue intelligence plan. When he asked what I meant, I replied that under army intelligence doctrine, the "commander" guided the intelligence effort by enunciating the "essential element of information"—the EEI. This enabled his intelligence staff to draw up a plan aimed at addressing the EEI, targeting their intelligence collection and analytical resources specifically to respond to the vital interests of the commander. I observed that McNamara's final remark had serendipitously given Colonel Winterbottom his EEI. Colonel Winterbottom barked that I should stick to my own frigging duties and let him worry about the god-dam intelligence plan.

The conference with McNamara also had its disquieting aspects. One was the tendency to "problem-solve" extemporaneously, on the spot. As a result, decisions were made without serious consideration of the conse-quences or of possible alternatives. Even agenda items carried over from earlier conferences seemed often to have been only superficially explored in the intervening months.

While this quick decision-making injected a sense of momentum, it didn't necessarily make for sound decisions. Secretary McNamara did not seem to be aware of—or disturbed by—the shallowness of some of the de-cisions. To some extent he may have assumed that the military staffs had done their homework. His ready acceptance of their judgments, views, and suggestions may have reflected misplaced trust in their professional-ism more than any desire on his part to rush through an agenda merely to create an impression of efficiency and decisiveness. For example, his deci-sions on the hamlet and village radios—whose swift resolution so pleased the conferees—seemed to me unlikely to make any measurable contribu-tion to security in the countryside. (District and provincial officials were still reluctant to send reinforcements dashing to beleaguered hamlets until well after dawn, when the enemy had usually broken off his attacks.) I formed the impression that McNamara was not well served by his "ex-pert" advisers, that they sometimes allowed themselves to be steam-rollered by not standing on their principles and professional beliefs.

Early in this 1962 trip to Vietnam, I visited the headquarters of the ARVN's field command, then headed by General "Big Minh." My purpose was to examine the potential of its intelligence staff to contribute to our project of analyzing the Viet Cong order of battle. To avoid the appearance of grandstanding, I refrained from calling on General Minh—the orchid fancier whom I had taken on a tour of Oahu four years earlier. But proto-col required that I at least see his chief of staff, the same Colonel Pham Van Dong I had met in 1954 in North Vietnam. He had then commanded the major ARVN training center at Quang Trung, just north of Haiphong.

In 1953 he had been the first Vietnamese officer to command a regimental-sized mobile group. We had hit it off very well together, partly because I had presented him with a bottle of Scotch which the army attaché's office had provided me for the occasion.

Dong greeted me warmly eight years after our first meeting but turned aside my compliment on his appointment to his present job. Resignedly, he observed that his career had not progressed significantly since our last meeting, that he had been bypassed by many who had been junior to him four years ago. He thought this was probably because of his political differences with the Diem government—he was not an insider. Dong told of having once been summoned to the palace in Saigon, where Diem said to him, "Colonel Dong, I am told you are preparing to make the coup." Dong said he had responded, "Mr. Diem, as a soldier, I am always prepared for action, but I do not make the coup." The colonel said I should note that he had not referred to Diem as "President" because he viewed him as "a usurper," having gained power illegally. I attributed Dong's apparent lack of respect to a pro-French bias; he was one of those senior ARVN officers who had served for years in the French Colonial Army. Many of them shared Dong's unhappiness with the Diem regime, and their general unhappiness was reinforced by what they saw as its heavy-handed, excessively rigid control of the military. The ARVN's leaders rarely displayed any great loyalty to Diem personally, nor to his coterie.

As our talk continued, Colonel Dong turned to contrasting the ARVN's situation in 1962 with that in the summer of 1954, when we had first met. Then, he said, the ARVN had no air force, no tanks, little artillery, no logistics. Then, the enemy was much more powerful: the Viet Minh had artillery, they had logistics, they had defeated the French at Dien Bien Phu. Now, everything was different. Now, he said, we have airplanes, we have helicopters, we have artillery, we have logistics; now the Viet Cong (here in the South) are weak—they have no artillery, they have no good logistics. "But," he said emphatically, "we will lose!" When I asked why, he said it was because "Mr. Diem" was blind—he would not allow the military to use the army properly, he would not let them fight the Viet Cong, he had given the American advisers, who knew nothing about Vietnam, too much influence. With "Mr. Diem" in charge of the government, there could be no victory.

Among Dong's laments was the recent veto by the senior American adviser to General Minh's field command of a carefully prepared plan for a national pacification campaign. As Colonel Dong described it, the plan envisioned an "ink-spot" strategy, concentrating military resources initially on securing the key population centers, ports, and lines of communication, and then gradually extending these solidly controlled areas outward, linking them up, and progressively pushing the insurgent forces back into increasingly remote areas where they could get no recruits or supplies, and where they would ultimately wither on the vine. (This was markedly similar to the "enclave plan" later put forward by, among others, General James M. Gavin, and rejected by General Westmoreland.) Dong explained that the adviser, a colonel, had rejected the concept because it required that most of the regular army units be employed in the pacification program rather than training to oppose a conventional invasion from the North. The adviser had criticized the field command's plan as being too cautious, overly passive, requiring too long to carry out, and surrendering the tactical initiative to the enemy.

Colonel Dong was markedly despondent and cynical about all this. He deplored a world in which an American colonel, with only fifteen years' military service, who in combat had never commanded anything larger than a battalion (during the Korean War), could veto such a well-staffed plan. General Minh, after all, had twenty-five years of military experience, against the very enemy now being fought, and had commanded forces in combat equal in size to an army corps—more than thirty-five battalions—during the 1955 actions against the paramilitary forces of the French-backed sects. The American colonel knew nothing of Vietnam and its people, and understood nothing about fighting a guerrilla force. But fate had decreed that he had the power to reject General Minh's plan. Life was hard indeed.

Shortly afterward, the field command was dissolved at MACV's urging, and the territorial commands were placed directly under the operational control of the ARVN general staff, which was also responsible for raising, training, and administering the ARVN. This change was the reverse of what had transpired during our own Civil War, when the direction of field operations was separated from the Union Army's general staff in 1864 and given to a separate headquarters in the field, headed by General U.S. Grant. This move had left the Union's general staff in Washington free to focus its attention on administrative matters while Grant fought the war. MACV's change saddled the ARVN general staff with the burden of directing field operations on top of its substantial administrative responsibilities.

When DIA approved Colonel Winterbottom's formal request that my stay in Saigon be extended for thirty days, General Harkins called me in to see him. He said he wanted to see "what a GS–15 intelligence specialist from DIA looked like." We chatted briefly, and then he asked that I call on him again before my departure. I agreed. In this "exit" interview he described to me his plans for keeping the Vietnamese army in the field to mount offensive operations during the coming rainy season, expressing the hope that the ARVN, with the support of American helicopter units, would be able to operate continuously despite the effects of the rains on road traffic. Wishing him well in this scheme, I expressed doubt that the projected operations would seriously impede the enemy's developing capabilities. When asked why, I said it was unlikely his intelligence staff would be able to target the enemy forces effectively. He seemed little disturbed at my candor and asked the basis for my views. I told him bluntly that his intelligence effort did not seem to be shaping up, that it could not yet inform him adequately about the enemy situation. I went on to say that his intelligence chief, Colonel Winterbottom, apparently did not understand what he was up against, and did not seem up to the task of pulling together the kind of intelligence that MACV needed to do its job. I told him there was also a gross lack of coordination among the Vietnamese intelligence services, both in the field and in Saigon; that procedures for handling captured documents and prisoners were inadequate on all sides. I observed that the resources to do the job were either on hand or could be gotten hold of, but that Colonel Winterbottom did not seem to know how to go about it. If General Harkins wanted good intelligence on the enemy, I suggested, he should begin by finding a more effective man to head his intelligence effort.

Always the calm, cool, and hopeful gentleman, General Harkins took all this in stride and said that perhaps I was overstating the case. But, he said, if there was indeed a problem, perhaps he and I could work on it together, I in Washington with the resources of DIA, and he in Saigon by guiding Colonel Winterbottom. Between the two of us, Harkins said, we should be able to improve the intelligence situation. I was unconvinced that he trusted my views, but I promised to do what I could, wished him luck, and departed for Washington.

On my way back to Washington after ninety days in Vietnam, I was asked by the commands at CINCPAC and USARPAC to stop over to discuss the state of MACV's intelligence effort and what assistance, if any, the commands in Hawaii might provide. My temporary duty in Saigon had not, of course, been on behalf of DIA as an institution; I had simply been loaned to MACV at its request. And Colonel Winterbottom certainly had no interest in having me act as an agent on his behalf. The chief of CINCPAC's intelligence staff, an air force brigadier general, pressed me to explain why I depicted MACV's intelligence effort as flagging, and what I thought ought to be done about it. I suggested that the first step should be to replace Colonel Winterbottom with someone better qualified to direct an intelligence effort in what was essentially a ground war—and a counterinsurgency situation at that. The officer showed no great shock at my suggestion, and we went on to discuss other possible steps. I learned later that the CINCPAC intelligence staff sent a back-channel message both to Colonel Winterbottom in Saigon and to air force intelligence in Washington, advising that I apparently was out to get Colonel Winterbottom.

Because the word was out that he was "under attack," the air force closed ranks behind Colonel Winterbottom. He was given several additional extensions to his "temporary duty," and in the end he served longer as intelligence officer than the normal one-year tour, and longer than either of his two immediate successors. As a consequence, the MACV's intelligence capabilities languished throughout the command's first three years.

During my one-day stopover in Honolulu (on a Friday), Washington ordered me to report first thing Monday morning to the office of General Joseph Carroll, director of DIA. McNamara apparently had suggested that General Carroll visit Saigon to look into MACV's intelligence program and see what could be done to augment its capabilities. (The president and Secretary McNamara were at that time urging all leading officials in Washington to visit Saigon to see for themselves what was going on, and bring back reports; they wanted everyone involved in the program.) General Carroll wished to debrief me as the first step in preparing himself for such a trip; I was the only DIA official who had been to Saigon.

I reported to his office on Monday morning and found all of DIA's senior officers gathered. I was asked to describe MACV's intelligence setup, its plans and activities, and to assess its effectiveness, which I did in a matter-of-fact fashion, candidly expressing myself as I had done at CINCPAC. When I had finished, General Carroll asked for my recommendations for improving the situation, and I began, after taking a deep breath, with the suggestion that Colonel Winterbottom be replaced, again outlining the reasons why I believed he was unsuitable for the assignment. General Carroll asked what service Colonel Winterbottom belonged to; when I replied that he was an air force colonel, the general flushed but continued questioning me on other matters for another fifteen minutes or so. Finally he thanked me and dismissed me.

After the door closed behind me—as one of those who remained later told me—the general asked the assembled colonels and brigadiers who the hell that civilian thought he was to call into judgment the competence of an air force colonel. None of those remaining had the knowledge, the perception, nor the inclination to note in my defense that I was a professional senior intelligence officer, an army reserve officer, and a career-long specialist on Indochina and on counterinsurgency situations. None of them believed that I knew what I was talking about, or that I had the professionalism and experience to make the judgments I had expressed.

My criticism of Colonel Winterbottom was not the only reason for General Carroll's discomfort. My briefing had outlined some serious deficiencies which clearly needed correction. And Secretary McNamara would be looking to General Carroll to do something about improving MACV's intelligence potential; the matter could not simply be dropped.

DIA did not need a problem of that magnitude and complexity. The agency had been in existence less than a year and was still in the process of pulling itself together. General Carroll himself was not experienced in field intelligence activities; he had previously headed the air force's special investigations office, which was a far cry from counterinsurgency intelligence. But he decided to face up to the situation and formed a task force to prepare him for his upcoming trip, to look into the problems I had raised, and to prepare proposals to solve them for discussion with MACV. I was initially to be included in his entourage, and though I was dropped from the party shortly before its departure for Saigon, I played a lead role in the preparations. We established a "Vietnam situation room," in which we conducted a program of several hour-long briefings for General Carroll and his party before their departure.

The general left Washington well briefed; he and his staff were ready for a thorough review of MACV's intelligence posture and confident of constructive results. But the wind was taken out of his sails when he stopped in Hawaii en route for the requisite courtesy call on CINCPAC. Admiral Felt chose to remind General Carroll that Vietnam was on CINCPAC's turf, and that as theater commander *he* was responsible for intelligence in Vietnam. He noted curtly that he reported directly to the Joint Chiefs, and that DIA was not in his chain of command. Therefore General Carroll had no responsibility for or authority over intelligence activities in Admiral Felt's theater. The admiral said he trusted that General Carroll understood this and would conduct his visit to Vietnam accordingly.

When the general reboarded his aircraft for the flight to Saigon, he advised his staff that they would not be conducting a *review* of intelligence in Vietnam but would simply make an "orientation visit" to familiarize themselves with the situation there. And that's what he and his staff did. Soon after their return to Washington, DIA—and the rest of the Kennedy administration—became caught up in the Cuban missile crisis, and I am not aware that McNamara ever called General Carroll to account for his trip to Saigon. Thus DIA was able to escape any direct involvement in, or responsibility for, the performance of the military intelligence function in Vietnam.

DIA's peripheral posture with respect to Vietnam over the next year or so contributed to my decision to leave the Pentagon and seek employment with the Central Intelligence Agency. I was not anxious to revert to a narrow specialization on Vietnam. I had welcomed the expanded professional horizons that had been my lot during the previous six years. Added responsibilities, such as managing DIA's "situation room" during the Taiwan Straits crisis in mid-1962 and the Cuban missile crisis in the fall, had been particularly rewarding, both intellectually and professionally.

Moreover, it seemed clear to me that the United States was binding itself to an albatross in Vietnam, that our government was moving ever deeper into a bottomless morass, becoming overly committed in pursuit of unattainable objectives. I believed that our chief planners and policymakers were too prone to view the problem in an oversimplified, superficial fashion. They had no comprehension of the political and social dimensions of the struggle in Vietnam, no understanding of why the French had failed, and little inclination to learn. I also believed that the Korean War had demonstrated that we Americans lacked the patience to fight a protracted war in which the issues were ambiguous, as they certainly would be in Vietnam. If the French, who had ruled in Indochina for more than eighty years, had been unable to comprehend and cope with the yearnings and longings of the Vietnamese people, I was certain that we "pragmatic" Americans would be at least equally unsuccessful. Our unqualified support for Diem's fundamentally unsuited, inept, and unpopular regime augured against any hope for success. In these circumstances I believed the intelligence community would face a thankless, uphill battle in attempting to convey a sense of reality to policymakers who were certain to be frustrated in their determined pursuit of fruitless objectives.

Shortly after my return to Washington from Saigon in 1962, word reached Walt Rostow, then with the State Department's policy planning staff, that a senior DIA analyst had returned from Vietnam with critical views of the situation. His request that I brief him on the situation caused quite a stir in DIA, which agreed to Rostow's request, provided that he come to the Pentagon for the briefing. It was also decided internally that a DIA general officer (an air force brigadier) should sit in at the briefing session as "moderator"—and I was warned to avoid criticizing MACV. While I could offer my own views on the enemy situation, I would do it without suggesting any shortcomings in MACV's intelligence effort. In effect I was not to wash the military's dirty intelligence linen in the presence of outsiders. Thus effectively grounded, my briefing evidently was not as forthcoming as Rostow seemed to have expected. He left with an air of dissatisfaction; he was certainly no better informed than he had been before we met, and his understanding of the situation in Vietnam had not been advanced. I had not been able to discuss the realities of the situation without being critical of MACV's overly optimistic reporting in a way that would have displeased my "chaperon."

Although I was not directly engaged in analyzing the Vietnam situation for DIA, I could not avoid involvement on the periphery. My normal duties included participation in DIA's current intelligence review panel, which passed judgment on the quality of articles submitted for publication. My approach to this function was aimed at sharpening the analytical content—and thereby the usefulness—of all these articles, particularly those dealing with Indochina. I deplored DIA's tendency simply to summarize field reports without commenting on their importance or placing them in a strategic context.

I was especially concerned with the need to identify and comment on trends and patterns in enemy activity. We had a responsibility, I believed, for going beyond a mere recital of facts that resembled reports from the investment markets (the Dow was up, the Nasdaq was down). We ought to put the facts into a broader perspective and make comparisons (favorable or not) with recent trends. Because any such efforts at interpretation often brought into question the overly optimistic narratives in MACV and embassy reports, our efforts drew unfavorable complaints from the field and from elements in the Joint Chiefs and the Defense Department. As a result, we were instructed to refrain from analytical remarks that could not be directly attributed to the military command in Vietnam. If MACV failed to point out that there were more battalion-sized attacks this week than last, DIA was not to make any such observation. Even when the statistical data in the annex to MACV's weekly report clearly indicated an increase in the number of assaults on strategic hamlets, we were not to point this out to consumers of DIA intelligence summaries—unless MACV had explicitly noted that fact. General Carroll apparently had decided that DIA would be politically correct and would refrain from independent analytical or interpretive comment on the course of events in Indochina.

In the late summer of 1962, I became concerned with a stagnancy in MACV's order-of-battle holdings since the publication of their first data in April. Through back channels I queried the MACV intelligence staff on the matter. After a brief delay, they advised that their analysis indeed indicated that additional combat units, comprising several thousand men, now met the criteria for "acceptance," and that this would be announced after clearing the matter with General Harkins. Soon they advised that the general had rejected the notion that enemy forces could have increased while suffering the extent of losses being inflicted on them by friendly operations. Colonel Winterbottom had therefore decided not to add the new units to the order-of-battle holdings at this time, despite hard evidence of continued growth in enemy capabilities.

Astonished at this suggestion that a field commander's subjective views could lead to the suppression of hard intelligence of mounting enemy capabilities, I tried to move the topic into open command channels, hoping to flush the matter into the open where all concerned—intelligence staffs and other officials—could see what was happening. If DIA were not to be permitted an independent view of the situation, I believed it essential that some means be found to keep MACV from suppressing the facts. To distort reality with overly optimistic evaluations of the situation was one thing; to suppress hard evidence that would preclude others from making a proper interpretation was something else.

Citing evidence reflected in fragmentary MACV reports about the creation of new units, we formally asked MACV when these units would be reflected in their order-of-battle holdings. MACV replied that there was insufficient evidence to warrant a change in those holdings, contradicting what they had said earlier in the unofficial back-channel exchanges. Thus began what was to become a continuing MACV tendency—formally and deliberately—to understate the size of the enemy's military forces and hence his potential. I was deeply chagrined at my role in contributing to the concept of developing very rigid criteria before "accepting" specific units into the order of battle. We had done this in Saigon earlier that year primarily to persuade the Vietnamese—and inexperienced young American intelligence officers—of the need for a serious, systematic approach to the problem. Now MACV was turning this insistence on hard evidence against our efforts to stimulate more realism and dynamism in the analytical effort. We were not engaged in an academic exercise but in a real-world war, where the results would impact the scale of the effort needed to defeat the burgeoning enemy forces. This sustained controversy over the strength of enemy forces in Vietnam has not been resolved today, almost forty years later.

To be truly useful to policymakers, intelligence must be a warning system. Its primary value in a dynamic situation is to detect and report incipient trends and patterns, anticipate changes, be "ahead of the curve." Intelligence staffs should never be satisfied merely with reporting, analyzing, and interpreting what *has* happened; they must concern themselves with what *is* happening now, and where that seems likely to take us. MACV's overly rigid approach to the Viet Cong order of battle could only reflect past—sometimes long past—developments, not ongoing trends. There was always a substantial time lag between an enemy unit's first reported appearance on the scene and its belated reflection in MACV's order-of-battle holdings.

In the normal order of things, the military command in the field is looked to for authoritative knowledge on the enemy situation. After all, it is on the spot, close to the situation, has initial access to the requisite intelligence data, and presumably has the principal interest in judging the size, character, and capabilities of its adversaries. If that command underestimates the enemy, it must bear the consequences; the success of its mission demands that it get the enemy order of battle correct.

In 1958 I had arranged to have USARPAC assume responsibility for the North Vietnamese order of battle because no intelligence staff in Washington was paying attention to it. When USARPAC's concern dwindled, MACV became the only intelligence staff anywhere that was devoting serious resources to the problem. Its efforts were handicapped not only by the command's apparent indifference to the validity of its order-of-battle holdings, but also by the relative inexperience of most of the junior intelligence officers available, and their unfamiliarity with either Vietnam or the unconventional character of the war. This was exacerbated by the twelve-month tour of duty of MACV's personnel, and the reality that many officers had two different assignments during that tour—a situation scarcely conducive to developing either a deep familiarity with the situation or a profound institutional memory.

During the first half of 1963, as the Buddhist crisis began to grip South Vietnam, General Carroll frequently asked me for written comments on specific press accounts of deteriorating conditions in South Vietnam's countryside. These articles contrasted sharply, of course, with the glowing accounts of progress from MACV and the embassy. Written by competent journalists such as Malcome Brown, David Halberstam, and Neil Sheehan, these reports attracted considerable interest and evoked much consternation and anguish among leading officials in Washington. In each instance, after carefully checking all the data available to DIA, I prepared brief memoranda for General Carroll which generally concluded that while we could not confirm every detail in these press accounts, they were not incompatible with the data annexed in MACV's reports. The stories generally reflected a substantial erosion of security in the countryside, contrary to reporting from MACV and the embassy. I suggested that the difference might stem from a tendency by the newsmen to lift out of context, or dramatize or exaggerate the situation, or it might reflect a more realistic viewpoint than MACV and embassy reporting—and I alluded to MACV's interest in "accentuating the positive."

I assumed that external inquiries had triggered General Carroll's interest. After several successive instances in early and mid-1963, the general discontinued such requests. I was disappointed to learn through the grapevine that there was no interest higher up in any further rocking of the boat. The fact was that these journalists were actively visiting the countryside, observing operations, and talking with lower-ranking American advisers, such as Colonel John Paul Vann, who could see that the war was not going well in their areas and were upset with the MACV's complacency and distorted reporting.

The deciding incident leading to my determination to leave the Pentagon and DIA occurred in August 1963. Marine Corps Major General Charles Krulak, a special assistant to the chairman of the Joint Chiefs, requested that DIA prepare for him a special briefing map, showing the locations of key installations in Saigon along with friendly and enemy troop units in the vicinity of the city. We understood he wanted to take the map with him to a meeting at the White House. His request came to my attention, and having little to do that day, I decided to take on the project myself. It was the sort of requirement I had handled many times over the preceding fourteen years, and I welcomed the opportunity to do something concretely useful. Obtaining the necessary map sheets, I had our DIA graphics shop mount them on briefing boards and cover them with acetate overlays, obtained the locations of the military units from DIA's Vietnam analysts, and had the units posted on the map and the key installations appropriately labeled. I was confident of the accuracy of the information.

I personally delivered the map to General Krulak before the specified deadline, and initially he seemed quite pleased with it. He complimented me on the level of detail provided and asked if it was accurate. I assured him that it reflected the best information available in Washington, and the general, still smiling pleasantly, turned to thank me. I was, of course, in civilian clothes; seeing no name tag, he asked who I was, and I replied "Allen, sir." He seemed stunned—apparently because I had mentioned no military rank before my name. Then his eyes narrowed, and he asked if I was a civilian. His jaw dropped when I replied affirmatively. He asked if I had done the work myself, and I said I had. He asked if any military men had participated in the project, and I said no, but I could personally vouch for its accuracy. He seemed dismayed, even aghast. After a brief pause, he said perhaps he could get along without the map after all, thanked me blandly for my efforts, and asked that I take the map with me on my way out. This incident coincided with secret deliberations in Washington over whether we should support the overthrow of the Diem government by its military leaders. My guess is that General Krulak probably had intended to place such a map on the table to focus discussions of the issue at the White House.

The general's assumption of civilian incompetence was the last straw for me. It was bad enough that the competence of a uniformed strategic reconnaissance specialist to manage a military intelligence effort in a counterinsurgency situation was beyond challenge by a well-qualified civilian intelligence officer. But I was humiliated by this demonstration that key people in my environment could not credit an unknown civilian with successfully performing a task that could easily have been handled by a uniformed NCO. The general may not have wanted to take the time to ask about my military background and my career experience, but I found his arrogance insufferable. It was time, I concluded, to find a more congenial work environment, one in which an individual's work was assessed on its merits rather than on the basis of the color and cut of his suit.

That afternoon I made my daily trek to Langley, Virginia, where for two years I had been representing DIA at the CIA's intelligence summary meeting. After the meeting I asked a senior CIA officer with whom I had become acquainted whether his agency had any room for a professional intelligence officer. He asked what civil service grade I held, and when I told him, he replied that the CIA was not taking people in that grade in a lateral transfer from other agencies. When I said I would take a one-grade cut, he was surprised but said he would look into the matter. On returning to my desk in the Pentagon later that afternoon, I found a note saying he had telephoned. When I returned his call, he said he was sending me a package of papers to fill out. Less than two months later, I reported for work as a senior analyst on Southeast Asia in the CIA's Office of Current Intelligence.

Before leaving for the CIA, I sought meetings with DIA's director and deputy director, hoping to explain to them the reasons for my leaving, and especially my concerns about the continuing deficiencies in military intelligence on Vietnam. Neither of them was available, but I was received by the DIA chief of staff, Admiral Sam Frankel, whom I had known previously. He listened impatiently but politely as I explained my reasons for leaving, asked no questions, thanked me for dropping by, and wished me well at the CIA. He did not react when I advised him that I had agreed to a loss in grade in order to go to the CIA. It seemed apparent that the DIA hierarchy would not mourn my departure, presumably because it removed from the premises a potential source of embarrassment.

8
At the
CIA

AS A NEWCOMER to the Central Intelligence Agency, I was not immediately included in the inner circle of CIA Southeast Asia specialists privy to sensitive matters. I was aware that some Vietnamese generals had been talking of a coup, but I did not have the same access to CIA operational messages or to the most sensitive State Department cables that my branch chief had. Nevertheless, in the waning weeks of October 1963 one could sense that the Diem regime was near the end of its rope, and it was only a matter of time before it would fall. My branch chief was discreet, yet I sensed he had access to inside information. We discussed the situation frequently, and I told him that although I agreed with those who believed it was not possible to "win with Diem," I also doubted that we could win without him. I observed that Diem and his family tightly controlled all the strands of power, particularly the police, the key intelligence and security services, and the army's special forces, as well as the Presidential Guard. Removing Diem from the scene would almost certainly lead to the unraveling of that web. If Diem fell, the result would be comparable to the fall of Humpty-Dumpty, and it might not be possible to put the pieces together again.

Under the circumstances, I suggested, unless we had valid reasons for concluding that any successor regime was prepared to pick up the pieces and knew what to do with them, it would be counterproductive for us to encourage a coup. Only if a successor group offered real prospects for running things more effectively than Diem, and was prepared to take positive political action to create a broad popular base, could it hope to overcome the Viet Cong. In the absence of real assurance in this regard, I doubted that a change in government would be in our best interests in the long run. My branch chief agreed. Others with similar views had reached our policy leaders, he said; all we could do was hope for the best.

On my own initiative I spent most of one day late in October working with the CIA graphics shop to prepare a briefing map of the Saigon area, almost identical to the one I had prepared for General Krulak three months earlier, so that we would be prepared if a coup came. As it happened, we spent the wee hours of the next morning at the Agency's operations center following events in the developing coup d'état in Saigon. We prepared a situation report and briefing notes for the director's morning meeting at the White House, and he took with him the briefing map we had put together the day before.

One of my first chores in CIA had been to represent the agency in a briefing for the secretary of state in late October. The president apparently had nudged Dean Rusk to get more involved in Vietnam, and the secretary was planning to attend one of McNamara's periodic conferences. William Sullivan, then head of the interagency task force on Vietnam, chaired the briefing session, which was held in Rusk's office about 5 p.m. George Ball sat in on much of the session.

I inferred from Sullivan's introductory remarks that this may have been the secretary's first in-depth exposure to the Viet Cong problem. Sullivan began with a broad overview in which he described the Viet Cong as a collection of guerrilla bands composed of peasants who farmed by day and fought by night. Appalled at this gross understatement of the true character of the situation, I exchanged glances with a respected colleague from State's intelligence bureau sitting opposite me; his raised eyebrows suggested that he shared my consternation. It seemed that we had our work cut out for us. Our fears were confirmed when DIA's team of military briefers—my recent colleagues—proved only too willing to toe the party line as set out by Sullivan. As they ran down the compilation of enemy forces on their briefing boards and maps, they repeatedly apologized for referring to "regiments and battalions," observing that these were really only part-time guerrilla bands, not comparable to conventional military units. Coming at a time when intelligence had just confirmed that the enemy was evolving a divisional command structure for his main force units in South Vietnam, I thought this was reprehensible behavior on the part of the DIA briefers.

They were well into the briefing before I was able to get a word in edgewise. Referring initially to a reference they had made to the Hanoi–Viet Cong relationship, I described the Communist command and control system for the war in the South, the nature of Hanoi's support, and the accelerating buildup of regular military forces equipped with a variety of heavy weapons. Referring back to DIA's briefing charts, I made the point that although some of the enemy forces were indeed irregulars, as described by Sullivan and the DIA briefers, a growing proportion were regular forces organized into conventionally structured combat units built around and led by professional, well-trained, and veteran officers, NCOs, specialists, and technicians infiltrated from the North. Citing intelligence from special sources, I concluded by noting that the emerging, division-sized regular units were adding a new dimension to the enemy's capabilities. They could be expected to pose a serious challenge to a Vietnamese government and military establishment already seriously weakened by the Buddhist crisis. George Ball largely supported my remarks, and my State intelligence colleague reinforced them at several points. But Sullivan closed the session as he had opened it, suggesting that the situation was not as bleak as some of the intelligence people believed. Rusk may have gone on to attend McNamara's next conference, but thereafter he continued to let the defense secretary take the lead on Vietnam.

In the aftermath of Diem's overthrow, Viet Cong activity intensified throughout South Vietnam. Although MACV continued to accentuate the positive, it became increasingly difficult to mask the scale and scope of the enemy buildup that was suggested, in part, by MACV's own reports. Embassy reporting also took on a somewhat more realistic tone as it became evident that the situation in the countryside was much more serious than Washington had been led to believe. Secretary McNamara expressed to CIA director John McCone his concern over the situation in the countryside, and they agreed to survey the American and Vietnamese intelligence efforts to determine what might be done to improve our awareness of the true situation. McCone proposed that a join CIA-DIA team be sent to the field for this purpose. The secretary agreed, but the Joint Chiefs objected, presumably on parochial grounds that it would be inappropriate for a military command to submit to an "inspection" of its intelligence effort by the CIA. McNamara then asked McCone whether the CIA could undertake the task unilaterally, looking into those nonmilitary U.S. and Vietnamese intelligence activities that might be construed as being within the agency's purview. The main concern of both men was to find some way of getting a systematic reading on the true state of affairs in the countryside; they were looking for ways to improve intelligence coverage, particularly at the rice roots level.

CIA in January 1964 thus assembled a team of seasoned intelligence officers, all with prior experience in Indochina. I was assigned as the lone analyst on the team; the other members were veteran operations officers. Working with this group for more than two months was one of the most professionally rewarding experiences of my career.

In Saigon the CIA station arranged for us to be briefed by embassy, MACV, and Vietnamese officers at the start. Our mission was described to MACV as a survey of Vietnamese intelligence activities, primarily police. Because the ARVN's intelligence apparatus was represented in commands at the province and district levels, it would be necessary to have MACV's cooperation as we looked into police intelligence activities in the countryside. MACV recognized this need and agreed. With MACV's explicit approval, we also acquired access to the MACV and ARVN intelligence apparatus at all levels, from the capital in Saigon to the district level, and were thus able to accomplish exactly what McCone and McNamara had in mind.

Among those who briefed us was Major General Richard Stilwell, then operations chief of MACV, who arrived in fatigues and combat boots, having just returned by helicopter from a visit to the command post of a major ARVN operation in one of the Mekong Delta provinces. The general was enthusiastic about the prospects for a tactical success by ARVN regiments against a notorious Viet Cong base area, where they were believed to have trapped at least one—and probably two—Viet Cong battalions. Stilwell rhapsodized articulately at some length, describing the operation as a potential turning point in the war, and extolling the anticipated effectiveness of procedures for coordinating combined MACV-ARVN operations. Spotting me in the group, he quickly remembered a briefing I had given him at DIA in Washington several months earlier, whereupon he abruptly shifted the topic to a discussion of the "principal problem" in Vietnam—the Viet Cong's political-military "infrastructure." I had coined the use of that term in briefing him and other military officers who were en route to assignments in Vietnam.

Rarely have I had the substance of a briefing fed back to me so fully and accurately as on this occasion. The general repeated most of what I had said about the "tip of the iceberg" being the enemy's main force military units, but that these were supported by the larger portion of his force structure that lay below the surface—the political-military infrastructure, the party apparatus, the provincial, district, and village committees that directed the Viet Cong effort at the grass roots, the paramilitary guerrilla-militia forces, the "liberation" associations (women, old men, youth), and so on. I was buoyed by this apparent indication that there were now in MACV senior officers who really understood the nature of the Viet Cong threat. If this were the case, there might now be hope that MACV would adopt realistic programs in pursuing the war; that success might be possible after all! But after just a few minutes in this vein, the general reverted to the more conventional military stereotype, observing that while it was important to be aware of the enemy's infrastructure, the main target had to be his military forces, and that the war would be won by search-and-destroy operations like the one he had been describing earlier. He went on to recount other facets of this "most important" operation. A few days later that operation was terminated without any significant contact with the supposedly "trapped" Viet Cong battalions; they had slipped away almost untouched. Although extremely articulate and able intellectually to grasp the nature of a Communist insurgency, General Stilwell seemed nevertheless unable (or unwilling) to translate that understanding into a realistic and effective counterinsurgency strategy.

After these briefings our team divided itself into sections, a field team of two or three officers to examine conditions in each of the four military regions, and two of us to look into the national intelligence setup in Saigon. I was elected as rapporteur for the team, and it was agreed that I would monitor the activities of our regional teams from Saigon and suggest issues for them to look into. The regional teams would report their findings to me, and if they uncovered anything "interesting" in their areas, I was to be invited to come have a look. These informal arrangements worked out quite well in practice, and at the end of two months we had finished our task and compiled our report.

In the report we noted the lack of effective coordination among American and Vietnamese intelligence components in the provinces, and particularly the inadequacy of procedures for exploiting captured documents and prisoners. We documented our findings and recommended steps to alleviate these shortcomings, noting the need for a coordinated intelligence effort from the top down. We cited the example of the British procedures in Malaysia. To parallel this, a mechanism would be needed—in the national capital in Saigon and in each region, province, and district—charged with integrating the activities of all American and Vietnamese intelligence services, civil and military. We also suggested that joint interrogation centers be established at each level to facilitate timely and thorough exploitation of prisoners and defectors to meet the combined needs of both civil and military intelligence services.

We called for the embassy, MACV, and the CIA station to establish systematic procedures at the Saigon level for periodic, in-depth, joint appraisals of the situation in each of the provinces, doing several each month and repeating the process at least once a year. We suggested that consideration be given to reviving the concept of a joint U.S. evaluation center, directly responsible to the ambassador, to oversee the appraisal program and to undertake independent, overall assessments of the situation and prepare detailed studies of key factors such as infiltration, the enemy political and military structure, and North Vietnamese support.

Few of these recommendations were implemented in toto, though a number of them were at least partially effected at one time or another. Several factors inhibited their adoption. One was the unilateral CIA character of the team, which was highlighted by Ambassador Henry Cabot

Lodge during one of the McNamara conferences that occurred late in our visit. The ambassador had met with us for several hours the day before, and chose to laud the team and its informal findings in his opening remarks to the conference. Unfortunately he focused his remarks on a series of observations he had elicited from us that were critical of the way the war was being fought, and he attributed them to the "intelligence survey team." General Taylor, attending the meeting as chairman of the Joint Chiefs, was incensed at our apparent effrontery, noting that he understood the group was composed of CIA civilians and that the team's views on operational strategy and the structure of ARVN's military and paramilitary force structure were irrelevant. We—along with McCone and the chief of station—were chagrined that the ambassador has used the team's findings to support his own misgivings about the way MACV was fighting the war.

Another factor inhibiting the implementation of our recommendations was the turf war between MACV and the CIA station for control of intelligence. A CIA station chief nominally is the principal American intelligence officer in a foreign country. Under peacetime conditions he is responsible for coordinating all U.S. intelligence activities in that country. In time of war, however, the CIA is expected to pass its intelligence assets to the control of the American theater commander. In Vietnam there was no declaration of war. Although an American military command operated in the country, the ambassador remained—nominally at least—the chief of the U.S. mission there. General Harkins—and later General Westmoreland—was a member of the ambassador's "country team," just as were the head of our economic aid program, the U.S. information service program, and the CIA station chief. The situation was unique: the United States was engaged in active military operations, but we were not at war. MACV's intelligence staff was expanding rapidly and already was more numerous than the CIA station.

The issue of intelligence jurisdiction cropped up from time to time but was never fully resolved. MACV chafed at the CIA's relative autonomy within the U.S. "country team" and occasionally flexed its muscles in an effort to bring the CIA station under its control. The station chief, Pier de Silva, was a West Point graduate who had served in the army during

World War II but had become a CIA career civilian. He insisted on maintaining CIA's independence in Vietnam on practical grounds; he also seemed to gain some personal satisfaction from crossing swords with his erstwhile military cohorts.

In the end, the United States never achieved a fully unified command structure in Vietnam. The commander of MACV had no command authority over the Seventh Fleet or the Seventh Air Force combat elements supporting his operations; he never gained command authority over the ARVN; and he never won authority over the CIA station. Some elements of the station came under MACV control when those civilian components involved in pacification operations were merged into the CORDS program, but the remainder of the CIA station retained its autonomy within the country team. Ultimately, under the CORDS arrangement, coordination was achieved at the provincial and district levels through the creation of combined intelligence centers in which the interests of all U.S. and Vietnamese intelligence services were represented. But the effort never achieved the degree of integration and effectiveness the British had enjoyed in Malaya.

Our survey team had also noted that MACV intelligence was continuing to understate the size of the enemy forces and had not yet produced serious studies of enemy logistics, force structures, or infiltration. Its order-of-battle analysis focused almost exclusively on the enemy's main force units, a factor that contributed to MACV's focus on large-scale conventional military operations. The "main force war" appealed to our military men; it more closely approximated the military problems taught at our army schools than did the guerrilla forces and tactics that were the foundation of the Viet Cong effort at this period of the war. The expansion of Viet Cong main force capabilities reflected in intelligence reporting—and in the scale of enemy action—made it expedient for MACV to focus on conventional solutions to the war and to ignore the guerrilla problem.

General Taylor had objected to our team's criticism of this tendency, which was then evident in MACV's approach to almost every aspect of the war effort. In 1963, MACV had begun taking over the larger paramilitary programs that had been initiated by the CIA. In doing so, the military tended to transform these forces along conventional military lines. Covert operations, against the North under MACV auspices became small-scale, hit-and-run, commando-type actions; the Civilian Irregular Defense Groups were formed into companies and battalions that were used to garrison border posts or serve as mobile "strike forces"; the focus was no longer on defending Montagnarde villages. The former civil guard and self-defense forces (neither developed by the CIA) were finally brought under military control and formed into Regional Force and Popular Force (Ruff-Puff) battalions and companies. MACV preferred that these units be used for "mobile" operations rather than being scattered about in local security outposts. MACV consistently resisted efforts to maintain paramilitary forces for the static defense of villages and hamlets to protect the populace and "show the flag." Their policy rejected passive, garrison forces; they believed all friendly military units should be engaged in mobile, offensive operations, constantly on the move, keeping the enemy forces off balance, seeking them out and destroying them. The problem was that, until the enemy was found and destroyed, this policy left the local populace vulnerable to Viet Cong harassment, terrorism, and political-psychological action. A populace thus cowed would not voluntarily cooperate with U.S. and Vietnamese government forces that merely passed through occasionally, in contrast to the Viet Cong underground cadres who stayed in place.

These issues were constantly debated in Saigon. Many within the MACV structure, both in Saigon and in the field, understood the problem and voiced opposition to the U.S. military's conventional approach, but they were always in the minority. An example of the nature of this problem is reflected in an encounter I had with an American intelligence adviser in one of the northern provinces (Thua Thien) during the survey mission. This young captain, still recovering from serious wounds suffered when his jeep had struck a mine, was briefing me on the enemy situation in the sector's operations center, using his charts and maps to illustrate the numbers, composition, and locations of the Viet Cong forces. He made no mention of the guerrilla-militia forces, and these were not reflected in his charts, so I asked about them. He replied that all Viet Cong troops were guerrillas. Agreeing that they all employed guerrilla tactics, I noted that his data obviously reflected only main force and local force units, organized at the province and district levels, but that I presumed the Viet Cong also had in this province, as elsewhere in Vietnam, guerrilla and militia units organized at the village and hamlet level. He confidently said there were no such forces in his province.

I turned to a boyish-looking ARVN officer—the Vietnamese sector intelligence chief—who had been standing by patiently while his American adviser briefed me, and asked him about the guerrilla-militia forces. His uncomprehending look made it clear that he did not understand English, so I asked him in Vietnamese about the *dan quan* (people's force, or militia) and *dan quan du kich* (guerrilla troops). His eyes brightened, and, breaking into a knowing grin, he went to the blackboard and wrote out the numbers for each of these two forces in that province. As I quizzed him further, he broke these numbers down by district, then showed me the records he maintained to support his estimates for the strength of these guerrilla-militia forces in his sector.

The American captain was embarrassed and chagrined. With just two weeks remaining in his one-year tour in Vietnam, he had discovered only now that he had been wholly unaware of half the enemy's military strength in his sector. This was early in February 1964; for several months he had been responsible for "advising" his Vietnamese army intelligence counterpart on the collection and evaluation of intelligence on the enemy. He had also been responsible for keeping his superior—the American sector adviser—up to date on the nature of the enemy threat and on the strengths and vulnerabilities of enemy forces in their sector. He was also responsible for passing relevant information up the line to the American intelligence adviser at the division level. Yet this bright young fellow had not been able to communicate well enough with his counterpart to gain from him an understanding of the enemy's force structure. Saddest of all, he had not been provided with relevant information from MACV's intelligence staff in Saigon, which—two years after it had gone into business—had not yet gotten around to publishing and disseminating a handbook on enemy forces for use by its intelligence advisers to the ARVN.

On a visit in March to another sector (Quang Ngai Province) further south, I encountered a major surprise of another sort. I had been discussing the situation in the sector in front of a map with an overlay depicting enemy activity over the past month. As we were preparing to leave, I noticed a stack of such overlays on top of the table and happened to flip through them. As I did so, the "incidents" on the overlays took on an animated series of patterns. I repeated the movement at a slower rate and realized that they revealed an astonishing flow of enemy activity from outlying areas of most districts inward, toward the district towns. Most of the others present—Americans and Vietnamese—said they hadn't noticed such a pattern before, though one of the older Vietnamese NCOs nodded his head knowingly, with an expression of disdain on his face for the officers present.

We studied these overlays closely for a few minutes, and it became evident to all of us that the pattern had begun to take shape during the preceding summer months, and had accelerated substantially since the overthrow of the Diem government. The overall pattern was that of a tide rising against rocks in the water—or sand castles on the beach—sweeping from the foothills into the coastal plain and converging on each of the district towns. This pattern appeared to have intensified in November. It seemed as though every vestige of local security stemming from the strategic hamlet program in 1962 and early 1963 must have been swept away by this tide of activity. Each of these incidents of enemy activity had been duly reported as it occurred, but apparently the information had not been collated and studied; certainly no one had reported what we had stumbled on by a casual flip of the overlays. No one in Saigon at MACV or the embassy had reported the kind of erosion we could see so readily.

When I returned to Saigon, I wrote a report on what I had seen in Quang Ngai, which we radioed back to Washington. I commented that this was the clearest, and certainly the most vivid, illustration I had seen of the pattern of deterioration in the countryside. None of the other sector or district command posts I had visited during our survey kept their older overlays lying about for perusal by visitors, but the gist of most of the discussions I had there had suggested a similar increase in enemy activity and a general deterioration in local security. The overlays in Quang Ngai clearly indicated that the ARVN's position was becoming tenuous; I concluded that if the trend continued, some of the district towns would be cut off within the next few months. If this pattern was being repeated in other provinces, I suggested, the security situation in Vietnam had deteriorated far more seriously than had been reported, and in Quang Ngai Province the Viet Cong seemed to have undone any progress achieved by the strategic hamlet program.

A few days later the Pentagon asked MACV to comment on my report, which had been circulated in Washington. Their reply was prepared by Major General Charles Timmes, in charge of the military advisory program, who had visited Quang Ngai Province a few days before my visit. He cabled to Washington a lengthy, rosy rejoinder to my report, essentially recounting all the positive things ARVN was attempting in the province, and denying any lasting effects from the Viet Cong activity I had referred to. In a later conversation with this very kind, genial general, he admitted that he hadn't seen the series of overlays I had been shown, and that the advisers certainly hadn't seemed as greatly concerned as I was. He knew the situation was not "going well" in this province, which had been one of those under the complete control of the Viet Minh during the French war, but it had seemed to him no worse than usual. He thought I had been too harsh in suggesting the demise of the strategic hamlet program in that province.

The kindly General Timmes was a holdover from the "accentuate the positive" school. Later that year, he and I happened to be visiting ARVN's II Corps headquarters at Pleiku on the same day, and I sat in on the formal briefings presented to him by the feisty and demonstrative Vietnamese Corps commander, General Ton That Dinh, and his staff. The situation in II Corps late in 1964 was going very badly. ARVN units were suffering heavy losses and seemed to be losing their self-confidence in combat with enemy main force units, which were gradually constricting ARVN's freedom of movement in the highlands. But each time Dinh or one of his staff cited an unfavorable fact, General Timmes would quietly interrupt the briefing to offer a "silver lining" or some otherwise positive or encouraging remark. He reminded me of a one-man cheering section at a high school football game, urging a beleaguered, tiring defense to "hold that line, hold that line."

During the survey team's activities, one striking feature was the extent to which the American advisers at all levels rapidly became—despite their normally brief tenure—the prime source of continuity and stability in the counterinsurgency effort. In the Diem era there had been substantial continuity in government and ARVN personnel appointments. Officials generally managed to cling to their positions as long as they could avoid incurring the wrath of the Ngo family, often spending several years in a particular post. Some changes had occurred in the aftermath of the aborted military coup in November 1960, and a few shifts were made to prop up the tottering structure during the Buddhist crisis, but otherwise continuity had been a hallmark of the Diem regime.

After the Diem coup, however, wholesale changes occurred in most positions at almost every level. Following the second coup—just ten weeks after Diem was overthrown—when General "Big Minh" was displaced by General Khanh, a second set of sweeping changes occurred, and this pattern of wholesale "purges" continued after each of the successive changes of government that erupted during the turbulent period that ended in June 1965 when Generals Nguyen Cao Ky and Nguyen Van Thieu finally stabilized the military hierarchy.

Each new head of government in his turn had purged key military, police, and civilian officials to bring in people whom he trusted (and who were willing to meet his "price" for the job). And each of these subordinates then brought in his "loyal" friends and relatives into key staff and command positions under his control, and so on down the line. The city of Da Nang had five mayors and five police intelligence chiefs during the year following the Diem coup but was far from unique.

In such circumstances even the most recently arrived American advisers soon became "experts" on the local situation. On one occasion I was present at a provincial airport in the delta area when a newly appointed Vietnamese province chief arrived. He was met by his American military counterpart, who immediately led the new chief to a waiting helicopter for a quick visit to a district town where immediate action was required to counter a significant Viet Cong threat. The adviser briefed his new counterpart en route, and, on arrival at the trouble spot, saw to it that the province chief made the necessary (and appropriate) decisions before moving on to another trouble spot. There the routine was repeated before the pair returned to the province capital and the new chief was shown to his new quarters by his American adviser.

This was a period in the war when the turnover on both the Vietnamese and American sides was so turbulent that virtually all institutional memory was lost, particularly at the lower levels. It was a rarity in 1964 and early 1965 to find a Vietnamese who had been in the same assignment for more than three months, and few American military men remained in the same post for more than half a year. In my travels later in 1964 and 1965, I often encountered situations in which no official—American or Vietnamese—was aware of a specific incident of unique significance that had occurred in that locale a year or so earlier.

I remained in Saigon for a month or so, finishing up the team report and working on special assignments for the CIA station. These included providing CIA director McCone with morning briefings during his visit to attend the McNamara conference. He met formally with the full team one morning and seemed satisfied that we had accomplished what he had hoped. My chores finished, I departed Saigon in early April, having agreed to consider the station chief's suggestion that I return in June to succeed his senior analyst whose tour would then expire.

William Colby and others claim that we won the pacification war in the early 1970s, after the Communist guerrilla-militia forces and their political infrastructure in the countryside had been decimated following the defeat of their conventional military offensives in 1968 and 1969. This may be true, but how much sooner might this have been accomplished had the Vietnamese government mounted an effective political-action program, based on the need for a social revolution, backed by the resources of the United States?

9
Assignment
in Saigon

ON RETURNING TO WASHINGTON in early April 1964, after ninety days in Vietnam, I resumed my analytical duties in the Office of Current Intelligence while preparing for my "permanent change of station" to Saigon. Agency headquarters had concurred in this assignment. The normal CIA overseas tour was two years and included the accompanying movement of families. Saigon was becoming increasingly insecure, and it was evident that the U.S. mission was waiting for a major terrorist incident that would provide a pretext for evacuating American dependents and "clearing the decks" for action. Because of this, I was not anxious to uproot my wife and four young daughters for what was likely to be a short-lived transfer to Saigon, and then to be in no position to look after them when evacuation was ordered. Therefore I decided to go by myself for the two-year tour, with the proviso that I would be entitled to two trips home for consultation at headquarters and visitation with my family during my assignment in Vietnam. In 1965, after dependents had been evacuated, agency officers assigned to Vietnam went on an eighteen-month "unaccompanied" tour, without visitation rights.

My position in the Saigon station was somewhat unique for the agency. Intelligence directorate analysts were assigned to certain other CIA stations, but none of them was in an active war zone. My duties thus differed in some respect from theirs. My principal functions were to advise the station chief on substantive intelligence matters, to keep him abreast of developments in the situation, and to prepare assessments of the situation for his use in the U.S. mission or for cable to Washington. I responded to queries from analysts in Washington and worked with the station's officers as they processed reports from local sources to be forwarded to headquarters. I also worked with officers in the embassy's political section and with their able team of "province reporters"—young foreign service officers fluent in Vietnamese who "rode circuit" to groups of provinces, gathering and reporting information on commercial, economic, political, and security conditions. And I kept in touch with elements of our economic aid mission (USOM) and with the U.S. Information Service in Saigon.

I had almost daily contact with MACV's intelligence staff in Saigon and frequently contacted their intelligence advisers during my visits to the field. I worked similarly with the Vietnamese civil and military intelligence services both in Saigon and in the countryside. My duties included briefing visiting American and foreign VIPs, shepherding some of them on their travels about the country, and "backgrounding" journalists who could be relied upon to be discreet in their reporting.

As part of the mission's nascent "province assessment" program, early in my tour I volunteered to prepare such an assessment of the situation in Quang Nam Province. During a three-day visit there I met with local American and Vietnamese officials, and visited most of the district towns in the province. My military escorts and I had a couple of hair-raising incidents involving exchanges of fire. A few weeks later, during a visit to Long An Province, the sector intelligence adviser, seeing I was unarmed, handed me a concussion grenade to use "as necessary" as we passed through an area where there had been an ambush the previous day. As a result of these experiences, I routinely packed an automatic pistol in the attaché case I carried on visits to the field.

I worked closely, of course, with other CIA station officers, both in Saigon and in the outlying provinces. They knew aspects of the situation that did not find their way into intelligence reports but were useful as additional tiles in the mosaic of my understanding. I consulted with our people during trips to the provinces and debriefed them when they visited Saigon in connection with their field assignments.

My job, in short, was to learn as much as possible about the situation and to share that knowledge with those who had a need for it. I had about as much access to information on the situation as anyone else in Vietnam, with the exception of sensitive operational information known to the station chief and his key operations officers, and the back-channel communications exchanged between Washington and the embassy and MACV in Saigon.

My access to some special intelligence materials technically precluded travel outside metropolitan Saigon. But both station chiefs under whom I served understood that my usefulness as "substantive adviser" would be limited if I were unable to check on important developments in the field, and therefore they tacitly let me travel at my own discretion, on a "don't ask, don't tell" basis.

Having ready access to air transportation, I could spend up to a half-day in any but the northernmost provinces in the country and return to Saigon before nightfall, though I often remained overnight in some of the larger, more secure cities such as Hue, Da Nang, Pleiku, and Can Tho. Because of my relative freedom of movement, I was often able to act as the "eyes and ears" of my MACV colleagues, who were grounded by stricter observance of the travel restrictions.

The perspective in Saigon on key events in 1964 and 1965 naturally differed sharply from that in Washington. The Tonkin Gulf episode illustrates that difference. Because I had access to information about U.S. destroyer patrols off North Vietnam, and was also aware of the planned "covert" shelling by Vietnamese special operations forces of an enemy radar station in the Tonkin Gulf, I erroneously assumed that the left and right hands of our military commands (MACV and the Seventh Fleet) would know enough to stay out of each other's way—in other words, that the *USS Maddox* would be advised to steer clear of the "covert" action. But it wasn't. I was also astonished by the alarmist response in Washington when the North Vietnamese navy reacted to the *Maddox*'s appearance in the neighborhood on the heels of the attack on their island radar station. The ensuing engagement between the *Maddox* and the North Vietnamese patrol craft, one of which was sunk, was—I thought—only to be expected under the circumstances. It seemed apparent to me, from the sensitive intelligence available, that the Vietnamese craft were simply "investigating" the unexpected appearance on the scene of the American destroyer, and that the clash resulted in large part from a misunderstanding by the participants on both sides.

The North Vietnamese navy's reaction to the appearance in the area of a pair of American destroyers two nights later seemed much more cautious; there was no evidence that they actually intended to attack. Hence I was stunned by Washington's decision to retaliate for the second North Vietnamese "attack" by bombing North Vietnamese naval bases. I have always believed that our highest-level officials became confused in their reading of raw, unevaluated intelligence reports, and that they did not realize that some of the "flash" reports they were reading at the time of the second incident contained information that was forty-eight hours old and in fact pertained to the first attack on the *Maddox*. Reliable historians have rightly concluded, I believe, that administration leaders seized the opportunity afforded by their reading of the ambiguous evidence to create circumstances that would enable them to extract a blank check from Congress for further escalation of our involvement in Vietnam.

In Saigon I was not fully aware of the extent of the administration's preparations for further escalation. My departure from Washington in mid-1964 coincided with the beginning of intensive planning as the president and his senior advisers considered various new courses of action in Vietnam. Planning had continued through the fall. I had been aware of Ambassador Taylor's recommendation against Washington's desire to bomb the North in retaliation for the Viet Cong's November shelling of the air base at Bien Hoa, which had destroyed several recently arrived American light bombers. But I did not realize how eagerly the administration was seeking a pretext for a major escalation which might stabilize the shaky South Vietnamese government and possibly force Hanoi to step back from its support of the war in the South.

Hence I was equally startled by Washington's reaction to the mortar and satchel-charge attacks on two American compounds near Pleiku in February 1965, which led to the beginning of our sustained bombing of North Vietnam and to the introduction of U.S. ground combat forces.

The Pleiku incidents were just two of several hundred simultaneous enemy attacks and harassing actions that occurred that same night at the end of the annual Tet cease-fire period. The Viet Cong's post-Tet "high-points" of activity had already become a tradition in Vietnam. In 1965 several of these attacks were on a larger scale than before, and the incidents were more numerous. At Pleiku there were more American casualties than in any previous incident, but they were not the first attacks on American forces. I was far more impressed with the number of major incidents that night throughout South Vietnam, and was pulling together a report analyzing the pattern of enemy activity when I learned that Washington had decided to retaliate by bombing military barracks in North Vietnam.

National Security Adviser McGeorge Bundy was visiting Saigon at the time of the incidents at Pleiku. The next day a senior intelligence officer at MACV—a brilliant and competent army colonel—told me of Bundy's phone call to Washington from MACV headquarters the afternoon before, in which he exaggerated the significance of the Pleiku incident by tying it to his visit to Saigon—and to that of Soviet premier Aleksey Kosygin, who also happened to be in Hanoi that day. Bundy had returned that afternoon from a trip to Pleiku, where he had observed the damage and seen some of the American wounded being removed from the wreckage. Over the secure phone, an emotionally drained Bundy advised the president that Hanoi had "thrown down the gauntlet." In his view the Viet Cong had, in apparent collusion with the Soviet prime minister, deliberately attacked an American installation, knowing that Bundy was in Saigon, to test the American reaction. I later heard a respected American journalist relate how he had been summoned to the White House in the middle of the night by a distraught President Johnson who, shaken by his earlier conversation with Bundy, grimly stated his determination to "lean on those (bleepers), I'm gonna lean on them (bleepers) hard." Johnson reportedly commented emotionally that he couldn't simply stand by and let the enemy "pick off our boys in all those isolated little Alamos." He vowed to "bomb the (bleeping) North."

There was, of course, no connection between the 1965 visits of Bundy to Saigon and Kosygin to Hanoi, and the annual, post-Tet "high point" in

Viet Cong activity. Probably no one in Hanoi knew that the American airstrip at Pleiku and the MAAG advisers' compound were to be included among hundreds of targets that the Viet Cong attacked that night. Kosygin's trip to Hanoi had probably been scheduled before Bundy's was announced. When this post-Tet flare-up of military attacks had been planned, no one in Moscow, Hanoi, or Washington had any idea Bundy would be in Saigon that night. Indeed, on a visit a few days later to Pleiku, I learned that one of the Viet Cong sappers involved in the satchel-charge attacks on the MAAG officers' billets had been wounded and captured. During his interrogation he disclosed that he had been detached from his former infantry unit three months earlier and assigned to the sapper team organizing for this action. After joining this unit, he had repeatedly rehearsed his role in preparation for the attack.

It would seem, then, that our bombing of the North in February 1965 was a retaliation waiting for something to happen; the Pleiku attacks were a convenient trigger for intended escalation. We had carefully built up the capability to bomb the North from bases in South Vietnam; aircraft and crews had been deployed and were standing by. Administration officials were waiting for a justification to act, and the Pleiku incidents provided it. The situation in the South had continued to deteriorate steadily. The Viet Cong forces had been pounding the ARVN, which appeared to be stretched taut and on the verge of collapse in some parts of the country; defeat seemed inevitable in a matter of months.

Secretary McNamara in Washington and Ambassador Taylor in Saigon now believed that some dramatic new round of escalation was necessary to stabilize the shaky political situation in the South, restore Vietnamese confidence in ultimate victory, and make Hanoi pay a price for its escalating support of the Viet Cong. They were also eager to evacuate American dependents from South Vietnam and put the U.S. mission on a wartime footing. The situation had become truly grim, and escalation had become a foregone conclusion, a certainty.

In mid-December, when the specter of impending defeat was becoming increasingly clear, the acting chief of station, Gordon Jorgenson, asked me to prepare an assessment of the situation to be sent to Washington on his behalf. We discussed the situation over dinner and agreed that the war was nearing a critical juncture. He wanted to be sure that decision-makers in Washington understood the consequences of the choices they would soon be confronting. I prepared a cable reviewing in stark terms the apparent acceleration of the enemy's buildup in the South, the intensification of enemy military activity since the Diem coup, the steady erosion of Vietnamese government control in the countryside, the decline of ARVN combat effectiveness, and the continuing evidence of instability and disunity within the ruling military oligarchy in Saigon—all this supported, where appropriate, with illustrative anecdotes and facts. The estimate concluded that, unless soon reinforced by external forces, the ARVN seemed likely to be defeated in the near future. At the station chief's urging, I added his personal recommendation (with which I agreed), that the United States not intervene in piecemeal fashion. If we were to commit U.S. ground forces, we should do so in strength; only massive intervention from the outset would ensure success. We should demonstrate our resolve by declaring war, announcing a full-scale mobilization, and making it clear that our aim was the destruction of North Vietnam's capacity to pursue the war. Anything short of this, we concluded, would be interpreted by Hanoi as a lack of commitment on our part and would encourage the Communists to try to outlast us as they had the French. Nothing we had done thus far, we noted, had shaken their confidence in ultimate victory, and their success against the French was the basis for their sustaining confidence. If we continued down the road of "sending signals" by progressive escalation, we could not expect to succeed. This assessment was sent to Washington before the end of the year as the unilateral view of the CIA station in Saigon; it was not coordinated with other components of the U.S. mission.

Sometime early in 1965, Washington asked for a coordinated mission intelligence estimate of the situation, perhaps triggered in part by our earlier unilateral station appraisal. I prepared a draft along the lines of our earlier cable, updating it as necessary and modifying the language in places to coincide with that of other mission components. After circulating the draft, I convened a meeting of representatives of the embassy's political section, the economic aid mission, and MACV's intelligence staff to review the draft and seek agreement on its conclusions. Some negotiation was required, the MACV representative insisting on changes that weakened descriptions of the enemy's military buildup and the scope and scale of his future capabilities, and on the imminence of the ARVN's collapse. But we managed to find common ground for describing these matters without undue acrimony, and a copy of the agreed estimate was forwarded to the ambassador for his information, as a matter of courtesy, before being radioed to Washington.

I was summoned to Ambassador Taylor's office to review the estimate with him. We went through it paragraph by paragraph, he having made a number of marginal notes asking why we were saying this, what was the basis for that, what was the nature of the evidence to support that statement, and so forth. In virtually every instance I was able to explain the basis for the points in question, and he grudgingly withdrew his objections until we reached the concluding paragraphs. In this final portion, the assessment synthesized the preceding discussion on significant issues and trends, and projected the situation into the future.

At first the ambassador wanted to omit this concluding section entirely, suggesting it was unnecessarily repetitive of what had already been stated. I objected on the ground that the assessment would be viewed in Washington as incomplete without concluding judgments regarding likely future developments. After a surprisingly lengthy dialogue on this matter, the ambassador finally directed that two of these final paragraphs were not to be sent to Washington. When I protested their deletion, he said they simply painted the picture darker than he saw it; the paper had already made it clear that some trends were unfavorable, and he saw no need to discourage the people in Washington from facing up to the decisions they would have to make in the weeks to come. I protested that we had been asked to provide an agreed mission intelligence estimate, and that all the appropriate elements of the mission had been consulted and had agreed. He expressed surprise and disappointment that MACV's intelligence staff had gone along with the estimate. But Taylor was unmoved by my arguments, saying he would approve transmission of the estimate to Washington only if the designated paragraphs were removed.

So the estimate was sent to Washington without the offending paragraphs, which assessed the ARVN's diminishing effectiveness and future prospects, and North Vietnam's capabilities and likely courses of action—I believed these were the crunch issues. At some risk to his position, the station chief acceded to my urging and separately cabled the deleted paragraphs to CIA headquarters for the director, requesting that they not be circulated outside the agency. Some weeks later, while I was home for consultation, I was pleased to learn that the station chief had been protected, and that those responsible for drafting CIA estimates in Washington had been made aware of the contents of the deleted paragraphs.

Later in 1964, Hanoi apparently sensed the possibility of early military success and embarked on an escalation of their war effort. In an apparent miscalculation of our likely reaction, they must have assumed either that we would not introduce American ground combat forces to prevent the defeat of the ARVN, or that if we did decide to intervene, we could not do so quickly enough to match their ability to reinforce. In any event, they added a new dimension by changing the nature of their infiltration. Through 1963, infiltrating groups evidently consisted of command and staff personnel and technicians, not troop units. These specialists were sent to the South to serve as the core for the expanding Viet Cong insurgent effort. They were largely veteran southern troops who had been evacuated to the North after the Geneva Accords, where they were formed into regular units of the People's Army of Viet Nam (PAVN). They then spent the ensuing years in military training and political indoctrination as regular army personnel. Perhaps forty thousand of these had trekked back to the South via the Ho Chi Minh Trail by 1963, joining with stay-behind agents to form the skeletal framework and muscle for the Viet Cong command and control machinery. They also served as the core of Viet Cong main and local force combat units, which were fleshed out by southern partisans.

Some infiltration groups, for example, made up the cadre for combat battalions, including commanders and senior staff personnel down through the company level, as well as communicators, cryptographers, heavy-weapons specialists, key political "commissars," administrators, and logistics personnel. Such groups of up to 150 men were combined with several hundred experienced southern guerrilla fighters furnished by the local Viet Cong command structure to form new main force combat battalions. Other groups might form regimental command, control, and support units, and still others would provide the cadre for similar functions at the division level. In this fashion, dozens of main force battalions and regiments, and several main force division headquarters with appropriate support units, were created in the South.

Other cadre groups had consisted of experienced personnel of the sort needed to staff out the territorial command structure of the Viet Cong from the overall command headquarters located in the Cambodian border area north of Tay Ninh, down through their regional, front, and provincial command centers; some were even assigned down to district level. These included the many types of specialists listed above as well as experienced medical, ordnance, engineer, intelligence and security, special operations, psychological warfare, counterintelligence, and assorted administrative specialists.

Contrary to the common perception at the time, infiltration during the early and mid-sixties was not merely a way of replacing Viet Cong combat losses. These groups were in fact the means by which Hanoi underwrote the creation and expansion in the South of a well-organized, full-time regular military force to back up the Viet Cong's local and guerrilla-militia forces. Without this type of augmentation, the Viet Cong's people's war could not have gained the momentum that in late 1964 and early 1965 brought them close to victory.

In 1964, however, the pattern of infiltration began to change, as Hanoi began moving entire combat units of PAVN—organized and trained in the North—into South Vietnam. The flow of cadre groups continued in parallel with the movement of combat units, but by mid-1965 the bulk of those infiltrating from the North consisted of battalions, regiments, and divisions of PAVN.

Intelligence was able to judge fairly accurately the relative rate of flow of these infiltration groups, but there was a built-in time lag between the initial indicators of a specific group moving south and ultimate confirmation of its arrival. We never had a full count, of course, but we probably accounted for most groups over time. We were conscious in a timely fashion of general fluctuations in the rate of flow, but we could not be sure of the actual numbers involved in these fluctuations until months later. The presence of PAVN units in the South could be confirmed only by interrogating prisoners or capturing documents on the battlefield, and some units were in the South for six months or more before being positively identified in contact with friendly forces.

In intelligence terms, North Vietnam was a "denied area"; we had no embassy or consulates there, and no military attachés. Western journalists seldom visited the North, and travel by foreigners was tightly limited. It was very difficult to acquire information through "human sources." Most of what we knew was derived from Hanoi's broadcasts of official government and party statements and documents, and articles and editorials from the government-controlled press, including military journals. It was also difficult to follow in detail the activities of the North Vietnamese army in its home environment, though general patterns and trends were apparent. Thus the movement of several individual battalions—as distinct from cadre groups—into the northern provinces of South Vietnam in 1964 was not detected until several months after the event, when a number of prisoners corroborated the distinctive, all-northern composition of these units. Toward the end of the year, however, we detected signs that elements of PAVN divisions might soon be moving south.

Most Communist combat units sent to South Vietnam were created especially for that purpose by splitting them off from regular PAVN divisions. These units would, in effect, replicate themselves—dividing in two like an amoeba, each half containing a share of the officers, NCOs, and specialists of the parent unit. Then both halves were brought to full strength by drawing "fillers" from a variety of sources, for example from training centers or from local forces. After a period of unit training, one of these formations would be sent to the South and the other would remain at the unit's original base. This process continued from 1964 until near the end of the war, with some PAVN divisions cloning or replicating themselves every couple of years or so, some doing it three and four times—perhaps more—during the course of the war. This system provided a flow of fairly well-trained and experienced combat units in the mid-sixties, though the quality naturally declined over time as experienced cadre were repeatedly drawn off from standing units that remained in the North.

We recognized this interesting pattern fairly early on, and it was well understood within the intelligence community. Unfortunately this system of reinforcing the war in the South was never, to my knowledge, systematically analyzed. We never had a good feel for its full impact on the fighting quality of PAVN forces remaining in the North, nor of those coming south. We were aware in general terms of the impact each incoming wave of such units would have on the combat potential of enemy forces in the South. But we never had a good understanding of how long this system could produce effective reinforcements in the South, or to what extent it may have constrained the pace of Hanoi's ability to sustain the war there.

In any event, by the end of 1964, North Vietnam's 325th Division seemed to be in the process of replicating itself, and it was apparent that lead elements of the cloned division were moving south. The appearance of even a cloned PAVN division would represent a substantial reinforcement of the enemy's main force capabilities in the South, so we were anxious to confirm its movement, its composition, and the nature of its armament as soon as possible. We were concerned, of course, not merely with the impact of this individual division but what it portended in terms of Hanoi's intentions to keep pace with our escalation of the war. We also wanted very much to know its ultimate destination in the South as an indicator of where the ARVN's already weakening fortunes might be strained beyond the breaking point.

Accumulating evidence indicated that regiments of the 325th Division, moving through Laos, were heading for South Vietnam's highland provinces (II Corps). But several weeks went by without confirmation of their arrival. No formal contact had been established with these units, though there was an ominous, persistent pattern of actions west of Pleiku which suggested that border outposts were being "rolled up" by some unidentified force.

I was watching this pattern closely, in cooperation with senior officers of MACV's intelligence staff. Finally, sometime in February or March 1965 we decided that it would be wrong to wait for the newly infiltrated regiments to disclose their presence by mounting a surprise onslaught against some important position; it would be preferable to confirm their presence now through friendly initiatives. The intelligence advisers at II Corps were not cleared for the special intelligence on which our concerns were based, and the MACV officers with whom I was collaborating were not permitted to travel. We agreed that I should go to Pleiku and attempt to stimulate our advisers there into initiating appropriate action that would reveal the presence of the newly infiltrated units, thereby depriving them of the element of surprise when they attacked.

MACV's intelligence adviser in Pleiku was a former colleague from my army intelligence days, and he understood the problem immediately, even though I could not divulge the basis for my concern. Between us we persuaded the senior corps advisers that it would be useful to send ARVN ranger units on reconnaissance patrols into certain areas. When this was done, contact was made with the newly arrived PAVN regiments and their presence thus confirmed. Also confirmed, therefore, was a new pattern of infiltration by full-scale, major combat units from the North, armed with a new family of Soviet automatic weapons never before seen in the South. These included the subsequently omnipresent AK-47, which ultimately became plentiful even within Viet Cong guerrilla-militia units. Hanoi clearly had now begun rapidly to reinforce the capabilities of its forces in the South, almost concurrent with the introduction of American ground combat forces in the South. The preparations for this action, which began in the fall of 1964, actually preceded ours by several months. Some suggested at the time that Hanoi anticipated our escalation. It soon became apparent, however, that the Communists had belatedly decided to capitalize on the chaotic political instability in the South following the overthrow of Diem, trying for an early victory—a knockout blow—by committing PAVN divisions.

Thus the early months of 1965 saw a sea change in the character of the Vietnam War. We had begun systematic bombing of North Vietnam, concentrating on the lines of communication to the South. To protect the air bases in the South from which our combat aircraft were flying, we deployed American ground combat units. And North Vietnam was about to introduce major combat units of its regular army. General Westmoreland, now commanding MACV, urged the introduction of American ground forces to bolster the defenses of the base at Da Nang, but Ambassador Taylor initially opposed this move. It was a logical and in fact essential extension of our decision to bomb the North, since the ARVN was stretched so thin it was patently incapable of preventing the Viet Cong from approaching to within effective mortar range of any target in South Vietnam. I have never understood why this was apparently not recognized as a foregone conclusion in the planning stage in Washington, particularly after the destructive Viet Cong attack on the Bien Hoa air base the previous November. Now, a Marine battalion was landed at Da Nang from the Seventh Fleet, over the ambassador's objections, and was soon followed by other Marine and army combat units carried by air and sea from bases in Okinawa, Hawaii, and the United States.

These new elements in the equation generated another request from Washington for an agreed Saigon mission assessment of the situation in late February or early March. I varied the procedure on this second estimate, convening my interagency colleagues first to seek their views before attempting a first draft. Our second meeting to review my draft was more lively and time-consuming this time than before. MACV's intelligence staff had been augmented and its analytical potential improved. The military were also smarting from criticism that they had "caved in" too readily in agreeing to the earlier estimate. Nevertheless we soon found acceptable language to express our views on the state of the war and its future prospects, and again the agreed estimate was submitted to Ambassador Taylor—with quite similar results. The ambassador worried with me through the estimate as before, page by page, and when we reached the conclusions, paragraph by paragraph.

In this estimate we had come down hard in our judgment that North Vietnam would not be deterred by the introduction of American forces to protect air bases in the South. We believed they were determined to match our escalation; we were almost certain they would continue to support the war in the South despite our bombing of the North. The ambassador believed our judgments were too pessimistic, and again he insisted that critical portions of the conclusions be excised from the estimate. Once more the deleted paragraphs were transmitted separately by a back channel to CIA headquarters, with a plea that they be tightly held to protect us from the ambassador's wrath.

I highlight these episodes because they are unique in my professional experience. I know of no other situations in which a consumer of intelligence—in this case Ambassador Taylor—exercised direct editorial control over the content of intelligence estimates. Intelligence studies and estimates are of course subject to sometimes onerous reviews by succeeding echelons within the intelligence bureaucracy. At the national level in Washington, they have even been remanded by the U.S. Intelligence Board for wholesale redrafting after having been agreed to at the working level. But consumers of intelligence are not normally considered part of the production process. They are free to accept, reject, or ignore the judgments of their intelligence staffs, and very often do. Although professional intelligence officers are fully aware of the limitations of their role as advisers to the makers of policies and decisions, they are very protective of their privilege of formulating and expressing their advice in their own terms, whether the users follow it or not. Ambassador Taylor had another option he could—and, in retrospect, should—have exercised: allowing the full intelligence assessment to be sent to Washington as written, and forwarding separately his own comments. His views certainly would have carried greater weight than our estimate.

In accepting the assignment in Saigon, I had mistakenly assumed that from that vantage point my analysis of the situation might be more effectively heard in policy deliberations than if I remained in Washington. For years I had been told that my views were not as credible as those expressed by authorities in the field. After all, consumers would say, MACV and embassy officials were on the spot, closer to the problem, more fully informed, and in a better position to have a "true feel" for the situation than those of us far away in Washington. Moreover, being responsible for executing policies and programs, they were presumed—rightly or wrongly—to have an interest in not understating the challenges and obstacles standing in their way. So I had determined to go to the field, to become one of those reporting from the scene, and to gain greater credibility as a result. As it turned out, being in Saigon had no effect on the credence given to my analysis. It seems that the message itself was the problem, not the messenger. Few consumers of intelligence on Vietnam welcomed bad news, whatever its source. This became evident during my first consultation visit to Washington early in 1965, when some people I met with suggested that in Saigon I was probably "too close to the trees to be able to see the forest." Only in Washington, I was told, could one see the big picture. I have since concluded that there is *no* ideal vantage point for the intelligence officer. If he is not telling the decision-maker what he wants to hear, or if his analysis clashes with the assumptions of the consumer, his voice will be ignored or significantly discounted; he will have little influence on the direction of policy.

During my two-year tour in Saigon (June 1964–June 1966), I witnessed the impact of the war on Vietnam, its countryside, and its society. It sometimes seemed as though—to paraphrase the views of the military adviser in one city during the Tet offensive of 1968—we were "destroying the country in order to save it." Vietnam was indeed a civil war, being waged within the country we were trying to defend. There were northerners and southerners on both sides; many southern families were divided; most groups and factions had a foot in both camps; rural villages flew the Saigon government's flag during daylight hours and the flag of the National Liberation Front at night.

In such a struggle the application of American firepower was brutal and merciless; it could not distinguish between friend and foe. This firepower, whether delivered by rifles and automatic weapons, artillery shells, or bombs, was the essential ingredient of the "main force war" waged by the American military forces. Employing it liberally spared the lives of many American troops, and it usually overwhelmed the enemy. Airpower—and especially the B-52—was employed extensively in this main force war. The enemy had to concentrate his main forces to isolate and attack our strongpoints and fire bases. He had to undertake extensive logistical preparations, moving supplies into forward positions to support major attacks. MACV's intelligence became adept at detecting such preparations, and military planners became proficient in demolishing them. It became evident before the end of 1965 that the B–52 could become the great equalizer in the main force war; its massive bomb loads could pulverize enemy troop concentrations, field fortifications, artillery positions, command posts, ammunition bunkers, and supply caches. The enemy simply could not set up and sustain a large-scale operation in a limited area once their presence in that area had been detected.

The ARVN increasingly came to rely on the considerable advantage they derived from the overwhelming firepower of American air support. When it was freely available, it usually made the difference, turning threatened defeat into victory. The successful defense of Khe Sanh and Hue in 1968, Quang Tri and Hue again in 1972, Dak To and Loc Ninh in 1972, all demonstrated this. The ARVN might never have been defeated in 1975 if Congress had not changed the rules and effectively ended American involvement and the use of the B–52s in the final campaign of the war.

The B–52 was also effective in demolishing enemy base areas, ultimately forcing the Viet Cong to abandon their traditional command and supply centers in South Vietnam and to seek sanctuary in increasingly remote areas and across the border in Cambodia and Laos. The use of B–52s against Viet Cong bases and in support of friendly garrisons inevitably depopulated large areas of the countryside as the populace fled to areas not subject to B–52 attack.

A B–52 strike is a truly awesome event. One night at dinner in Saigon, conversation suddenly stopped, and I became aware that my adrenaline was flowing. Then I noticed that the shutters of the house had begun to rattle, and the drapes were fluttering. In the distance we could hear the faint, ominously deep, and sustained rumble of explosions. I had known that the first B–52 missions were scheduled for that evening, against targets some 35 miles from the city. But when a B–52 releases its load of 72 or more 750-pound bombs, everyone one within that distance of a strike is aware of it. Those as close as three or four miles are in for a terrifying experience. I later witnessed the impact of B–52 strikes no more than three miles away from where I stood, and from aircraft flying within less than ten miles of the strike; it was always an imposing sight.

B–52 strikes certainly impressed the people living in the countryside.

By 1968 more than a third of Vietnam's population were refugees, having sought shelter in formally established camps, or "squatting" in the slums of the major towns and cities. The countryside in areas adjacent to Viet Cong bases and in their operating areas was pocked by the pattern of huge, flooded craters formed by two- or three-mile-long sticks of B-52 bombs. Large areas were devastated by repeated bombings and depopulated by the flow of refugees toward safety. These trends had begun late in 1965 and were clearly defined by the time I left Saigon in mid-1966. The impact of this bombing on the livelihood of millions of people and on Vietnamese society as a whole was a terribly disheartening thing to observe.

By the late summer of 1964, CIA headquarters had decided to establish a new analytical component in the Saigon station, to do research on the Viet Cong's political-military infrastructure. The need for research and analysis on that target had been highlighted in our survey team's report earlier that year. I had believed that a joint CIA-MACV research group could best do the job, since the Viet Cong political and military control apparatus was interwoven. Moreover, the same source materials—documents and prisoner interrogation reports—were needed for both research tasks. MACV was unwilling to devote resources to the task in 1964, however, since it was only peripherally related to their main concern—main force combat units. And the CIA was reluctant to detach manpower to work with MACV on the task, believing that its resources could well become lost in the shuffle at the military headquarters. So the CIA station in Saigon was to work unilaterally, under my supervision, with resources to be provided from headquarters in Washington. By the end of the year, more than a dozen analysts had arrived to work on the project.

Our main interest was to establish a "political order of battle" on the Viet Cong political-military control apparatus, showing in detail the organization, composition, and location of its component elements and leadership throughout South Vietnam. We wanted a comprehensive picture of the Viet Cong structure in every province, comparable to that assembled by the British in Malaysia. This would obviously further everyone's understanding of the nature and scope of the insurgency. More important and practical, it would help target intelligence and counterintelligence operations designed to penetrate the enemy's political apparatus and disrupt its operations. Later it would become an important adjunct of countermeasures aimed at neutralizing the enemy's control apparatus, measures such as induced defections, capture, or elimination through combat operations or counterterror tactics (ambushes, booby-trapping of meeting sites, and so forth), in the much maligned and misunderstood PHOENIX operation.

Useful work was done by this research branch over the years, but it never reached its anticipated potential in gaining an understanding of the Viet Cong infrastructure. This was due in part to friction with the military, and also to the fact that few analysts brought with them to Saigon knowledge of the area and familiarity with the structure of covert revolutionary movements. Only a couple of these people were familiar with the concepts of military order of battle. Most were experienced economists or analysts of foreign governments. No textbooks were available, so it took some months before these analysts gained enough familiarity with the subject matter to be productive, and almost all left at the end of their eighteen-month tours. But their work did lay the basis for successful intelligence and security operations later in the war, and it stimulated the military to devote more attention to these aspects of the enemy problem. At the working level, our research prompted a number of our military intelligence advisers and analysts to take an interest in the enemy's paramilitary and security forces, which had been largely ignored because of MACV's primary focus on the conventional Viet Cong and PAVN military forces.

I spent a bit of my time in Vietnam escorting visiting VIPs—senior CIA officers and a number of foreign visitors—to their appointments with civil and military officials in Saigon, and on tours to their areas of interest elsewhere in the country. My job was to ensure that they had maximum access to those aspects of the situation that interested them, within the limited time allotted. Between these junkets and my own travels, I saw much of the Vietnamese countryside, visiting twenty-six of the forty-four provinces (and flying repeatedly over the remainder) and most of the major American and Vietnamese military commands. I had countless meetings and discussions with senior American and Vietnamese officials at all levels and was exposed to just about every aspect of the ongoing war.

I also had an opportunity to observe over time the progressive Americanization of South Vietnam. Aside from the bomb craters and destruction, even more visible was the spread of American bases and depots. There had been fewer than 500 Americans in Vietnam when I first visited the country in 1954; there were some 25,000 when I began my two-year tour in mid-1964, and ten times that number when I left in June 1966. At the time of my last visit in 1968, more than a half-million Americans were there. I witnessed the burgeoning of huge American bases at Da Nang, Qui Nhon, Nha Trang, Pleiku, Bien Hoa, My Tho, Long Binh, and Cam Ranh Bay. I observed the spread of the American and Vietnamese "fire bases." I saw elements of the American 25th Division disembarking from giant jet and turboprop cargo aircraft at Pleiku, many of them having flown nonstop from their home base in Hawaii; an entire brigade with the bulk of its equipment was airlifted into Pleiku in just two weeks. I saw the queuing up of American cargo vessels at the ports of Da Nang, Qui Nhon, and Cap St. Jacques—as many as 35 ships at each location awaiting an opportunity to tie up for unloading.

Also evident were the scores of hilltops flattened to accommodate fire bases, countless acres of land cleared around U.S. bases to provide open fields of fire against enemy attacks, and hundreds of square miles of defoliated terrain along the roads and waterways to deny cover for potential Viet Cong ambushes. The impact on the economy of the crater-filled rubber plantations, paddy fields, and stands of hardwood trees was incalculable. It was rare after the mid-1960s to make a two-hour flight over Vietnam without witnessing a B-52 flight or one or more tactical air strikes, or a formation of a dozen or more helicopters lifting troops into combat, or columns of military vehicles moving along roads or across open fields.

I also observed at ground level—as I had at Tarawa during World War II—the debris of war; the death and mutilation of soldiers and civilians in the towns and cities; villages being rocketed and bombed because someone there was thought to have fired at an aircraft passing overhead, the villagers fleeing into nearby fields, wailing and flailing their arms helplessly.

Although interesting from an intellectual or academic point of view, Vietnam was altogether disheartening and demoralizing for nearly everyone who experienced it. One was never far from the war, even in the heart of Saigon. Terrorist bombings, mostly targeted at American-occupied facilities, including civilian restaurants, were frequent. When dining out, one acquired the habit of consciously looking about for suspicious packets or satchels before ordering a meal. When an explosion was heard, conversation turned to speculating about its approximate location and likely targets in that area. On many nights we were awakened by the rumble of American medium tanks en route from the docks through the city to the military camps in the countryside. One watched from rooftop vantage points many a spectacular display by American aircraft dropping flares to illuminate areas of enemy activity just beyond the outskirts of Saigon; these were often followed by helicopter gunships and aircraft bombing and strafing. On more than one night, ARVN helicopters circled continuously low over Saigon as troops participating in an attempted coup maneuvered through the streets. One learned to steer clear of throngs of anti-government demonstrators parading through the streets, hastening into the safety of air-conditioned quarters to escape clouds of tear gas.

Early one dark morning in 1966, while breakfasting before going to MACV to attend a predawn rehearsal of the intelligence staff's morning briefing for General Westmoreland, I heard a small explosion from the direction of downtown, followed by small-arms fire. Shortly thereafter, at MACV headquarters, there was a flurry of activity and excitement generated by reports of an "attack on the Brink BOQ" by a Viet Cong "armored" vehicle. A firefight was continuing with terrorists in the area. I was forced to make a slight detour en route to the embassy to avoid driving through this action. As I passed the scene two blocks away, I saw tracers from a number of automatic weapons, and several American military jeeps with M-60 machine guns racing to that area. The firefight continued for almost an hour before quieting down.

The episode had started with the explosion of a "bicycle bomb," parked by a Viet Cong terrorist across the street from a U.S. military bus stop. When a passing cab driver gunned his engine to get out of the way, his jeep was fired on by guards at the Brink Hotel across the street. Guards at another American military billet down the street fired back, believing they were being fired on by terrorists. Soon there was a continuing fusillade as dozens of armed Americans exchanged fire with one another. Passersby in the early morning rush hour were hit. A large dump truck carrying civilian laborers crashed into a light pole alongside the Brink, and a dozen or so unarmed women in the back of the truck were killed—this was the enemy "armored" vehicle rumored to have been in the "attack" on the BOQ. By the time it was all over, two dozen civilians had been killed and as many more wounded. No "enemy weapons" were found, no terrorist bodies. The lone terrorist who had parked the bicycle apparently had gotten safely away before his small bomb exploded. On my way back to my own quarters at lunchtime, driving through traffic still jammed by the incident, I managed to count 147 bullet holes in the front end of the dump truck that was still lodged against the light pole alongside the Brink BOQ. It had been several hours before anyone had gotten close enough to the truck to see the bodies of the dozen women laborers who had bled to death in the back of the vehicle.

My most traumatic experience was the terrorist car-bomb attack on the American embassy in March 1965, which killed more than a score of people outside the building and two inside, including a secretary in the CIA station. The station's front office was devastated—a half-dozen of its people, including the station chief, were so seriously hurt they had to be medically evacuated to the States. Two agency officers were totally blinded by flying glass; sixty other CIA personnel and embassy staffers inside the building were less seriously injured, most returning to duty the next day. I suffered multiple contusions and minor lacerations of the scalp and face, and a mild concussion; I had been standing by a window less than twenty-five feet from the bomb. Those of us not evacuated were allowed a few days R&R in Hong Kong some time later, and the CIA wounded were later awarded the Medal for Exceptional Service—the agency's equivalent of the military's Purple Heart.

In January 1966 I accompanied our deputy station chief to Bangkok where we attended one of the periodic SEACORD meetings, at which U.S. political-military programs in Southeast Asia were reviewed and coordinated among the missions in the region. Among those attending such sessions were our ambassadors to Laos, Thailand, and Vietnam, our senior military commanders in those countries, and the theater commander, CINCPAC. One of the principal agenda items at this meeting was the pause in the U.S. bombing of North Vietnam then in effect. General William Momyer, Seventh Air Force commander, briefed the conferees on his command's operations over the previous few months, proudly displaying charts that showed how the number of sorties had remained relatively constant despite the bombing pause over North Vietnam, and how the tonnage of bombs dropped had declined only slightly. Admiral U. S. G. Sharp, then CINCPAC, expressed surprise, sternly remarking that the figures should have declined substantially. Momyer eagerly observed that they might have, but that he had successfully urged his squadrons to intensify operations over Laos during the pause over North Vietnam, and they had responded well. Admiral Sharp spoke reprimandingly, noting that one reason for the bombing pause had been the depletion of our reserve of bombs and the reduced flow of bombs through the pipeline; the bombing pause was supposed to allow the pipeline to be replenished and the recently stepped-up manufacture of bombs to bring the flow back up to the normally required levels. The intensified bombing of Laos was defeating the purpose of the lull. Momyer apparently still did not get the point, and launched again into an explanation of how, despite the lull, he was maximizing the effectiveness of his command, flying as many sorties and dropping almost as many bombs as before. Admiral Sharp asked what the hell he was bombing in Laos, and Momyer eagerly replied that the missions were chiefly against targets of opportunity along lines of communication, though adverse weather conditions meant that most bombs had to be jettisoned into the free bomb zones—that is, into areas where there were no known friendly forces. Admiral Sharp flushed and became quite agitated, observing that this was a gross waste of precious resources; that bombing of Laos was of secondary importance at best; that no ordnance should be expended there unless it was directed against important, confirmed military targets; that we weren't in business to turn the jungles of Laos into toothpicks; and that ordnance expenditures had damned well better be reduced during the bombing pause if Momyer expected to have anything to strike with when the pause ended. General Momyer started back once more into the breach, undauntedly protesting that he hadn't simply kept his aircraft idle during the pause; that he had demonstrated his command's ability to maintain a high sortie rate even with North Vietnam off limits, and it was his duty to make maximum use of his resources to support the war effort. An explosion from Admiral Sharp was narrowly averted when General Westmoreland gently reached up and pulled Momyer by the arm back down into his chair, allowing the chairman quickly to move the meeting on to the next item on the agenda. I am not sure General Momyer ever understood the basis for Admiral Sharp's wrath.

This conference was also notable for an exchange that took place during a reception when General Richard Stilwell, now commander of American forces in Thailand, presented to Bill Sullivan, ambassador to Laos, a toy submachine gun meant to symbolize MACTHAI's proposal for a plan to provide direct military support to Sullivan's (and the CIA's) "secret war" in Laos. Sullivan deftly cut the articulate general down to size, noting his disappointment that the much-touted MACTHAI proposal was—as he had feared—a sham, a toy, rather than representing any useful military support. Stilwell's gambit was a dismal flop.

When Ambassador Lodge returned to Saigon to succeed General Taylor in the summer of 1965, he called in the CIA station chief and warned that he would hold him responsible if the Viet Cong seized the embassy and took the ambassador hostage. Lodge said he realized he was their prime target, and he was prepared to defend himself, displaying a Magnum .357 that he kept in his desk drawer. But he said it was the CIA station chief's job to see that he didn't have to use his gun. (It was actually the job of the embassy security officer and the Marine guard detachment.) Lodge said he wanted to be briefed regularly on the Viet Cong threat to the embassy, on their capability to attack. He wanted a map kept in his office that showed the locations of friendly and enemy units in the Saigon area so that he could be aware of the extent of the threat at any particular time. He wanted the station chief to keep him informed of any changes in the Viet Cong subversive organization and sapper forces in the Saigon area.

The station chief asked me to prepare the map and keep it updated. In light of unpredictable access to the ambassador's office, we prepared two maps. One was placed in his office, the other in mine where we could make the changes, switching when the opportunity afforded. The ambassador seemed obsessed with this topic during his second tour in Vietnam, and his behavior in other areas was equally erratic.

At one point I prepared a brief memorandum for the ambassador from the station chief, reporting an important pronouncement by Hanoi and noting that it was intended to keep him abreast of developments. The whole thing comprised two very short paragraphs of six to eight lines each—I had long since discovered that the ambassador had an extremely brief attention span. That afternoon I was summoned to the ambassador's office, where he gruffly asked what the memo was all about. Perplexed, I explained that it had seemed to be an important development in Hanoi's attitude, and we thought he should be aware of it. Why? he demanded. Because we wanted him to be aware of its importance in case the matter came up in his discussions with senior American or Vietnamese officials over the next few days; we thought he would find it useful to be able to demonstrate familiarity with the development. What did we expect him to do about the development? he asked. Nothing specific, I replied. We had sent it to him merely for his information. What did we want him to do with it? he barked, growing more riled. I had some private thoughts about what he ought to do with it at that point, but, restraining myself, I simply suggested that if he initialed it to acknowledge having seen it, I would be happy to relieve him of any further responsibility in the matter. He initialed it, threw it across his desk to me, and directed that I not send him any further pieces of paper that did not require his action. He was a very busy man and had no time to waste on matters about which he could do nothing. I promised to keep that in mind, and was dismissed. At that stage in his second tour, he was not a pleasant man to deal with.

With the increasing buildup of American military forces, the ambassador's role in Vietnam was eclipsed by that of the military. As ambassador, Maxwell Taylor had been able to exercise effective control over his former protégé, General Westmoreland, and of course Taylor's military views carried considerable weight with the administration in Washington. Lodge, however, had little interest in military aspects of the war and a limited grasp of military strategy. He seemed easily bored by such matters and frustrated by his inability to influence the direction of affairs in Vietnam. Although nominally the chief of the U.S. mission, he had little control over its principal business—the conduct of the war.

In December 1964 the Vietnamese military "Young Turks" had abolished a civilian council whose existence had been carefully nourished by the embassy as one means of legitimizing the military oligarchy. Ambassador Taylor had summoned the errant military leaders to his office where he dressed them down in the fashion of a West Point upperclassman dealing with plebes. Several of them had stood their ground, attempting to justify their action and expressing little regret. Later, as they left the embassy, the scene was recorded in a number of press photographs, many of which were distributed internationally.

Some months afterward I was in the office of General Thi, the I Corps commander, and noticed a framed enlargement of one of these photos on the credenza behind Thi's desk, featuring his face bearing a wide grin. I asked the significance of the picture. He replied that it reminded him of one of the proudest days in his life, when he and his colleagues had stood up to Ambassador Taylor and had made it clear to him who was running the government of South Vietnam. General Thi was one of many senior Vietnamese officers with whom I talked over the years who recognized the need for a social revolution in Vietnam. He raised the issue at this meeting and asked my advice and American support in bringing it about. He and the other generals, he said, were not interested in window-dressing such as the civilian council which they had created and then dismissed. Vietnam needed a government and political program that would meet the political and social aspirations of the people. The Viet Cong, he said, wanted to change society. The people wanted this too, but the people did not want the Viet Cong to be the agent for change. They feared the Viet Cong, believing they would be harsh and cruel masters; the people wanted an alternative to the Viet Cong that made sense, one that offered hope. The only alternatives they had known were the French colonialists, the autocratic Diem regime (which was not interested in a real social revolution), and the succession of military governments since Diem, which had offered no program. General Thi, knowing I worked for the CIA, pleaded for advice. If we Americans wanted to save Vietnam, he and many of his fellow officers would be pleased to help, but they needed political guidance. All I could tell him was that I would see that his message got to the proper American authorities.

Although I personally hoped that something might be done, I believed that nothing would come of it. A year earlier, a group of us in the station had drafted a proposal for serious political action in the wake of the second or third coup after Diem's overthrow. We recognized that without an organized political base, the generals could not attract popular enthusiasm. The only thing they had going for them was the general revulsion against the Viet Cong among the people, based on fear of their harsh methods. It seemed merely a matter of time before that attitude might change, and that peace under the Viet Cong might be perceived by a majority as preferable to a continuation of the stresses of war.

We had proposed an effort to create a mass, revolutionary political movement, systematically organized at the grassroots level in the hamlets, villages, and towns, and in the wards of the cities, incorporating the military and civilian components of the government at all levels, pledged to an enlightened platform to be adopted by a national convention, operating under the leadership of one of the more charismatic military leaders but open to all interested groups (except the Viet Cong). This political machinery could use patronage and party largesse to win friends, backed by an effective political-psychological program to influence attitudes. It was a large order, but the experienced political-action specialists in the station thought it was feasible under the right political combination of American covert action and "Boss Daley" political machine knowhow, with Vietnamese leadership and political-social input.

Washington had no serious interest in the proposal, and the political section of the embassy was skeptical. They believed it would be difficult to conceal the American hand in such a covert program, and there was reason to doubt that the Vietnamese military leaders would sort themselves out in a way that would permit them to work within such a framework. Some of us felt these views were overcautious, but the decision was made to forgo such action. I did pass on General Thi's views this time around, but it met with the familiar rejection. Many of us felt that Vietnam could not be saved without such a counterrevolutionary movement. We were not convinced it would work, but we were sure that nothing else would. As in the equation with Diem, we would not necessarily win with it, but we could not win without it.

By the end of my tour in Vietnam, I was fatigued from debating the course of the war with scores of participants and observers, counseling and encouraging newly arrived, earnest young CIA officers destined for service in the provinces, and debriefing their predecessors preparing to return to the States. I had officially "backgrounded" Joseph Alsop and more than a dozen other visiting journalists, briefed a number of senators and congressmen and other visiting VIPs—including Henry Kissinger and Clark Clifford—at breakfasts, lunches, or dinners; exchanged information with CIA officers managing and instructing paramilitary training centers, where tens of thousands of Vietnamese "Rural Development" cadres were trained for pacification duties; worked with dozens of CIA case officers and their supervisors in Saigon and in the provinces, and with scores of American and Vietnamese military officers at all levels. Finally, I had spent hundreds of hours in a variety of aircraft and helicopters, flying through thousands of miles of air space over Vietnam—with no opportunity for collecting frequent flier miles.

Thus my two-year tour was spent observing, reporting on, and analyzing the many facets of the war in Vietnam, attempting to illuminate and clarify the understanding of those responsible for making decisions on American policy. I finished the tour with the feeling that my efforts—and those of my colleagues—had been for naught. We were far more deeply entangled in the quagmire when I left Saigon than when I had arrived.

10
Escalation

MACV'S INTELLIGENCE EFFORT finally moved into high gear with the arrival of the army's major General Joseph McChristian in mid-1965. An experienced intelligence officer who had just completed two years as head of army intelligence in the Pacific, McChristian brought to his new post a comprehensive understanding of the role of military intelligence and of the resources and structure that would be required for the task at MACV headquarters. He had served as an intelligence officer on General Patton's Third Army staff in World War II, and I had known him during his assignments to army intelligence in the Pentagon.

In Saigon he inherited an inadequately organized staff of about three hundred people. With the stimulus afforded by Secretary McNamara's direct interest, and support from DIA's General Carroll, McChristian got the required resources and quickly built a full-scale military intelligence organization to meet the needs of General Westmoreland. By the time McChristian left Vietnam, about three thousand military intelligence personnel were serving MACV.

There were marked qualitative improvements as well. Under McChristian's tutelage, MACV's intelligence activities improved substantially. Great progress was made in managing a more effective exploitation of prisoners and captured documents in both American and Vietnamese channels. Improved analyses supported combat operations. The entire intelligence effort took on a more professional tone. McChristian achieved closer collaboration with the ARVN's intelligence effort by establishing combined U.S.-Vietnamese military centers for analysis, the exploitation of captured documents, and the interrogation of prisoners of war. The quality of some analytical work continued to be inhibited by the twelve-month limit on military tours, which foreshortened institutional memory, and some U.S. Army field elements expressed frustration at the apparent concentration of intelligence resources in Saigon. Nevertheless McChristian's efforts put MACV seriously into the intelligence business for the first time, and I applauded him for it.

When my tour in Saigon ended in June 1966, I returned to Washington, stopping en route at the American missions in Singapore, Bangkok, Hong Kong, Taiwan, and Tokyo, and at the CINCPAC command in Hawaii, to report on the situation in Vietnam. After several weeks' leave I was assigned as deputy to George Carver, who was CIA director Richard Helms's Special Assistant for Vietnamese Affairs (SAVA). Our staff, which reported directly to Helms, was charged with overseeing all agency activities—analytical, operational, and support—related to Vietnam, and coordinating those activities with other departments and agencies in Washington. SAVA was designated at the central contact between CIA and the outside world on Vietnam, and we represented the agency in most interagency deliberations on Vietnamese matters.

Our modest staff operated a situation room, which was a focal point at headquarters for all sorts of data on the war, and included maps and charts displaying the locations and activities of both friendly and enemy forces in Vietnam. We worked closely with those elements of the CIA's intelligence directorate responsible for producing analyses of various aspects of the war, and we were in close touch with the rest of the intelligence community. The staff also included several officers working on special activities which did not fit readily into the prerogatives of other agency components.

George Carver was very much an activist—a bright, highly articulate, and energetic "operator." He relished meeting challenges and overcoming obstacles, and was intensely dedicated to the cause of defeating the Communist-led insurgency in Vietnam. His early agency career had been in operations, and this was reflected in his "can-do" problem-solving approach to his work. This contrasted with my own more circumspect, deliberative style. I regarded myself primarily as an analyst, not an operator, and I was inclined to strive for an objective viewpoint. My preference was to look at the implications and consequences of our policies and actions, and to likely "enemy" reactions, without advocating a particular policy or program. While Carver stressed the possibility of success in a given course of action or situation, I tended to focus on what our adversary might do to offset that course of action. Carver was inherently optimistic while I was regarded as a Cassandra, seeing only the pessimistic side of things. Naturally, I considered myself to be more realistic.

We both understood our differing perspectives and generally managed to work in a complementary fashion, each of us helping keep the other honest. For example, I was in Carver's office while he was briefing Averell Harriman and Cyrus Vance before their departure for the 1968 Paris peace talks. George stopped abruptly in the midst of a lengthy monologue setting out his optimistic views of the situation to acknowledge my presence. Telling our visitors that I saw things differently, he invited me to present the other side of the picture, which I did.

Our differing outlooks sometimes made our relations with other agencies awkward. Some interagency groups preferred Carver's activism and positive outlook and were unenthusiastic about my substituting for him in their deliberations. Indeed, some viewed me as not a "team player," mistakenly believing I saw the opposition as being ten feet tall; I knew full well they averaged under five feet eight, but I insisted they were muscular, slippery, skilled, unified, and dedicated to their task.

Because of the continuously controversial character of the administration's Vietnam policy, both Carver and I developed constituencies with which we were comfortable. On occasion, outsiders would ask which one of us reflected the agency's view on Vietnam. The answer was: neither, or both. The "CIA view" on any issue or problem—operational or substantive—was that of the director as expressed by himself, or in papers he had approved, which usually reflected the reconciliation of many disparate views. When an authoritative opinion or position was required in a new situation or on a new topic, we canvassed the interested people in the agency in order to work up a consensus or a majority view. If on my own, I tried to suppress my personal prejudices and give the best, most objective answer I could, consistent with what I knew or believed to be the views of the director and other appropriate senior officials of the agency. This was not always easy; I know that my objectivity may have been more "pure" on some occasions than on others. We devoutly believed that the agency should not be perceived as having a particular axe to grind, that its usefulness was diminished to the extent it took sides in policy disputes. We knew our role was to use our knowledge and experience to illuminate the discussion, to shed light on the factors affecting our courses of action and on the likely consequences of the options under study.

Carver and I discussed such matters freely between us and with colleagues at the working level both within and outside the agency. I had never personally discussed this matter with Director Helms and did not know he was aware of our differing viewpoints. Early in 1968, however, Helms called both of us to his office to say that he had just talked to Clark Clifford, the newly appointed secretary of defense, who indicated that he wanted to continue the weekly meetings McNamara had set up with Carver as CIA's senior Vietnam specialist, and in which I had substituted for Carver on several occasions. Helms said he wanted the two of us to go together to Clifford's office for the initial session; he told Carver that he wanted me to have equal time during the discussion. His purpose apparently was to show Clifford that the agency did not have a monolithic viewpoint on Vietnam, then let Clifford decide which outlook he was most comfortable with. This was a distinctly "Helmsian" solution to the problem. As it turned out, Clifford expressed no preference, and Carver handled most of the meetings with the defense secretary.

My first chore upon joining Carver's staff was to review a major CIA study, several hundred pages long, dealing with North Vietnam's "will to persist" in the war. Carver thought this task would bring me up to speed on the agency's current analytic views and on its capabilities for dealing with what was then, and continued to be for years, the dominant issue confronting the intelligence community. McNamara had asked Helms for such a study, and Carver had orchestrated the preparation of contributions from the various analytical components of the intelligence directorate. The basic purpose was to parse out all the factors affecting North Vietnam's determination to continue the war. The paper included separate sections analyzing the political stability of the Hanoi regime, its relationship with the Soviet Union and China; the impact of our bombing on Hanoi's capability to support the war in the South; the economic and manpower resources of North Vietnam; Hanoi's views of the prospects for success in the South; the strengths and weaknesses of the government in the South; the status of the pacification program; the prospects for Vietnam's military forces; and the nature and extent of Soviet and Chinese aid to North Vietnam. Almost every conceivable aspect of the war was covered. The various contributions were synthesized into an "executive summary," but they were also included separately.

The thrust of the judgments in this study was that Hanoi's efforts to pursue its aims had been complicated and made more expensive by our bombing program, and that Hanoi could no longer hope for an early victory because of our massive military buildup in the South. Nevertheless North Vietnam's ability to reinforce the Viet Cong's military capabilities in the South was far from exhausted; our bombing program could inhibit—but not prevent—such reinforcement; the destruction of North Vietnam's industrial capacity would have little effect on the outcome of the war because it contributed little to the war effort; and Hanoi could rely on the Soviet and Chinese for necessary arms and supplies. Therefore we believed that Hanoi remained confident of victory over the long term and was prepared to continue the war indefinitely, despite the possibility of even greater military pressure by the United States.

I was impressed with the thoroughness and comprehensiveness of this paper. It was a highly professional piece of work, contrasting markedly with the less sophisticated and narrower military intelligence products I had been reading in Saigon for the last two years. It was the first in a series of such papers thereafter prepared more or less quarterly and intended primarily for Secretary McNamara's consumption, though copies were passed also to a few other senior policy officials in Washington. Over the ensuing years, the CIA refined its analytical methodologies on some of the subject matter and expanded its analysis to include additional topics, but this first study was fundamentally sound and perceptive in its analysis, and its judgments generally stood the test of time.

Shortly after reading the paper, McNamara asked Director Helms if he could meet weekly with CIA's top expert on Vietnam. Carver was assigned that responsibility and made an appointment with McNamara for a Monday morning meeting. The defense secretary sent over a list of topics he hoped to consider in such meetings. On the day of the first meeting, however, Carver was out of town, and it was agreed that I would go in his stead.

McNamara greeted me cordially when I arrived at his office at 10:30 as scheduled. After we were seated, he asked which agenda item I had chosen for the morning's meeting. Embarrassed, I replied that I was not aware he had submitted a prospective agenda and was not prepared to discuss any particular topic. I apologized for the slipup and assured him that George Carver would come prepared the following week. When I stood to leave, McNamara motioned for me to stay, saying he had set aside a half-hour to talk about Vietnam that morning, and that perhaps we could usefully talk about the general situation. The secretary said he had read our lengthy study a few weeks earlier and had found it very interesting. I said I had reviewed it just after returning from two years in Saigon, and that I thought it was the most comprehensive study on Vietnam I had seen in the seventeen years I had been following the situation there. This piqued his interest; he hadn't realized there was anyone in the government who had worked on Vietnam for that long a time. He asked about my career, where I had served, and when.

A few minutes later he said that with all my exposure to Vietnam, I must have some thoughts about what we might be doing wrong in the war. I demurred, saying that as an intelligence officer it was not my place to critique our policies; my job was to illuminate policy deliberations, not to second-guess decisions or criticize their execution. He said he understood that, but surely, after seventeen years of looking at the situation, I must have some opinions as to whether we were doing the right thing, and he wanted to hear them. I continued to demur, but McNamara insisted, saying he wasn't asking for agency views, that he would take responsibility

for any objections that Director Helms might express about my responding to the secretary. He wanted to know what I would do if I were sitting
in his place.

Any further fencing would only waste more of his time, so I decided to
respond candidly. Emphasizing that I was expressing my personal views
and not those of the CIA, I said I would stop the buildup of American
forces, halt the bombing of the North, and negotiate a cease-fire with
Hanoi. He asked if that would not simply lead to a takeover of South Vietnam by the Communists, and I acknowledged that it certainly would, over
time. He asked how America could justify its involvement if, in the end,
we failed to preserve a non-Communist government in the South. I said
obviously we could not justify our actions if we confined the solution to
Vietnam exclusively. But if we put the problem into a broader regional
and international context, it might be possible to develop a regional solution that would be palatable to our country, one that would be more satis-
factory than continuing the current costs of the war to both sides. At this
point the allotted half-hour had ended, but, noticing the time, McNamara
directed his staff to cancel all appointments before lunch.

Resuming the dialogue, he asked how I envisaged such a regional solution being worked out. I hadn't thought this through beforehand, but
speaking off the cuff I referred him to the 1954 Geneva Accords, which
had reflected a consensus between all the interested parties except the
United States and Diem. I expressed the conviction that Hanoi had intended generally to abide by that agreement, which provided for the
ultimate unification of Vietnam after elections in 1956, and for the "neutralization" of Laos and Cambodia. He asked whether Hanoi had not attempted to undercut the agreement in Laos from the outset. I said Hanoi
had to some extent reacted to our attempts to "purify" the areas under
Laotian government control, which had not been consistent with the
agreement, just as Diem's crackdown on Communist agents in South
Vietnam after 1955 had not been consistent with the agreement. I noted
that "neutralization" of Laos and Cambodia did not imply an absence of
Communist attempts at subversion, but that it referred to nonalignment
of the governments there and an absence of big-power intervention.

McNamara then asked if my concept of neutralization wouldn't guarantee ultimate Communist control of Cambodia and Laos. I said that geopolitical factors made those countries susceptible to subversive penetration from Vietnam, but it might be possible to combat these effects through some combination of local political action, effective international supervision of any agreement, and the fostering of regional cohesion and cooperation. He asked why I was ready to risk the subversion of those countries—to allow the dominoes to fall—within the framework of a negotiated settlement. I replied that the risk of Communist domination in that fashion seemed no greater than under our present course of action, because there was no guarantee that our present efforts would produce victory; indeed, I was not convinced a military victory was possible. I suggested that if our aim was to destroy North Vietnam, that was a different matter, because we had means that could be used toward that objective that we were not then employing. But if we limited our aim merely to fighting to save South Vietnam and preventing the other countries from falling "like dominoes," I was not sure we could succeed. A limited objective implied that we would use only limited means, and limited means might not produce decisive results. If we were not prepared to commit the resources necessary to defeat North Vietnam, it seemed preferable to me to move to negotiations and cut the high costs of the war for both sides.

McNamara observed that I apparently assumed we could not win the war. I replied that it was not an assumption but a calculated judgment. I saw no evidence that the weight of our military effort would cause Hanoi to abandon the war, and I saw no reason to believe that any level of bombing of the North—short of nuclear devastation—would force the Communists to quit; they had not held the cities during their war against the French, and they didn't need them to fight us in South Vietnam. All they needed to continue the war was manpower, of which they still had an adequate supply (and the Chinese might make up any future deficit); arms, which their Soviet and Chinese allies apparently were willing to supply in sufficient quantity; and determination. Apparently they had convinced themselves they could outlast us, just as they had the French, and I saw little we could do to disabuse them of that conviction.

Returning to the subject of negotiation, the secretary asked why I thought Hanoi was ready to negotiate and would do so if we stopped

bombing now, since our bombing pauses thus far had produced no over-
tures. I suggested that a definitively declared bombing halt would produce
a different result from an apparent "pause" or nominal restraints on the
areas we bombed. He asked what terms I thought Hanoi would demand. I
said they would insist on the total withdrawal of U.S. forces from Vietnam
and ironclad guarantees on procedures for reunifying the country. He
asked how we could be sure they would live up to an agreement. I said we
could be no more sure of them than they of us; that having been robbed of
the fruits of their victory at Dien Bien Phu, they would certainly demand
far more assurance this time, and they would be tough negotiators.

Again he asked how we could publicly accede to such a solution after
all we had invested in our support of South Vietnam. I referred again to
the regional and international context. I suggested that if we included all
of Southeast Asia in any settlement, we might find an acceptable quid pro
quo. China and the Soviet Union, perhaps Japan and England as well as
Burma, Thailand, and Malaysia, and perhaps even Indonesia and the
Philippines ought to be brought into the solution. We should demand a
cessation of the Communist-backed insurgencies in Burma, Thailand,
and on the Malaysian border in exchange for a cease-fire in Indochina. We
could demand the withdrawal of Communist forces to remote enclaves in
both Laos and Cambodia, as well as within South Vietnam, noting that the
Communists would not agree again to a withdrawal of their forces from
the South. We could insist on a comprehensive system of international inspection to prevent (or at least inhibit) infiltration into Laos, Cambodia,
Thailand, and Burma. In exchange we would have to agree to withdraw
our forces from Vietnam, though we could insist on the right to maintain
forces in the region, perhaps as part of an international deterrent/reaction
force in Thailand. The Communists might well reject some of these
points at the outset, but I believed they would be flexible once they concluded that we would not block their ultimate assimilation of South Vietnam.

We discussed these points for an hour and a half before McNamara
broke off for a lunchtime appointment. He seemed genuinely interested
throughout, and as I left he remarked that he had welcomed the opportunity to explore facets of the problem that normally did not arise in other

meetings. He said he looked forward to renewing the discussion the following week. I reminded him that George Carver would be back by then, and that his views differed somewhat from mine.

This was the only protracted, one-on-one exchange I had with a cabinet member during my career. At the time I was a mid-level intelligence officer, experienced in dealing with my sub-cabinet-level counterparts. I'm sure I wasn't as articulate in expressing myself as the above reconstruction of the meeting suggests. Conscious of my position relative to the secretary, I was also aware of the uniqueness of this opportunity to express my views. The meeting may not have made a lasting impression on McNamara, but it was unforgettable for me. I will always wish that I had anticipated the course the meeting would take and had prepared for such a discussion.

I briefed Director Helms on the gist of my session with the defense secretary upon my return to Langley, and discussed the meeting at some length with Carver before he went to the second session. George said he thought I had gone overboard in my remarks; Helms did not react significantly. In retrospect I wish I had written an account of that session and circulated it widely within the government. That I did not do so was because, as I indicated in my remarks to the secretary, I did not believe it appropriate for a CIA officer to be initiating policy suggestions. The line an intelligence officer walks in this area is narrow and tricky. If I had known how much longer (seven years) it would be before we negotiated a final settlement with Hanoi, I certainly would have pursued the matter further at the time. But then, if our leaders had known what we were getting into in Vietnam, they too might have acted differently.

After my return from Saigon, I had represented Carver at a meeting of the principal interagency working group, which was chaired by William Bundy, assistant secretary of state for Southeast Asia. This group's role included coordination of the interagency work required to support the consideration of policy options on Vietnam by the National Security Council. New options had been proposed, and at this meeting State, Defense, the Joint Chiefs, and the CIA representatives were to pull together specific papers related to these options. I was asked to provide a CIA paper on the likely Communist reactions to these options. I remarked that it would help me, as one who had been away from Washington for a couple of years, if those present could refer me to a basic paper that outlined our purpose in Vietnam—our overall policy, the objectives we were pursuing—so that I could put these new options in perspective.

My colleagues seemed puzzled by this query. Surely, they said, everyone knew that we were trying to defeat North Vietnam's aggression and to preserve a non-Communist government in the South. I said I understood the latter as an explicit objective but was concerned about the former. The discussion at the meeting had suggested to me that there were a number of inconsistencies and ambiguities between the kinds of actions we were discussing and "defeating" North Vietnamese aggression.

Several of those present became impatient, suggesting that how we got to where we were was not the issue; the question under study was what needed to be addressed. Others questioned my motives, suggesting that I was fighting the problem, or challenging the relevance or soundness of the options under study. I said I would drop the matter if they would simply steer me to those earlier studies that must have spelled out our objectives and the strategic basis for the decisions that brought us to this point in the war. After heated discussion, the group acknowledged that there was no single paper that would solve my apparent problem, and the chairman suggested that it might be useful to establish a group to study the matter and produce a clear statement of our current objectives—and that I should chair that group.

On returning to headquarters I reported to Director Helms the various tasks assigned to the agency, mentioning that I had been asked to head a subgroup to define U.S. objectives in Vietnam. He was taken aback at this notion. Although sympathetic to my interest in understanding our aims in Vietnam, he objected to the idea of the CIA playing a leading role in defining those aims. We should be asked simply to provide the intelligence needed to support such deliberations. We could even offer personal opinions on the matter, if asked, but we should contribute little more than that.

Helms was right, of course; I should have fended off the group's gambit. I notified Bundy that I could not follow through on the task, and the matter was dropped. I had the impression that my colleagues were relieved; most of them seemed to consider it an unnecessary, even feckless diversion from the task of winning the war. I personally wondered how we would know whether we were making progress if we had no clear idea of what we were trying to accomplish. No serious study aimed to define our objectives and outline a strategy for achieving them until early 1969, when the Nixon administration embarked on a series of policy reviews. The first National Security Study Memorandum (NSSM) of Henry Kissinger's National Security Council faced up to the issue.

Sometime in October 1966, Secretary McNamara asked the director if CIA could develop a practical method for measuring progress in the pacification program. None of the various measurement systems he had seen had impressed him as getting to the root of the basic issue—how the war was going in the countryside. Were we winning or losing, and was there a realistic way of measuring this? McNamara's memo was passed to me by the director, in Carver's absence, and our staff was given about a week to prepare a response.

I was familiar with MACV's initial approach to measuring who controlled what in the countryside, having participated in its inception four years earlier and having followed its evolution since then. That concept had addressed the status of individual villages with rather generally defined criteria, based solely on our analysis of information available in Saigon that had not been systematically gathered for that purpose. The provincial reports produced separately by MACV and the embassy were narrative in form and lacked the systematic application of consistent criteria. The Marines in I Corps had devised an interesting matrix that systematically measured the status of several factors at the village level in the areas where they were working. But these data were essentially measures of specific inputs to the pacification programs; they gave little feel for their impact on the enemy. This had been the problem with reporting on the Strategic Hamlet program in the early sixties: the data simply reflected inputs, and there had been no systematic measurement of con-

ditions in the hamlet after it had been certified as meeting the initial
criteria for the program. Thus the only measure of "results" was the ever-
increasing cumulative total of "completed" hamlets, with no reflection of
their subsequent history, whether they continued to meet the criteria, or
whether their status was eroded as a result of enemy activity.

Secretary McNamara specifically asked that we look at the system
being used by the Marines. I invited two officers from the operations directorate to my office for a "brainstorming" session. One was a seasoned
officer whom I had known as a senior trainer and adviser at our training
center at Vung Tau. The other I had known in Saigon as one of the
brighter, more energetic and capable of our young case officers working in
one of the provinces in the Mekong Delta.

Together we reviewed the existing evaluation methods and criteria,
noting the best features of each. While the Marine Corps pacification effort in areas occupied by their troops in I Corps was concentrated at the
village level, the Vietnamese government's program in the remainder of
South Vietnam was being implemented on a hamlet-by-hamlet basis.
Government pacification teams were assigned to work within a specific
hamlet, not in a village at large. In Vietnam, a village comprised a number
of hamlets, which were sometimes scattered over an area of twenty-five
square miles or more, much as in an American township. It was often the
case that in a given village, some hamlets (usually those nearest a road or
major canal) would be under quite firm government control while more
remote hamlets in the same village would be "out of bounds" for government forces and fully under Communist control. Hamlets located between these two extremes would be under varying degrees of influence by
both sides. Our evaluation system was designed to measure these distinctions with as much objective precision as possible.

With this in mind, and using a blackboard, we devised a matrix which
expanded on that being used by Marines, ultimately settling on eighteen
factors to be measured. Half these factors were associated with specific
"inputs" into the government's pacification program: schools built,
medics trained, hamlet self-defense elements trained, hamlet chiefs
elected, police in place, sanitation projects completed and so forth. The
other half reflected results or "output": proximity of Viet Cong activity

against or near the hamlet, extent to which the hamlet chief actually spent his nights in the hamlet rather than slipping off to a more secure location, level of activity by self-defense elements, extent of government information program, levels of activity at school, effectiveness of hamlet medical aid station, and so forth.

We decided against a simple "yes-no" evaluation and chose to establish five grade levels for each of these eighteen factors. This meant defining specific indicators, or criteria—as objectively and clearly stated as possible—that would express the degree of progress or success achieved with respect to each factor. This produced a matrix that would be relatively simple to fill in by those responsible for making the evaluation. Since each of the eighteen factors being measured related to specific objectives of the government's current pacification program, the completed matrix would, in effect, provide a picture of the degree to which those objectives had been met in any particular hamlet.

Over the next few days we bounced the concept off a number of other experienced CIA officers, refined the criteria or "indicators," and then coordinated the proposal with appropriate CIA components.

McNamara approved our concept immediately and pressed Helms to begin the evaluation as quickly as possible. We had not addressed the subject of who would actually execute the evaluation program; we had assumed it would be the military. It would have been inappropriate for the CIA to formally evaluate the effectiveness of the programs of other U.S. government agencies. Although the CIA contributed substantially to the Vietnamese government's pacification program, the U.S. economic aid mission and the U.S. Information Service also had major roles. On the Vietnamese side, the police and the ARVN played major roles, and the program was managed and supervised by the government's province and district chiefs, who commanded all Vietnamese military and police operations in their respective locales, with the assistance of their MACV advisers.

The CIA's information-gathering activities were aimed at what our adversaries were doing, not at what U.S. agencies were doing abroad. Only MACV had resources in place to implement such a program. The CIA had only one or two officers in each of the 44 provinces, whereas MACV had 100 or more, including an advisory team in each of the 240-odd districts.

There were some 13,000 hamlets in south Vietnam, 300 or more in each province and as many as 60 in each district.

McNamara wanted Americans to do the evaluations; he and others in Washington were still smarting from the exaggerated claims the Vietnamese had generated for the strategic hamlet program. Director Helms made the case to Secretary McNamara that only MACV could do the job and should be charged with responsibility for the program. McNamara agreed but insisted that the system be put into effect as soon as possible.

Over the next week or so we hurriedly coordinated the concept with other agencies in Washington. Some of these were miffed that McNamara had turned to the CIA for an independent look at the problem rather than having it staffed through one of the interagency working groups. We briefed Bob Komer, then working on Vietnam for the National Security Council at the White House. He was skeptical of its usefulness and expressed doubt that the system would produce reliable readings of the status of pacification. He suspected that those doing the evaluating would tend to see things in the best possible light—which, of course, was indeed likely. We agreed this would be a problem with any such endeavor, and that was why we had made the criteria as objective as possible. The system would be more useful in indicating trends than in documenting with absolute accuracy the status of each individual hamlet. Within a year Komer would become the American "pacification czar" in Vietnam, as deputy commander of MACV for civil operations and rural development support, with ambassadorial rank. As such, his duties included oversight of this Hamlet Evaluation System.

The Joint Chiefs were uneasy; they were suspicious that the CIA was somehow moving into their bailiwick—that by devising the system we were trying to look over the shoulders of the military. They knew that MACV had been working to come up with a system on their own, and they didn't like the idea of one being imposed on them by McNamara and the CIA. Obviously they had little choice in the matter and conceded that the system should be tested in the field. The Chiefs insisted, however, that a Joint Chiefs colonel accompany me to Vietnam to oversee the testing and presumably to keep an eye on me. Because of McNamara's urgings, we completed the coordination in Washington quickly, we compiled and printed the necessary instructions and evaluation forms, and I departed for Saigon early in November.

I stopped briefly in Honolulu en route to brief the CINCPAC staff and Marine Lieutenant General Krulak, then head of the Fleet Marine Force, Pacific. CINCPAC had no problems with the concept. General Krulak, as might be expected, thought we should have stuck with the Marines' system; he was convinced their approach to pacification was sound and should be the model for the entire pacification program in Vietnam. And, of course, he believed the evaluation system ought to concentrate on the village level, not on the individual hamlets. I said I appreciated his views, and I assured him that the results of the Marines' pacification effort at the village level could be readily determined by aggregating the scores of the individual hamlets in the village. He was dubious but recognized that with McNamara's blessing there was little use in debating the issue. Since he apparently did not recall our encounter in the Pentagon three years earlier, on this occasion I escaped unscathed.

My Joint Chiefs chaperone joined me in Honolulu, and we flew on to Saigon. We briefed a meeting of the "Country Team," chaired by Ambassador Ellsworth Bunker, and with its pro forma approval moved ahead to the tests. Working with the MACV staff, we selected four districts in differing parts of the country. Key members of MACV's advisory teams in those locales were brought in to Saigon to be briefed. We then gave them packets of instructions and evaluation forms, and they returned to their subsectors.

During the week we spent a day in each of the four districts and at the headquarters of the provinces in which they were located. There we interviewed as many American and Vietnamese officials as we could, in order to gain a feel for the status of the pacification effort in the areas being evaluated in the tests. Thus equipped, we were in a better position to deal with the test evaluations.

We reviewed the results with American advisers at each echelon up the line, and we were satisfied that they reflected a reasonable degree of consistency in the way the evaluators had applied the criteria. MACV wanted further refinements over time. We agreed. The Country Team decided to inaugurate the Hamlet Evaluation System at the beginning of the new year.

After two weeks in Saigon, my Joint Chiefs escort and I departed for Bangkok where, at McNamara's suggestion, we briefed the mission on the evaluation system. The Country Team there found it mildly interesting but far too complex and resource-intensive for their needs, which was certainly true. So the colonel and I headed back to Washington, having set in motion a program for evaluating the progress of pacification in Vietnam that would continue for more than seven years and consume thousands of man-days of work by countless young army officers. But the results of their efforts were never utilized to their full potential.

Almost immediately the principal interest at higher levels in Washington was the aggregate pacification score for the country as a whole. The question most frequently asked was, "What's the average score for the month?" When told that the average score for all hamlets in Vietnam in a given month was, for example, 2.661 (on a scale of one to five), the next question was invariably, "How does that compare with last month?" If told the previous month's score had been 2.652, there were sighs of relief—pacification was making progress! If the previous score had been only 2.643, there were gasps of ecstasy. Never mind that an aggregate score masked significant moves in every direction among the eighteen different factors in thirteen thousand hamlets. The Viet Cong might well overrun a hundred hamlets at one end of the country during the month, but this could be offset by marginal improvements in several thousand other hamlets, so the significant setback would not be evident in the essentially meaningless aggregate score. High-level policymakers were not interested in the details, of course, and were happy to accept the aggregate score as a useful "index" of the status of pacification.

In the CIA, however, we continued to be interested in developing some means for using the Hamlet Evaluation System (HES) as a tool for analyzing trends and patterns in the war. Virtually all reporting from Saigon on activities related to the war was geared to a common factor: geographic locale. Air strikes, enemy harassing attacks, patrol engagements, friendly and enemy troop dispositions, supply caches, command post locations, original homes of refugees, former locations of defectors and prisoners, positions of artillery units and locations of their targets, ambush positions, helicopter landing pads, elephant sightings, locations of province capitals, district towns, hamlets, outposts, major combat actions—the sites of all these things were unfailingly reported in terms of a common system of geographic reference points, the Universal Transverse Mercator (UTM) grid system used by our military forces. But there were separate computerized accounting systems for every conceivable kind of activity, including the locations of the hamlets in our new evaluation system. Because these computer files were developed by several different agencies at different times for different purposes, using different computers and equipment and different programming languages, they were essentially incompatible; they could not readily be used on a single computer system. The only common element they shared was the use of the UTM to identify the location of what was being reported.

For some months in 1967 we considered developing some means to permit detailed and comprehensive analysis of all these geographically based data files. Using the data from HES as the basic file, it would be valuable—and feasible—to compare the trends reflected in its monthly reports with data on other activities in the vicinity, such as air strikes, friendly and enemy troop movements, combat operations, refugee flows, enemy activity, and so forth. If these could be overlaid on maps for study in varying combinations, we believed it would be possible to find explanations for fluctuations in the HES scores in individual districts and provinces, to determine cause-and-effect relationships among these various kinds of activities. Indeed, it might be possible to identify patterns and trends in the war that were not otherwise apparent in the statistical and narrative reporting from the field.

The potential usefulness of this type of analysis was almost exciting. Collating all of this data for visual presentation might make it possible to anticipate the consequences of friendly or enemy action and thus provide, among other things, a management tool for the pacification managers in the provinces as well as a planning tool for military operations. It might be possible to ascertain where things could be expected to go well and hence to reinforce programs in those areas. Conversely it might be possible to anticipate where reverses could be expected and to reduce temporarily the commitment of additional resources in those areas until conditions improved. With a computer-driven geographic plotting device and a minicomputer, available at the CIA and through outside contractors, we got a promising start in analysis and comparison of the data. But we were unable to obtain necessary additional funds (about $400,000) from the Washington bureaucracy for software because we could not demonstrate a post-Vietnam application for it. Thus we were unable to pursue this potentially powerful analytic tool to fruition; the bureaucracy proved too inflexible.

This episode illustrates the shortsightedness that afflicted most departments and agencies in Washington during the Vietnam War. Even after the United States had deployed a half-million men to Vietnam and was spending more than $100 million a day to wage the war, in many places there was a deep-rooted reluctance to shift bureaucratic gears for the long haul, to adapt normal peacetime structures, methods, and practices to this new reality. Most elements of the Washington bureaucracy tried to cope with the burdens of the war within a business-as-usual framework, attempting to "ad hoc" their way along, and only grudgingly (and temporarily) shifting resources from cherished programs to support war activities. Budget processes generally moved along routinized paths, and it was not easy to push through "extraordinary" supplemental adjustments to meet unanticipated short-term needs. All agencies tended to minimize the impact of the war on their longer-term plans and programs. Few people believed that our entanglement in the Vietnam War would continue for another eight years.

I am not suggesting that our ill-fated computerized analytical scheme would have altered the outcome in Vietnam. But it might have given managers and planners a better picture of what was happening in the war, and perhaps keener insight into why. Countless computer programs in use today can do what we were hoping to do in 1967. But there was little interest then in changing our ways of doing business in order to accommodate unanticipated requirements, even if they were related to a major—albeit undeclared—war effort.

Word of our efforts toward integrating data from various sources to permit better analysis of the war reached the White House in the spring of 1967, where it attracted the interest of Walt Rostow. As the prime Washington consumer of the monthly HES score, Rostow sometimes harried us with anticipatory phone calls when the monthly tally from Saigon was due. HES, however, measured only progress in the pacification program, and provided (through related census data) the status of population control. It did not otherwise evaluate the progress of the war. The body count was widely seen as another useful measure, but its real value was limited because of doubts concerning its accuracy, and because the enemy's morale and combat effectiveness were affected by other factors as well. Indeed, from Rostow's point of view there were too many factors to take into account, and too many separate data bases to permit the average high-level official readily to judge overall trends in the war. He asked the intelligence community to address the problem and to see if there might be some way of weighing the relative value of the various indicators to produce a single index that would faithfully reflect the status of the war.

Carver asked me to organize a working group to tackle this problem, and suggested we convene in a retreat environment to enable the group to apply its undivided attention to the issue. About a dozen of us—Vietnam analysts and data systems specialists from State, DIA, the National Security Agency, and the CIA—closeted ourselves at an agency-owned country house for a week, where we studied data bases, talked data systems, and brainstormed the problem in pastoral isolation. Several times we thought we might be approaching a solution, only to arrive at a dead end. We finally concluded that any index we might produce would be essentially meaningless. Just as the popular single HES score masked considerable turbulence within the pacification program, so a single "war index" would likely conceal significant shortcomings in key aspects of the war effort. Some of these failings might require urgent command attention, but they might well be overlooked because of the focus on a single index. We readily identified a number of factors as being crucial to any understanding of trends in the war, but we could not agree on a method of accurately weighing their relative significance in the context of a single measure of progress in the war. Thus my task force failed in its mission—probably just as well.

The last, best opportunity to create a solid political base for the Saigon government was lost with the Vietnamese national elections in the fall of 1967. Having persuaded Vietnam's military leaders of the need to establish a legitimate basis for their government—which had, after all, overthrown both Diem and his constitution—the American embassy patiently shepherded the Vietnamese through the steps necessary for the development and promulgation of a new constitution. Under the constitution, elections were to be held to choose a president and vice president to succeed the military junta, as well as a new national assembly. Unfortunately for our Vietnam War policy, American concern for this process was directed more to appearances than to realities. Both Washington and the embassy in Saigon were more interested in the favorable impact the procedure would have on international opinion and on public opinion in the United States than in its impact on the real politics of the Vietnam War. We were more concerned with form than with substance. Most senior American officials overestimated the domestic political value that would accrue to the Saigon government from merely relegitimizing the non-Communist government in the South. They believed—or merely hoped—that this would make it more attractive to people in the South as an alternative to the Viet Cong.

Some of us in the CIA were convinced that this was a vain hope. We believed that those who already opposed the Viet Cong would continue to do so regardless of the complexion of the ruling military oligarchy, and that the fence-sitters, skeptics, and uncommitted would cynically view any elections as so much eyewash. The mass of the populace would believe there was little difference among the choices they were offered—that the junta almost certainly would manipulate the results to ensure that one of its members was duly anointed to head the new government.

The people also understood that free elections under a Communist-controlled government would be even more unlikely. But for them, that was not the real point. Neither side offered them anything to hope for, only a continuation of the war until one side or the other won. One side— the Viet Cong—they perceived as hard, cruel, and vindictive—but also as defending the ideals of Vietnamese independence and nationalism against outside intervention, Western imperialism, and "neocolonialism." Even the staunchest anti-Communist Vietnamese felt a sense of xenophobic pride in the way the Viet Cong were holding up in the face of the powerful American military forces, and in the Viet Minh's earlier defeat of the French. They recognized that the American-supported government was fending off the imposition of a brutal, harsh Communist regime. But they regarded the junta as dominated by the commercial, educated, and military elite, all of whom were subservient to the American "imperialists." The Saigon government was making no positive appeal to the people at large.

It seemed to some of us that the coming elections could be used to galvanize popular attitudes in support of a political program that appealed to the basic yearnings and desires of the people. This would have required the junta to create a realistic, positive political platform and a mass political movement dedicated to its achievement. The French had never attempted any political effort of this sort. The Diem government had never formulated a political platform with widespread popular appeal, and its organized political base was fatally narrow. The 1967 elections seemed to present a context for offering to the Vietnamese people an effective, counterrevolutionary alternative.

For such an effort to succeed, it was essential that the Vietnamese themselves provide the leadership, impetus, and socio-cultural-political content. A program based largely on American ideals would have little appeal; its success would depend on its appeal to Vietnamese values. The Viet Cong leadership had proven adept at organizing and stimulating mass support, but the Saigon government lacked the skills, political mechanisms, and resources to do the same. It would need American help to make up for these deficiencies, and this assistance would have to be provided covertly. American support for a program of the requisite scale would have been impossible to conceal, but the extent of our involvement might have been successfully camouflaged.

It was clear that we would have to take the initiative, establish contact
with sympathetic members of the junta, and explore possibilities along
the lines of my earlier discussion with General Thi. The CIA had people
familiar with political-action programs of the kind that were needed.
When we floated the idea to Ambassador Bunker, however, he rejected it
out of hand. He insisted that although we had set in motion a constitutional, democratic electoral process, the United States could not "play
God" by injecting itself into that process in any way. The Vietnamese
would have to work out the practical, political application of the process
among themselves. If they developed a concept that seemed worth supporting, we might consider some means of backing them. But we could
not take the lead; if such an American role was ever discovered it would
destroy everything we had been able to accomplish thus far.

Some of us believed that, in order to protect our investment, we had
to go beyond "civic action" and concentrate on "political action" to ensure that the resulting constitutional arrangements were nurtured and
protected. But Ambassador Bunker believed we should not attempt to
shape or influence the way the Vietnamese generals carried out the political process.

As the time for individuals to declare their candidacy drew near,
members of the junta put out feelers to determine whether and when the
Americans would announce their endorsement of Prime Minister Ky.
Among the Vietnamese it was a foregone conclusion that any candidate
backed by the military junta would be elected to the presidency, and it was
widely assumed that their candidate would be the former air marshal.

For more than two years Ky—as prime minister—had been managing
the day-to-day business of the South Vietnamese government. General
Thieu was the nominal chief of state, but his duties had been largely cere-
monial. Although junior in military rank to Thieu, Ky actively presided
over the government, managing its day-to-day operations. In this he had
enjoyed the backing of a majority within the ruling military junta, including all those of northern origin. Under the new constitution, the president would be the chief executive, and the vice president would be
virtually powerless.

Ambassador Bunker steadfastly insisted that the United States should not endorse any candidate for the presidency. To do so would be an un-warranted intervention; the Vietnamese leaders should be permitted to sort such things out for themselves. This would demonstrate to their own people and to the outside world that the new constitutional processes had worked freely and smoothly to legitimize the government. It would also clearly show that the government in Saigon was not an American puppet. It would show that the Vietnamese had reached a new level of political ma-turity and sophistication after four years of instability and military rule. In effect, the *form* of self-government was all-important; we had no con-cern for its political substance.

Ky's stewardship, and its acceptance by the junta, had brought relative stability and continuity to the Saigon government for the first time since the overthrow of Diem. Despite his flamboyant demeanor, Ky exuded a personal charm and charisma that appealed to many, Vietnamese and Americans alike. He had some of the political attractiveness of a Magsaysay, the late Philippine president, and he clearly enjoyed more popularity within the military forces and urban classes than his peers. He also seemed to have more potential than the other Vietnamese officials for leading a popular counterrevolutionary movement. His reputation as a womanizer, however, diminished his standing in Bunker's eyes, and it was clear the ambassador believed South Vietnam would be better off under someone else's leadership.

Bunker instructed all members of the American mission, in their con-tacts with the Vietnamese, to make their neutrality toward the election absolutely clear. Although CIA officers complied strictly with the ambas-sador's orders, many of my colleagues and I in Washington chafed at the indecision and delays this produced. Time was of the essence if the Viet-namese were to undertake a major political-action program of the sort we believed essential. The sooner the Vietnamese settled on a candidate, the better the chances of getting a suitable program in place. But the adminis-tration in Washington embraced Bunker's view that the United States should express no choice in the matter. Thus there was no real enthusiasm outside of the CIA for a massive political-action program, and no interest in pressing the generals to push things along.

When the generals duly met to choose their candidate for the presidency, most observers anticipated a rubber-stamp endorsement of Ky. During the meeting, however, Thieu cleverly raised the question of the American embassy's apparent neutrality with respect to Ky, noting that this could be interpreted as a lack of confidence in the prime minister. If the Americans were satisfied with Ky's leadership, would they not endorse him and make this known through their contacts with members of the junta?

Ky was stung by Thieu's suggestion that the Americans had no confidence in him, and his backers in the junta were perplexed. To the oriental mind this was the obvious meaning of our reluctance to support Ky. The generals could not name as candidate a man whom the Americans were unwilling to endorse. They were indecisive but finally agreed to adjourn and canvass their American contacts on this vital issue.

When they reconvened the next day, the generals unanimously acknowledged the Americans' strict neutrality. Thieu then announced that he had decided he must run for the presidency, insisting that the Americans preferred him to Ky, that this was the signal they were sending by their silence on the matter. Ky recognized the cleverness of Thieu's gambit, but he was powerless to argue against it. Because the generals—at American insistence—had agreed earlier that there should be but one military slate, Ky could not contest Thieu in the elections. The junta recognized that the military must maintain a semblance of unity and cohesion in order to preserve the constitutional process. Ky had greatly aspired to the presidency; now, seemingly deprived of that opportunity by Thieu's obduracy; he threatened to withdraw from politics altogether and return to duty with his air force. But his colleagues, recognizing the value of his popularity and wishing to preserve a façade of unity, prevailed upon him to accept the vice presidential candidacy.

By not "intervening" in the Vietnamese electoral process, the United States thus effectively dictated its outcome. There can be little doubt that our neutrality permitted Thieu's emergence. This outcome effectively foreclosed any possibility of a major political-action program following the elections. Washington would not likely have approved it even if Ky had emerged as the presidential candidate, though some preparatory steps had been taken. But such a program was clearly not an option under Thieu's leadership.

Thieu was a native of the southern portion of central Vietnam. He was not interested in mounting a social revolution. A proven survivor, he had risen largely through intrigue and manipulation, outlasting the other officers of his generation (he had begun his military career as an officer in the French Colonial Army). Thieu was not a dynamic natural leader; he was almost totally lacking in charisma. Like most southerners, he distrusted the more dynamic, forceful northerners who dominated the junta and the Vietnamese military forces. Thieu was intelligent and "mature" (a decade older than Ky), and he impressed some Americans as a passably competent administrator—albeit inclined to move sometimes with painful slowness. His discretion served him well; Bunker was more comfortable with Thieu than with Ky, unaware that neither general was exactly puritanical in character.

But General Thieu wanted no part of a mass political movement. Even with himself as its torchbearer, there could be no guarantee that he would not lose control of it to a potential rival. Thieu was not a man to trust the masses, and he distrusted democracy as well. He had relieved several of our Vietnamese instructors at the CIA's Vung Tau training center because they had injected some unapproved political content in their classes as a means of motivating the students. A successful political-action program was contingent on the leadership of someone like Ky, or with whom Ky could work effectively. By pursuing Bunker's strict policy of remaining aloof from the electoral process, the United States lost its last real opportunity for helping to undergird our war effort in Vietnam with a well-organized political base. In itself such a base would not have guaranteed victory, but without one, defeat in the long run was inevitable.

11
The
Public
Opinion
Campaign

VEXED AT growing public criticism of the war on the home front, the administration embarked in the summer of 1967 on a major campaign to convince the American people, and their elected representatives, that we were on the right track in Vietnam; that the administration's policies were sound and were producing favorable results; that there was, indeed, "light at the end of the tunnel." This new, concerted campaign was orchestrated from the White House situation room by an interagency working group. Under the chairmanship of the president's National Security Adviser, Walt Rostow, the group comprised the public affairs and legislative liaison chiefs of the White House staff, State and Defense departments, the U.S. Information Agency, and a CIA representative—usually George Carver but often myself in his place. The agency's role in this group involved two legitimate intelligence functions. First, our presence enabled us to provide information on the general situation in Vietnam, particularly on Communist propaganda trends and Hanoi's likely reactions to our attempts to influence world opinion. Second, the CIA was responsible for carrying out covert psychological actions—both "black" and "grey"—to complement the USIA's task of influencing opinion in foreign countries.

The objective of this task force was to win public and congressional acceptance of, and support for, administration policies and programs in Vietnam. The group drew up a strategy aimed at achieving its goal before the end of 1967, and devised and orchestrated a plan to implement that strategy. Meeting weekly, it reviewed programs and activities and updated tactics to deal with the evolving situation. I attended a number of these meetings and found them among the most distasteful and depressing sessions of my entire career.

The effort was in large measure foreign to my outlook as a professional intelligence analyst. I had been conditioned to strive for objective truth in my work, for honesty in selecting the evidence to be employed, and for personal integrity—and that of the institution for which I was working—in formulating my judgments. This working group seemed to me the antithesis of those standards. Its function was to manipulate public opinion and to alter popular perceptions so that they would coincide with what the administration wanted the public to believe. There was no consideration of objective truth, honesty, or integrity in performing these tasks, and surprisingly little concern about credibility.

These are, of course, routine functions in the process of "molding" public opinion, and they are part of virtually all advertising programs, political campaigns, and commercial and government "public information" activities in our country. It would be foolish to condemn all these practices as "immoral," though I would suggest that conceptually there is an implied amorality. But the approach followed by this special working group in 1967 struck me as crossing well over the line into immorality. On many occasions the truth was grotesquely and deliberately distorted in order to make a point.

I dreaded these meetings because I frequently found myself a minority of one in my passion for at least a modicum of honesty in the deliberations. I would interject the view that a given position or statement was unsupportable by the evidence, or vulnerable to exposure by our adversaries or the media as artificially contrived, fanciful, or even false. I also would point out how Hanoi could be expected to refute a particular claim or trump a weak propaganda gambit. On such occasions I would be brought up short by impatient suggestions that I "get on the team," or questions about "whose side" I was on. More than once the chairman prefaced a proposed tactical ploy with an acknowledgment that there was "no need" for me to speak to the matter because my views in such cases were "sufficiently known."

True, in large measure my remarks reflected my fundamental skepticism about the war in Vietnam. At the same time I believed an opinion-shaping effort had to be credible to be effective; it could not be credible if much of it could be exposed as untruthful. My "unhelpful" contributions were consistently brushed aside; the other participants in the meetings obviously believed in what they were doing as strongly as I disbelieved in it. I was merely a minor burr under the saddle of a program whose aim was to reassure the public that their president was pursuing a wise and effective course in Vietnam.

Early in this campaign, in Carver's absence, I took a phone call at work from Rostow, who said he urgently needed a CIA study of progress in the pacification program in Vietnam. I asked whether he was asking CIA for an assessment of pacification trends, and he said no, he simply needed a paper that would show progress. I said I didn't think CIA could do an objective paper that would show only progress; my sense of current trends was that were serious problems with the pacification effort in some areas. He said he was aware of that, but the president needed a summary that would help him convince a number of congressmen and other White House visitors in coming weeks that the pacification effort was on track. I replied that any summary of the pacification effort as a whole would have to present the bad news along with the good. Rostow impatiently argued that I knew as well as he did that there were forty-four provinces in Vietnam, and that while there might be setbacks to the program in some areas, others would show progress. He wanted a summary of events in those areas where it was meeting with success.

Clearly upset by now with my apparent recalcitrance, Rostow said he didn't care about the provinces where the results were unfavorable; he was simply asking for a summary of where developments *were* favorable. At this point I suggested that he wasn't really asking for an intelligence paper, that what he wanted was something the U.S. Information Agency, the Defense Department, or the Joint Chiefs might produce. He protested that they would never be able to meet his short deadline, and he objected to my apparent reluctance to meet the president's urgent need for information. Hot under the collar by this point myself, I replied that, on the contrary, it was because I wanted to help the president that I could not be a party to "cooking the books" in the manner he was suggesting.

After Rostow slammed down the receiver (or so it sounded to me), I realized that I had just told the White House to buzz off. In effect I had jeopardized both my own career and the agency's carefully nurtured reputation for responsiveness.

I went to see Director Helms to alert him to the fact that I had refused to give Rostow what he asked for. After briefing him on the conversation, I told the director that if we were forced to produce such a study, I would resign; I could not be a party to it. Helms assured me that if we were in fact forced to do such a paper, I would have to get in line behind him, because he would be the first to resign.

Rostow, however, was not to be denied. He made another approach to the agency, bypassing our office and asking the CIA's intelligence directorate to produce a paper on the subject. The Office of Current Intelligence was asked to prepare a summary of indications of progress in pacification, as an attachment to a memorandum sent to the White House over Helms's signature. The forwarding memorandum—which I saw a few days later—stated that, as requested, there was attached a summary of portions of recent reports from Saigon reflecting progress in pacification. Its second paragraph noted, however, that the summary omitted other statements in those same reports that reflected adversely on the program or showed setbacks in certain areas, and that the attached summary should not be construed as an analysis of overall trends. At the White House, the covering memo, with its caveats, was removed from the attachment, which was sent into the president with a slip initialed by Rostow stating, "At last, Mr. President, a useful assessment from the CIA."

When I saw a copy of Rostow's note affixed to the summary, I was incensed. First, I resented his insinuation to the president that the CIA was not normally useful in supporting White House intelligence needs. Second, I resented Rostow's bypassing of normal business channels in order to get subordinate elements of the agency to do his bidding. It was just the sort of back-channel maneuvering that years later got several CIA operations officers into trouble for supporting Ollie North's activities in the Iran-Contra business without the knowledge and approval of their superiors.

The administration's public opinion campaign was designed by the interagency working group to peak with visits to Washington in November 1967 by Ambassador Bunker and General Westmoreland. The intent was to pull out all stops with the media—multiple appearances on the Sunday TV talk shows, for example—to beat the drums for the "light at the end of the tunnel" message. Favored journalists were given exclusive interviews and "inside information" to ensure an appropriate crescendo of favorable publicity in the windup of the campaign. As part of this effort, data on the alleged virtual elimination of the enemy's main force units in the III Corps area were given to Joseph Alsop, which he gleefully published.

The director occasionally asked me to meet with Alsop and serve as a sounding board for his forthcoming articles. Helms's aim was to keep Joe from "wandering too far off the reservation"—to discuss matters relatively freely and objectively as a means of "keeping him honest." I lunched with Alsop as he rehearsed his column on the alleged demise of the enemy's military potential in III Corps. I told him the story was absolute nonsense. Although it was consistent with MACV efforts to downplay enemy capabilities so as to imply progress in the war, this particular information was a gross distortion of reality. Joe insisted he had gotten it from a member of Westmoreland's entourage, that it had the general's confidence, and that indeed it was based on an intelligence study. I told Alsop I knew that, because I had read the report on which he had based the column. It had been written by Lieutenant Colonel William Benedict, a former army colleague with whom I had worked in the Pentagon as well as on MACV's Viet Cong order-of-battle project in 1962, and who was now intelligence chief of the U.S. 1st Infantry Division in the III Corps area. Benedict was a good man but sometimes given to flights of fancy; his analytical work had always needed careful supervision and review. He had briefed Westmoreland in Saigon on the analytical piece in question, and

"Westy" had included him in his entourage for the Washington trip. Since the administration's public opinion campaign had been closely coordinated with the embassy and MACV, Westmoreland had quickly recognized the value of this particular item as one that would support the image the White House wanted to project.

The gist of the paper was that, of the thirty-three enemy main force battalions present in the III Corps area at the beginning of the year, all but three had been destroyed or otherwise put out of action as a result of aggressive U.S. and South Vietnamese operations; the three remaining battalions were cowering in sanctuaries across the border in Cambodia. As I told Alsop, the story was unsupported by credible evidence. Indeed, substantial evidence from very reliable sources showed that there had been a significant reinforcement of enemy main force capabilities in III Corps during the year. MACV had not yet acknowledged these reinforcements because to do so would necessitate a politically unacceptable increase in the assessed strength of the enemy forces. Thus the thesis portrayed in Alsop's projected column and backed by General Westmoreland was not only wrong but dead wrong. Alsop scoffed; he knew a "good story" when he saw one, and he published his column.

I looked up Benedict a day or two later and castigated him for such amateurish and sloppy analytical work. He shrugged, saying that, after all, it was one way of looking at the problem. He chuckled when I reminded him that a good intelligence officer looked at the evidence on both sides of the question. That was probably true, he said, but that approach could ruin an otherwise interesting story. He dismissed my obvious dismay with his statement that the piece had, after all, earned him a trip home to visit his family.

I met Benedict again, at the command post of the 1st Division north of Saigon, in the immediate aftermath of the Tet offensive. His analysts briefed me for two hours on their reconstruction of enemy troop movements preceding, during, and since the initial onslaught on Saigon during the Tet holidays. Basing their analysis primarily on interrogation of prisoners captured during these operations, as well as on captured documents and other evidence, they showed how the equivalent of five full enemy divisions—some forty-five main force battalions—had slipped through and around friendly forces to get between them and their Tet offensive targets, the major American installations at Bien Hoa and Long Binh, and in Saigon, and virtually all the provincial and district capitals in the III Corps area. After these briefings—which impressed me as a good bit of analysis, comprehensive and thorough—Benedict and I went back to his tent to relax over cigars and a quick brandy while waiting for a helicopter to arrive to return me to Saigon. "Well," he said, apologetically, "I really f—d that one up, didn't I, George?" I replied that indeed he had. The thirty-three main force battalions in the III Corps at the beginning of 1967 had not been reduced to three, as he had suggested and as Alsop had parroted to the American public. They had in fact, been *reinforced* by one-third to a total of forty-five, all of which had participated actively—and with considerable impact on the outcome of the war—in the III Corps area.

American policies on Vietnam during the Johnson administration were coordinated and decided at several levels within the national security bureaucracy. The primary forum for policy development was the interagency working group chaired by William Bundy of State. Attendees at meetings of this group varied over time and depended in part on the topic under consideration. Bundy was bright but tended, I thought, to nudge the consensus toward action along impractical lines. He seemed not to be overly concerned with consequences, more willing to accept the easy tactical "fix" rather than to weigh the issue in terms of strategic realities. Bundy's deputy, Philip Habib, was often present; he was consistently one of the more realistic, practical voices in the group's deliberations, a man with shrewd political instincts, usually able quickly to cut through to the heart of a matter. The Department of Defense was represented by a variety of bright young "policy wonks," who were often insightful and excelled at constructing a case on either side of an issue. Among these was Morton Halperin, who, then as now, often played a devil's advocate role, a brilliant academic who enjoyed trumping the other fellow's card in a debate. These Defense representatives were innovative, able to identify and articulate any number of "quick fix" options at the drop of a hat, always positively action-oriented but flexible, and highly adept at brainstorming.

The Joint Chiefs were represented by General William DuPuy, a bright, articulate officer who was an effective spokesman for the military viewpoint—the positive, optimistic outlook. Others often appeared from the Joint Chiefs as well as from the NSC staff, USIA, and USAID, and "straphangers" from State. I represented the agency at dozens of meetings of this group.

The principal group met more or less regularly, and on call, to deal with broader issues or urgent matters, or to review the status of ongoing staff actions and special projects, oversee the work of subgroups, debate options under consideration, parcel out work assignments on new policy options, and decide on options and recommendations that would be passed to higher levels for further consideration or approval. The work of the group's committees was not particularly systematic; many major policy options bypassed them altogether and were worked out privately and informally by group members. Sensitive operational matters were handled through other channels, to which Bundy was usually privy. The psychological warfare (public opinion campaign) working group that met at the White House under Rostow led an entirely separate existence. And different combinations of people were involved in matters related to sounding out Hanoi on the possibility of negotiations.

The highest policy level was the "Tuesday Lunch" group, which usually included the president, Secretary of State Rusk, Defense Secretary McNamara, the chairman of the Joint Chiefs, and (after the fall of 1967) the director of the CIA. One of the duties of Carver's staff was to prepare Helms for these sessions, pulling together briefing papers and background studies on issues and options likely to be considered, and commenting on the bureaucratic interests and related manueverings. Carver received some feedback on these sessions, but Helms very much respected LBJ's passion for secrecy on policy deliberations.

The policy process as I experienced it under the Johnson administration is best characterized during this period (1966–1968) as ad hoc and episodic rather than systematic, deliberate, and structured. I have already described my futile attempt in 1966 to determine our objectives and our strategy for achieving them. The dismantling by the Kennedy administration of Eisenhower's mechanism for coordinating National Security

Council policy planning and operations substantially reduced the effectiveness of the foreign policy and national security decision-making process in Washington. Although the Eisenhower NSC process was often inflexible and cumbersome, it had nevertheless introduced a useful degree of deliberation and had formally integrated intelligence considerations into the making of policy. In retrospect, some refinement of that process was certainly desirable and would have been far more beneficial than its virtual demolition. The baby need not have been discarded with the bath water. Since Johnson, administrations have moved erratically toward building an effective coordinating mechanism, but with only occasional success. Under President Nixon, Kissinger engaged the national security bureaucracy in a structured approach to policy review and deliberations, but key decisions were often made without being vetted through this machinery. Carter and Zbigniew Brzezinski followed a generally similar pattern, but the Reagan administration seemed to be somewhat less structured. President George Bush and Brent Scowcroft introduced a useful innovation by creating a Deputies' Committee, which served as a filter for details and thereby allowed the principals to concentrate on broader issues.

I was involved in the national security decision-making process under six administrations (Truman through Carter), and was on its periphery in the Bush and Reagan administrations. In retrospect I believe the Eisenhower process was the most effective. In the absence of a reasonably systematic approach, our policies tend to be excessively dominated by aggressive individuals or organizations, or by the interplay of bureaucratic politics, rather than by rational deliberation of national interests, resources, the interests of our allies, economic considerations, and the consequences of various options. Without systematic consideration, the focus shifts to day-to-day tactics and stratagems, neglecting long-term strategies and consequences, except when entirely new administrations come to power and go through the rigors of a policy review process. This ad hoc syndrome and its inadequacies are reflected in the Bay of Pigs operation, the Dominican Republic intervention, and the Cuban missile crisis (where we were fortunate), as well as in the full course of our Vietnam involvement, especially after 1960.

12
Counting
the Enemy

MACV'S INTELLIGENCE STAFF in Saigon stuck to its conservative approach to estimating enemy order of battle into 1967. Its holdings on the composition and strength of main force enemy units continued to lag somewhat behind reality on the battlefield; several months often passed between the initial identification of a new unit and "confirmation" of its presence in the form of two valid prisoners of war or captured documents. The estimated strength of accepted main force and local force units also tended to be on the low side, because body counts were subtracted from the estimated strength of enemy units known to have been engaged in combat, without any provision for the likelihood that those losses would be made up over time by replacements. Although in CIA we had misgivings about these matters, we consistently deferred to MACV's analytical preferences. These were, after all, more or less "conventional" military forces, and we recognized that, as the responsible military command in the theater, MACV was free to judge how it wanted to calculate the enemy's military strength.

Beginning late in the fall of 1966, however, intelligence analysts in Washington came to realize that the strength of the enemy's paramilitary forces—characterized as guerrilla-militia elements—had increased substantially during the preceding few years. We knew that MACV had paid little attention to these irregulars since initially estimating their strength in

1962 at about 100,000. Indeed, their estimate had declined somewhat because of the belief that these forces must also be suffering losses. The guerrilla-militia forces were the ones most frequently encountered in the Vietnamese government's ongoing pacification program, the struggle for control of the populated areas in the countryside. The ill-fated Strategic Hamlet program had been designed to protect the rural populace from incursions and depredations by Viet Cong irregulars. Seeing Strategic Hamlets as a major threat to their position in the countryside, the enemy mounted a major counteroffensive which brought the program to a standstill by mid-1963 and steadily pushed it back while the Vietnamese government was distracted by the Buddhist crisis. After the overthrow of the Diem government in November 1963, the Viet Cong intensified their efforts to extend their control and influence in the rural areas, gaining access to well over a million additional peasants. From this expanded population base they busily recruited additional guerrillas and "self-defense" militia to consolidate and protect their new holdings. From this same source they were able to reinforce the local force units at the district and provincial levels to support their growing irregular forces in the rural villages and hamlets.

Meanwhile the CIA station in Saigon was becoming more deeply involved in the pacification program, working with Vietnamese officials at the national and provincial levels to develop new methods and techniques to sustain—and ultimately expand—the government's presence in the countryside. These activities naturally heightened the CIA's interest in coping with the Viet Cong's paramilitary forces and covert political apparatus—the infrastructure at the lowest levels. The Saigon station's collation branch, which focused on the political apparatus, was one response to this interest.

In order to get a better handle on the guerrilla-militia forces, the Vietnamese Affairs Staff in Washington in mid-1966 assigned an eager and capable young analyst to the task of examining the hundreds of translations of captured Viet Cong documents forwarded by MACV. This analyst, Sam Adams, soon found among these documents plausible evidence of the extent to which these forces had been increased. Working under my general supervision, Adams discovered enemy reports from a number of provinces accounting for guerrilla-militia forces at several times the strength reflected in MACV's order-of-battle holdings for those provinces. By the fall of 1966 he had accumulated evidence that clearly indicated an increase in these forces to a total of well over 200,000 in the year 1965. These and related documents provided a more comprehensive understanding of the composition of the Viet Cong's interrelated secret control and security apparatus at all levels, and confirmed that these also existed in greater numbers than reflected in MACV's current estimate of the enemy's strength.*

These new findings were duly noted in a number of memoranda distributed by the CIA in Washington in late 1966 and early 1967, and were reflected in the agency's initial draft in the spring of 1967 of a special National Intelligence Estimate. This estimate addressed the "Capabilities of the Vietnamese Communists for Fighting in South Vietnam." When the draft was circulated to other components of the intelligence community, the higher numbers it proposed for the enemy's order of battle in South Vietnam sparked one of the most heated and prolonged controversies in the history of American intelligence. Previous estimates, reflecting Washington's acquiescence in MACV's numbers, had totaled just over 300,000, including some 120,000 in main and local forces, 40,000 in administrative and service components, 90,000 guerilla-militia troops, and some 60,000 "political cadre." The draft estimate proposed a new total of 500,000, with most of the increase accounted for in the guerrilla-militia category.

When representatives of the intelligence community convened to discuss CIA's draft, the DIA spokesman, indicating he was reflecting MACV's views, rejected the proposed increase in enemy strength. DIA had sought MACV's comments on the draft and stubbornly defended the field command's position throughout the coordination sessions. After two months of fruitless wrangling, in an unprecedented move to break the deadlock,

---

*Adams's book, *War of Numbers* (South Royalton, Vt., 1994) is a detailed, candid, and sometimes emotional account of his central role in the "numbers controversy" on Vietnam, and of his exhaustive efforts thereafter to right the "treasonous" wrong he perceived in its outcome.

MACV was invited to send a delegation to Washington to participate in the discussions.

Although MACV's representatives indicated they were willing to adjust their numbers for individual components of the order of battle, they could not agree to an increase in the total strength of the enemy's forces. The conferees did agree to split the guerrilla-militia forces into two separate categories (i.e. guerrillas and militia), and tentatively agreed to list all of the force components under two headings, "military" and "other." When the talks broke off in late August, the figures in the draft estimate had been adjusted as below:

Military

Main and Local forces	121,000
Administrative and Service	40,000–60,000
Guerrillas	80,000–100,000
Sub-total	**221,000–281,000**

Others

Political cadre	90,000
Irregulars (Militia)	120,000
TOTAL	**431,000–491,000**

The spreads in the numbers reflected continuing differences in CIA (the high side) and MACV (the low figures) estimates for those categories. DIA and MACV rejected any notion of totaling the numbers for the two broad categories—military and "other"—insisting that the order of battle should include only military components. The CIA, on the other hand, insisted that all these components should continue to be included in an overall total, as in previous estimates; to stop doing so, the CIA felt, could give consumers a misleading impression that the enemy forces had been reduced. DIA supported MACV's insistence that continuing to list a total of the two broad categories would give an erroneous impression that the enemy's strength had increased. The CIA and others believed that omitting the combined overall total would fail to reflect the substantial buildup in the enemy's paramilitary force level since 1963.

Some have suggested that the CIA's position on the order-of-battle issue was a blatant, bureaucratic power play aimed at gaining a dominant role over the Pentagon in interpreting the Vietnam War. I know of no one in the agency who regarded the issue in that light. Strange as it may seem to cynical outsiders, most of those I worked with were motivated essentially by a principled quest for honesty and truth, in accord with the biblical exhortation inscribed over the entrance of the CIA's headquarters building: "Ye shall know the truth, and the truth shall make ye free." The record shows that a number of military intelligence officers in Saigon and in the Defense Intelligence Agency agreed with the CIA's position in this dispute.

This fundamental controversy posed an extraordinary dilemma for the intelligence community, whose embarrassment was compounded when word of the dispute was leaked to the press. This development confounded top levels of the administration, which was fully engaged in the campaign to demonstrate progress in the war and thereby eliminate Vietnam as a divisive issue in the coming presidential election. The U.S. mission in Saigon played a major role in this campaign through its Joint U.S. Public Affairs Office (JUSPAO), which orchestrated press relations for both the embassy and MACV. The Country Team in Saigon was officially marching in lockstep toward Washington's goal of demonstrating "light at the end of the tunnel."*

Ambassador Robert Komer (Westmoreland's civilian deputy for pacification) cabled Washington on August 19 that ". . . any explanation as to [wide discrepancy between MACV and CIA figures] would simply lead press to conclude that MACV was deliberately omitting [militia] category in order [to] downgrade enemy strength. Thus credibility gap would be further widened at a time when in fact we are moving toward much more valid estimates." Three days later General Creighton W. Abrams, Westmoreland's military deputy, discounted the military capacity of the mili-

---

*In his memoir, *In Retrospect*, Defense Secretary McNamara observed that the extended dispute over these numbers was "well known to CIA Director Dick Helms, the president, and me, and the other senior government officials. It aroused deep emotions. . . . The issue became where to draw the line when reporting 'enemy strength.' Westy excluded more of the irregular forces than did some of his intelligence officers and some CIA analysts. . . . I leaned toward the more inclusive (and larger) estimate."

tia. In his message to General Earle Wheeler, chairman of the Joint Chiefs, Abrams went on to note: "The press reaction to these inflated figures is of much greater concern. We have been projecting an image of success over the recent months, and properly so. Now, when we release the figure of 420,000–431,000, the newsmen will immediately seize on the point that the enemy has increased about 120,000 to 130,000. All available caveats and explanations will not prevent the press from drawing an erroneous and gloomy explanation as to the meaning of the increase. All those who have an incorrect view of the war will be reinforced and the task will become more difficult."

Meanwhile, in the midst of the dispute on numbers, MACV's recently arrived intelligence chief, Major General Philip B. Davidson, Jr., was asserting his personal control over the command's order-of-battle estimates. In an August 15 memorandum he outlined new procedures to be followed "for determining OB on a weekly basis. . . . What we have got to do is to attrite main forces, local forces, and particularly guerrillas. We must cease immediately using the assumption that these units replace themselves. We should go on the assumption that they do not, unless we have firm evidence to the contrary. The figure of combat strength and particularly of guerrillas must take a steady and significant downward trend as I am convinced this reflects true enemy status. . . . Due to the sensitivity of this project, weekly strength figures will hereafter be cleared personally by me."*

Four days later General Davidson advised the DIA representative to the discussions in Washington with the CIA that ". . . Further consideration reveals the total unacceptability of including the strength of the self-defense forces and the secret self-defense forces in any strength figure to be released to the press. . . . The figure of 420,000, which includes all

*General Davidson, Westmoreland's intelligence chief 1967–1968, rationalizes the MACV point of view on the numbers controversy in his *Secrets of the Vietnam War* (Novato, Calif., 1990). His views contrast sharply with those of General Bruce Palmer, who wrote that "on balance, the Agency did a good job in assessing the situation in Indochina during the 1965–74 period. Its overall intelligence judgments were generally sound and its estimates mostly on the mark." Palmer also judged that the CIA was closer to ground truth on the order-of-battle issue than was MACV.

forces including SD [Self Defense] and SSD [Secret Self-Defense], has already surfaced out here. This figure has stunned the embassy and this headquarters and has resulted in a scream of protests and denials. . . . In view of this reaction and in view of General Westmoreland's conversations, all of which you have heard, I am sure that this headquarters will not accept a figure in excess of the current strength figures carried by the press. . . . Let me make it clear that this is my view of General Westmoreland's sentiments. I have not discussed this directly with him, but I am 100 percent sure of his reaction. . . ."

Adding further fuel to the fire, MACV's intelligence staff had formally briefed the press that month on its belief that the war had reached a "crossover" point with respect to enemy strength. The enemy's losses in South Vietnam, this thesis maintained, were now exceeding his ability to replace them, and if current trends continued, he would soon run out of troops. This judgment was derived by comparing enemy losses—derived from MACV's body count—with the estimated flow of troops infiltrating from the North and the rate of recruitment in the South.

Unfortunately, all the numbers in this equation were "soft." The body count was notoriously inaccurate; it often included any unidentified body on the battlefield, such as innocent bystanders, and was frequently inflated by adding a guess as to the number of dead who had been carried off by the departing enemy. Allowing for some consistency in these exaggerations, the body count was nonetheless useful as a rough measure of trends in the intensity of combat, and of its relative cost to the enemy. With respect to "inputs" that would offset these losses, MACV had no real basis for estimating the number of recruits being added to the forces in the South, apart from an occasional report indicating that a local force unit had drawn replacements from militia units. These were never frequent or timely enough to permit more than the roughest guesstimate of what the current—or relatively recent—overall trend might be.

As for infiltration, MACV's figures were based on a strict bookkeeping exercise derived initially from hard but incomplete evidence of specific infiltration groups, which had to be confirmed—and fleshed out—over time by prisoner interrogations and captured documents. It was often six months or a year before the accumulated evidence would permit a conclusive judgment as to how many troops had infiltrated from the North in any given month. The rate of flow fluctuated markedly with the seasons, and in accordance with the enemy's strategic planning, and such changes became evident only well after the event.

Thus, although the crossover thesis was interesting and potentially significant, its validity was not readily discernible on a real-time basis. Yet MACV suggested in August 1967 that the crossover point had been reached, and they represented this as a key indicator of "light at the end of the tunnel."

This crossover thesis was an inevitable result of Westmoreland's strategy of attrition, which was also clearly reflected in General Davidson's new procedures for order-of-battle analysis. If losses exceeded input, it was only a matter of time before enemy military forces would be annihilated. Depending on whether the curve accelerated, leveled off, or declined, one might even project when the enemy would run out of manpower. This kind of pseudoanalysis obviously fostered the "light at the end of the tunnel" and "we're on the right track" psychology in Saigon and Washington, and helped set up the stunning impact of the Tet offensive.

The argument over the crossover point was dismissed by some observers as another trivial debate over semantics. But to some of us it was much more than that. If attrition was indeed our fundamental goal in Vietnam, and if progress toward that goal was to be measured by a declining curve in the strength of the enemy's force level, it seemed to many of my colleagues that the losses should be applied against a much larger force basis than the numbers reflected in MACV's order-of-battle listing. Subtracting losses from a smaller, incomplete force level would misleadingly foreshorten the apparent time required to complete the attrition process. Many of us believed as early as late 1966 that time was running out on the patience of the American people with an indecisive war, and that our "will to fight" was likely to evaporate long before that of the Communist leaders in Hanoi. There were far more of the enemy than MACV's estimated 248,000 that had to be attrited.

Under normal procedures, fundamental disagreements on national estimates were handled by setting forth the majority view in the text and placing the dissenting view in a footnote. Director Helms, however, made it clear early on that he was unwilling to follow that procedure in this instance. He believed it would be inadmissible for the intelligence community to split on so basic an issue as military order of battle, and he would not countenance a dissenting footnote by either side. The director was clearly dismayed at the impasse, observing repeatedly that reasonable men ought to be able to resolve such a dispute, and more than once urging us on the Vietnamese Affairs Staff to "work it out."

In September, George Carver led a delegation from Washington, which included representatives from INR and DIA, for a final conference on the issue at MACV headquarters in Saigon. MACV's delegation, headed by General Davidson (and with Westmoreland's public affairs officer, Brigadier General Winant Sidle, in attendance), refused to budge during three days of sometimes bitter debate. Carver wired Helms: "So far our mission frustratingly unproductive, since MACV stonewalling, obviously under orders. . . . Variety of circumstantial indicators . . . all point to inescapable conclusion that Gen. Westmoreland (with Komer's encouragement) had given instruction . . . that VC strength total will not exceed 300,000 ceiling. . . . Root problems as we all recognize lie much more in political public relations realm than in substantive difference." Carver later told me that at a private dinner that evening, Ambassador Komer bluntly insisted to him, "You guys just have to back off, that's all there is to it. You've got to back off."

Biting the bullet, Carver that night redrafted the offending portions of the estimate. His carefully crafted "solution" acceded to MACV's demand that the "other" categories—the militia and political cadres—not be included in the listing of the enemy's forces. He agreed to MACV's lower figure (35,000–40,000) for the administrative services, and to a figure of 70,000–90,000 for the guerrillas. These numbers, combined with 119,000 for main and local forces, produced a new total for enemy military forces of 224,000–249,000. The political cadre were listed separately at an agreed level of 75,000–85,000. No figure was provided for the militia, who were effectively "marched out" of the agreed order of battle. A statement was included in the narrative text of the estimate that there may have been as many as 150,000 "other" paramilitary (irregular) troops in 1966, but these had suffered substantial attrition since that time and were not now in-cluded in the military order-of-battle total.

In a personal session with Carver the next day, General Westmoreland readily agreed to the proposed changes. Carver wearily cabled Helms that he had "squared the circle" and that the dispute was resolved. Many of us in CIA were unhappy with the solution. I personally felt that we had sacri-ficed our integrity by acceding to MACV's disingenuous cooking of the books, that we had corrupted the objectivity of the intelligence process by yielding to what would today be described as a "politically correct" settle-ment of the issue. After some reflection, however, I recognized that we had worked ourselves into a no-win situation, caught between a profes-sional rock and a political hard place. Convinced that we had been right in principle, I toyed briefly with the idea of resigning in protest but rejected such an act as a futile gesture. Swallowing my professional pride, I deter-mined to press on with other business, hoping for success the next time around.

Director Helms apparently also had misgivings about the final out-come of the issue. Although he approved the revised estimate on Novem-ber 14, 1967, he forwarded it to the president with a covering memo, in which he wrote: "The new estimate is sensitive and potentially controver-sial primarily because the new strength figures are at variance with our former holdings. . . . I have considered not issuing this Estimate and after considerable consultation, believe this would be a mistake. . . . In short, the charge of bad faith or unwillingness to face the facts would be more generally damaging than the issuance of this document which can stand on its own feet."

Sam Adams was professionally and personally enraged over the out-come, and embarked on a crusade to avenge the alleged "sell-out" by the agency. It consumed him for the remaining twenty years of his life. His perseverance generated two full-scale investigations by the CIA's inspector general of Adams's assorted charges of malfeasance and treason by top agency officials, including Director Helms. Ultimately forced out of the agency on grounds of insubordination (for deliberately violating specific instructions against circulating his personal memoranda outside the agency), Adams carried on his campaign in public. *Harper's* magazine in

1974 published a lengthy article written by Adams, which contained still classified information; a year later he stimulated the House Select Committee on Intelligence to include his charges on its agenda for hearings dealing with the CIA's performance. The committee called William Colby (then the CIA director), George Carver, and me to testify, but under Congressman Otis Pike's chairmanship, the committee's probe on the Vietnam issue was relatively flaccid, short-lived, and inconclusive.

As a result of the *Harper's* article, CBS became interested in Sam Adams's story and produced a "CBS Reports" ninety-minute documentary, "The Uncounted Enemy: A Vietnam Deception," on the issue. The broadcast charged the military with conspiring to mislead the president, the Congress, and the American people on the truth about the war in Vietnam. At the urging of Adams and CBS, I had acceded reluctantly to be interviewed for the show, stipulating that I would not be a party to any attack on the agency for its role in the matter. Excerpts from my interview, and those of a number of other military and civilian intelligence officers, lent weight to the Adams-CBS contention.

After the show was broadcast in 1982, General Westmoreland filed suit for libel and defamation of character against Adams, CBS, Mike Wallace, and the show's producer, George Crile. In preparation for the trial, Westmoreland's attorneys subjected me to seven days of deposition hearings. CBS called me—and about a dozen other CIA and military intelligence analysts—to testify during the trial, which took place during the winter of 1984–1985. The three days I spent on the witness stand were unforgettably stressful; Westmoreland's attorneys were relentless in their efforts to destroy my credibility. In the end, General Westmoreland's lawyers, who were running out of funds, were dealt a mortal blow when the judge ruled that they must explicitly disprove CBS's allegations. Westmoreland withdrew the lawsuit before it went to the jury, in exchange for a statement by the network that it had not meant to question the general's loyalty or patriotism, which he chose to construe as an apology.*

A year or two after the trial, my former colleague, Colonel Gaines

---

*For a candid view of the complex trial from a juror's perspective, see Patricia M. Roth's *The Juror and the General* (New York, 1986).

Hawkins, whose earnest testimony had helped CBS's case, chose to end his battle with cancer by suicide. When we had met in New York after the trial, Gaines had exuberantly hailed me as "the pro's pro." I had never seen a more conscience-stricken man, however, than the Colonel Hawkins who in 1967 had dutifully, but with obvious pain and remorse, defended MACV's position at the order-of-battle conference in Washington. He told me privately at the time that he personally agreed with the CIA's numbers and that he deeply regretted that circumstances—his job—required that he rebut them. Gaines's loyalty as a soldier outweighed his own profes-sionalism as an intelligence officer in 1967, but I believe he earned absolu-tion through his forthright testimony during the trial.

Sam Adams died prematurely in 1988, still unreconciled to his defeat in the dispute over the 1967 estimate. Sam was a very likable fellow, an avid, hardworking, painstaking researcher who was utterly convinced of the validity of his findings and implacable in defending them. But his un-suppressed enthusiasm led him to remove hundreds of classified docu-ments from agency files and sneak them out of the headquarters building. These papers, which he took home and at one point buried in his neigh-bor's yard, formed the documentary basis for his continuing campaign. He became tragically quixotic in his twenty-year quest for redemption, which ended only when he was stricken by a massive coronary attack. I suspect that those who knew him well would agree that Sam, who was an honest man, died of a broken heart.

13
The
Tet
Surprise

AS CARVER'S DEPUTY, I was usually only on the periphery of the Johnson administration's repeated attempts—through a variety of diplomatic and covert channels—to send signals to Hanoi about the possibility of negotiations. These activities were regarded as highly sensitive, and information about them was tightly held in Washington. I was aware of most of these because of the need to act on Carver's behalf during his absence, but I was not involved on a daily basis when he was available to deal with them personally.

The White House obviously was willing to negotiate an end to the war which included an end to Hanoi's aggression and the withdrawal of its forces from South Vietnam. Hanoi's position was the mirror image of ours—they were prepared to negotiate a result under which the United States discontinued its support for the Saigon government and agreed to withdraw its forces from Vietnam. Neither side, in effect, was willing to accept a settlement that did not ensure "victory."

After early 1966, Hanoi had repeatedly made it clear through all channels, overt and covert, that talks could begin only after Washington "unconditionally" stopped bombing the North. In the autumn of 1967 an apparent approach through CIA sources in Saigon gave us new insight into the current thinking of COSVN, the Communist headquarters for South Vietnam. This exchange of "signals" reflected a nuance on the Communist side not previously evident to most of us. The COSVN contact suggested that negotiations would be possible only when the Communists were convinced that the U.S. government had concluded that victory was unattainable. Limited bombing "pauses" or restrictions were insufficient; only an unequivocal, unconditional cessation of bombing, and an announced intention to withdraw U.S. forces, would demonstrate that Washington had abandoned the aim of victory. Without any such manifestation that our attitudes had changed, there was no prospect for negotiations.

I insisted at the time that this message seemed to be a legitimate "clarification" of Hanoi's view, that they were trying to make the Johnson administration understand why its earlier probes and tentative bombing pauses had been fruitless. At the end of January 1968, Hanoi launched the massive Tet offensive, which dramatically underscored the fact that an American victory in Vietnam was still a long way off.

The Tet offensive was an intelligence failure in so far as we failed to anticipate the full scope and nature of the onslaught, and we wrongly assumed it would come at the end of the Tet holiday, rather than in the middle of the cease-fire period three or four days earlier. The fact that we *had* predicted a massive offensive throughout South Vietnam on an unprecedented scale for late January, however, and that American and Vietnamese commanders had been warned of its imminence and were planning to meet the anticipated offensive, is seldom noted. Why did we miscalculate its scope and nature; why didn't we expect an attack on *all* the important urban centers, province capitals, and district towns? Why didn't we expect it *during* the holiday period?*

Our failures resulted from a number of factors, the most important being that we did not think the Communists believed the time was propitious for a general uprising. Their evolving strategic scenario reflected an unrealistic assessment on their part of the prospects for success. We had

---

*A detailed and informative examination of the intelligence community's performance is contained in Captain Ronnie Ford's *Tet 1968* (London, 1996).

seen some reports which suggested that they believed the coming offensive would be climactic; they were briefing their units to the effect that it was intended to produce a general uprising in the cities that would lead to the overthrow of the government and the seizure of power by the Communists. After a number of such reports, some analysts in the CIA station in Saigon examined the thesis that Hanoi had concluded that a "general counteroffensive and general uprising" was then a feasible option. Their analysis of the arguments in support of this thesis was not persuasive to many of us in Washington. We thought the Viet Cong must have been misled by their agents in the cities, or that they were merely psyching their troops up for a major effort in the more conventional military offensive we believed was coming. There was no evidence to indicate unusual unrest in the cities, or aggressive Communist agitation of the sort that could be expected to precede an "uprising." Yet the leaders were telling their troops that the people would indeed "rise." It sounded phony, and most of us were not convinced.

Because we rejected the notion that a rising was imminent or might be instigated, we could not anticipate that the offensive would take the form it did. It made no sense for the Communists to attempt to overrun all the major population centers in the absence of a real "rising" by the people, because the sheer weight of the military power of more than a million American and Vietnamese troops would certainly crush the offensive. Even if there had been a massive, popular uprising, we doubted that the Communists could have long maintained control of any city, given our overwhelming military power at that time.

Since we did not believe that conditions met the criteria for such a rising, as set forth in the Communists' doctrine for revolutionary war, we dismissed the possibility of an attack on the population centers as not being a viable option. More likely, most of us thought, was an unprecedentedly massive offensive along more traditional post-Tet lines, involving widespread assaults on and bombardments of allied military bases, airfields, command posts, outposts, and pacified hamlets, combined with an effort to culminate the siege at Khe Sanh with a victory. Much of the activity of the Tet offensive was indeed conducted along these more traditional lines. MACV's post-Tet analysis estimated that only a fraction of the enemy's available forces—roughly 85,000 troops—were committed in the offensive. This is sheer nonsense and is based on an excessively narrow definition of the term "committed." The assault on the cities and principal towns, to which this figure relates (and even there it understates the real strength of the forces involved), was only one facet of the onslaught that extended over a period of two weeks or so in January–February 1968. Concurrent with this effort were attacks on or bombardments of nearly every major allied base and supply installation in Vietnam, attacks on hundreds of hamlets in the countryside, and an active siege of Khe Sanh. In addition, main force and local units were deployed to intercept and block allied troop movements reacting to the offensive. MACV's figure of 85,000 (or less) makes no allowance for any of the forces involved in these other activities. The fact is, virtually all the Viet Cong and PAVN forces in South Vietnam participated in active combat operations during the Tet offensive. I believe the number may actually have totaled as many as 400,000, including hamlet militia troops integrated into main force and local force units for the purpose. Unfortunately, no intelligence service in Saigon or Washington undertook a comprehensive postmortem study of this matter to establish in detail the identity, strength, and specific activities of *all* enemy forces committed during this politically decisive campaign. Such a study, based on prisoner interrogations, captured documents, and other relevant intelligence, would have been a boon to military historians.

The reasons why we did not expect the offensive during the Tet holidays are relatively straightforward. First, the enemy traditionally observed the annual Tet cease-fire, using the period to prepare for a major "high-point" of activity immediately afterward. Second, since they knew we would be expecting a major offensive at about that time, it did not occur to us that they would seek surprise by moving the attack forward to the cease-fire period. Again, the kind of offensive we were expecting did not require much stealth and secrecy; only the surreptitious entry of sapper units into towns and cities required that kind of "stealth," and they could have moved in throughout the period of Tet. The Tet offensive was unprecedented; the only way—in any endeavor—to achieve real surprise is to do the unprecedented. The only way to anticipate surprise is to anticipate the unprecedented. This is not easy, even when one has all one's faculties carefully attuned.

When we received initial word at CIA headquarters of the Tet offensive, I had just concluded briefing Phil Habib and Nicholas Katzenbach of State on the impending offensive, showing them the maps in our briefing room on which we portrayed the movements of major enemy units based on hard evidence from technical sources. It was the only place in Washington where these deployments were systematically plotted so that the patterns of developing concentrations were evident. Habib and Katzenbach were depressed by the thrust of my briefing, because I had emphasized the overwhelming and unprecedented weight of the military forces being assembled in various places for the onslaught, and the map vividly depicted this; it left no doubt as to the massive character of the attack. As we stood in front of the map saying our goodbyes, an officer rushed up to me saying, "Mr. Allen, sir, the embassy in Saigon is under attack." Habib chuckled, suggesting I have my troops knock off the horsing around. The officer earnestly persisted, exclaiming in his best "Pearl Harbor" warning tones, "This is no drill, sir; the wire tickers report that the embassy is under attack and the VC have penetrated the compound," and he offered a wire-service report detailing this. Habib's jaw fell, and he turned ashen grey. He seemed to realize immediately the significance of this development—that the wind had been taken out of the administration's sails; the "light at the end of the tunnel" had been turned off; the administration's policies had been derailed from "the right track."

General DuPuy brought the chairman of the Joint Chiefs and a number of other top military officers to our situation room during the first few days of the Tet offensive, to brief them on the situation using our unique maps of enemy deployments, until DIA was able—with our help—to duplicate the maps for use in the Joint Chiefs' facilities in the Pentagon.

The order-of-battle issue reemerged after the Tet offensive. The CIA was unconvinced by MACV's early estimate that only 84,000 enemy troops had participated in the massive onslaught; this figure never changed. Vietnam's major urban centers—Saigon, Hue, and Da Nang—plus 36 of the 44 provincial capitals, and at least 64 of the 242 district towns, were assaulted by the enemy.* In addition, virtually every major air base, military garrison, and supply installation was hit, and hundreds of village centers

---

*William J. Duiker, *The Communist Road to Power in Vietnam* (Boulder, Colo., 1981).

and hamlets were attacked, raided, or harassed. Government military forces generally recoiled from the rural areas to protect the administrative centers (and their families); the Viet Cong later claimed they had dealt the pacification program a serious blow by "liberating" more than 1.5 million people in rural hamlets. This was reflected in the Hamlet Evaluation System assessments for the end of February 1968, which showed a decline of 15 percent in the number of secure hamlets.

Pre-Tet intelligence clearly indicated that the enemy planned an all-out military effort aimed at producing a "decisive" victory. Although many PAVN main force units apparently were held back from the initial assault, they had been deployed forward into positions from which they could intercept and engage U.S. and ARVN units that might be sent to reinforce beleaguered points, and their heavy-weapons units helped bombard numerous targets. But virtually all the Viet Cong forces—main force, local force, guerrillas, and militia—appear to have been committed in the offensive, whether formally identified by MACV intelligence or not. This was evident from the weight and breadth of the attacks, and from their impact on the situation throughout South Vietnam.

I am no more convinced now than I was at the time of the Tet offensive that the Communists actually expected to seize power and win the war through a single massive stroke—a general offensive and uprising in January 1968. Some in Hanoi and COSVN may have hoped for this result, and the concept was certainly touted by their political and psychological warfare agents in the South to stimulate their military forces to a heroic pitch. In many towns and cities, these political cadres did openly attempt to stimulate demonstrations against the regime, which were readily crushed. But I believe their real expectations and aims fell short of a *climactic* victory; rather, they wanted to change the direction and focus of the war.

I believe their aims were: to demonstrate that the victory Washington was pursuing in Vietnam would be prohibitively costly; to demoralize the American and Vietnamese publics; to stimulate political action against the war in the United States; and to create conditions for moving the struggle from the battlefield to the conference table. Their intention was indeed to mount a psychologically crushing blow, but not necessarily to achieve military victory; their aim was to convince us that a negotiated settlement was a more feasible option for us than military victory, that we could not block the unification of Vietnam.

The consensus among Hanoi's leadership may have allowed for either outcome—that by mounting the all-out effort they might end the war and be able to seize power, but that they were consciously prepared to accept the lesser outcome of moving toward negotiations. The Viet Cong had carefully coordinated the "negotiation track" with their military effort against the French, timing their final assault on Dien Bien Phu to coincide with the opening of the 1954 Geneva conference in order to achieve maximum psychological effect. They could have finished that battle some days earlier had they wanted to. In 1968 I believed that Khe Sanh was not simply a decoy to draw MACV's forces out from the cities but was an essential complement to the Tet offensive. Given the pattern of the enemy's military effort, and their doctrine, they would not have expected the Khe Sanh battle to be *the* tactically decisive blow. The Khe San siege and the Tet offensive were parallel efforts, rather than a feint followed by a real blow. They intended to take Khe Sanh and wanted very much to do so. Had Khe Sanh fallen coincident with, or in the wake of, the Tet offensive, it would have added to the crushing psychological weight of the offensive. It was the only place in Vietnam where the Communists could hope to overrun a significant American garrison (four or five battalions). The battles accompanying the Tet offensive elsewhere would have involved a war of maneuver, in which they knew that the Americans would be more effective; there would be no real hope of destroying a major American force in the open. But Khe Sanh was isolated and under siege, as the French had been at Dien Bien Phu, and the Communists hoped to repeat the pattern of that earlier triumph.

They knew that militarily Khe Sanh would be more than a sideshow, as Dien Bien Phu had been. But they also knew it would involve only a fraction of the total military forces on either side. They did hope to draw major American forces from other areas into the region, to meet the threat posed by their buildup there—and they succeeded in forcing General Westmoreland to shift the weight of American ground forces to the north.

This reduced the size of our forces in other areas, but not sufficiently to leave the cities unprotected and vulnerable to the Tet attacks. Their strategic aim was thus very similar to that at Dien Bien Phu—to inflict a strategically crushing blow on the home front (this time American instead of French) with their attacks on the cities, followed by a significant tactical defeat at Khe Sanh. Westmoreland's counterblow at the enemy forces surrounding Khe Sanh denied Hanoi the frosting on its strategic cake.

The enemy had grossly underestimated the destructive firepower that Westmoreland would be able to employ to defend the Marine base at Khe Sanh. Strategic Air Command B-52s alone dropped more than 100,000 tons of bombs in the vicinity of Khe Sanh in a 60-day period, thoroughly demolishing the PAVN siege operation. PAVN's attempted assaults were effectively met by artillery and tactical air strikes on a scale dwarfing what the Communists had experienced at Dien Bien Phu. Their command post for the campaign in nearby Laos was destroyed and its staffs put out of action. The enemy simply could not ready an effective siege in the face of MACV's firepower. As it turned out, a victory at Khe Sanh was not essential to the final outcome of the spring campaign, though had it occurred it would have spurred the U.S. move toward peace talks.

I believe the Communists were not wholly disappointed by the results of the Tet offensive. Although they suffered horrific losses and were tactically defeated at every turn, the military offensive achieved its strategic purpose. It led the Washington establishment to conclude that victory was unattainable at an acceptable cost, and that the time had come to move the principal arena for the struggle from the battlefield to the negotiating table. I believe Hanoi had concluded that this option would produce more favorable results for them than would an indefinite continuation of the war. Hanoi's leaders did not wish to face the prospect of a continuing U.S. military buildup; they had decided to halt the progressive escalation of the U.S. military involvement. They calculated that they could not win militarily in the South in the face of the American military power then in place there; it would be too costly to continue the struggle at the level of intensity it had reached. Regardless of whether the crossover point had been reached, they preferred not to continue waging a war of attrition on the scale of 1967. Their leaders were prepared to recognize—to them-

selves—that there were limitations to the effectiveness of "national liberation struggles" if America was willing to commit large enough forces to
make them too costly. But they were not acknowledging defeat; there were
still ways for them to break the stalemate on the battlefield by moving
Washington to the negotiating table. They were fully aware of the growing
dissatisfaction with the war in the United States, and they believed it
could be exploited in the same way they had fostered opposition to the
earlier war in France. The diplomatic-psychological initiative now offered—at least for the time being—the most attractive option.

This entire question of the motives behind Tet warrants serious study.
I suspect, though, that it may prove to be one of those perennial—and un-
resolvable—controversies of history.

After the initial shock wore off, concern mounted in Washington over the
impact of the Tet offensive on our military and pacification programs. In
the CIA we decided to take a quick reading, so it was agreed that I would
go on a two-week mission to "assess the damage," visiting key areas
throughout the country, interviewing appropriate American and Vietnamese officials at various levels, and "seeing for myself." As I readied my
departure, the administration decided to send an interagency team
headed by General Wheeler of the Joint Chiefs and including Phil Habib
and General DuPuy. I was designated as the CIA member of the group,
though I went on ahead to gather data. I visited most of the major cities,
including Can Tho, Saigon, Bien Hoa, Nha Trang, Ban Me Thuot,
Pleiku, and Da Nang; continued fighting in the citadel at Hue precluded a
visit there. I talked with senior American and Vietnamese officials about
what had transpired in their areas during the offensive, and its impact on
our war effort. I met with Ambassador Bunker and other embassy officials, and talked to members of the intelligence staff at MACV. I also interviewed President Thieu and Vice President Ky to see how they were
reacting in the aftermath of the attacks.

I called first on Ky, accompanied by a senior CIA operations officer. Ky
was dispirited and dejected, and disgusted with Thieu's performance,
deriding his alleged lack of leadership in the crisis. He was discouraged

that he had been given little to do, and he spoke of the need to restore confidence, to inspire people to pick up the pieces. He spoke openly, repeatedly, and vehemently of his growing belief that Thieu must be overthrown, and suggested that he, Ky, would be willing to do it. When we briefed Ambassador Bunker on this meeting, he was appalled that we had not peremptorily told Ky to refrain from a coup, insisting it was not in the American interest. We apologized as best we could, pointing out that Ky obviously was not ready to move, that at best he was floating the idea to find out what the American reaction might be, and that in any case we had been uninstructed. Bunker growled that we should have known what the U.S. reaction would be and should have made it clear to Ky that he was talking nonsense. We reported our interview to Washington and, of course, sent word back to Ky that the United States would not be happy if he were to depose Thieu.

The next day we returned to the palace to call on President Thieu, whose offices were at the opposite end of the long corridor from those of Ky. Thieu spent most of the interview railing against his vice president, turning most of our questions about the Tet offensive to the issue of Ky's irresponsibility, disloyalty, and incipient treason. He knew, of course, of our visit to Ky the day before. Thieu was correct in his assessment of Ky's attitude, but his obsession with Ky at the expense of dealing with the myriad of problems that needed his attention in the aftermath of Tet seemed incongruous to us. As Thieu ranted and raved about his vice president, his demeanor conjured up images of the Emperor Nero and his legendary fiddle. We reported this interview too to Bunker and to Washington.

After about ten days in post-Tet Vietnam, I drafted an overall assessment, documenting how the ARVN's self-confidence had been shattered; how ARVN regular and paramilitary forces had abandoned wide areas of the countryside to the enemy, seeking refuge in numbers in the cities and towns, and thus rolling back the pacification program; how American advisers were now unable to get the ARVN to move back out to counter the enemy's gains; how the Vietnamese populace had been demoralized by the ferocity and ubiquitousness of the enemy's attacks and the apparent inability of one million Vietnamese and American military troops to protect even the inner core of the major cities; and how the Vietnamese leadership seemed to have lost its grip on reality in the aftermath of the offensive and was not effectively addressing the critical situation. I also noted that although the enemy had suffered heavy losses, their forces appeared to be regrouping and could mount further large-scale offensive action in a matter of weeks.

In fact it was not until May that the Communists were able to mount a second major blow—the "mini-Tet" offensive, which, had it occurred before Tet, would have been on an unprecedented scale. It was, however, only a pale shadow of the Tet offensive. This was followed in August by a third major convulsion, again smaller than the two previous efforts but on a significant scale nonetheless. Losses were extremely heavy in both of these subsequent offensives, and it was obvious that the enemy could not hope for an uprising or for any military "victory" in these later surges. I believed these were intended primarily to reinforce the trauma inflicted by the initial offensive rather than to produce a military "victory" on the battlefield. They were aimed at keeping us inclined toward the negotiating track; having gotten our attention at Tet, the Communists wished to retain it until we arrived at formal negotiations.

My post-Tet assessment was a rather pessimistic part of the report of General Wheeler's special task force. I did not participate in any general deliberations of this group and did not review their report before it was submitted in Washington. I was aware that they were taking a sober but hopeful view, and were recommending significant reinforcement of our military effort in Vietnam.

I was disturbed when my views came to the attention of Joe Alsop, who wrote a series of columns attempting to portray the Tet offensive as a glorious and decisive victory of American arms, and denouncing the views of "foolish analysts" who suggested otherwise. I had been forced to debate the issue with him at a "background" lunch and found him intractably and almost shrilly espousing the optimistic thesis that the Communists had been ruined by the Tet offensive; that they had staked everything on a single throw of the dice and had lost. I disagreed. Although it was true that the Tet offensive had been a tactical-military disaster for them, I did not see it as a blunder. Yes, they had gambled for the highest stakes, but I denied they had been dealt a death blow, insisting that they retained substantial military potential (which they later demonstrated). I noted that Alsop had "destroyed" the enemy two months before Tet, to no avail, and that the "ghosts" of those killed at Tet might prove to be as effective as the ghosts of those whom he had written off before Tet.

I was, however, convinced that Tet was likely to prove to be psychologically decisive. The image of near victory carefully nurtured by the administration in the fall of 1967 had been destroyed; it would be impossible to persuade the American people again that we were "on the right track." Had it not been for that overblown psychological campaign in the fall of 1967, Tet would not have had quite the traumatic effect on American opinion that it did. But having been told that the war was almost won, and then to be confronted with the drama of Tet on television, the American people would not be so malleable in the future. The administration had lost any hope of credibility on Vietnam. The siege of Dien Bien Phu had brought to power in France a government committed to ending the war without victory, and it seemed to me that the Tet offensive would have a similar effect in the United States.

I was also convinced that the confidence of the South Vietnamese military and civilian populace in ultimate success had been dealt a death blow. Most Vietnamese then and there came to the gut realization that a Communist takeover was only a matter of time. They had—over the preceding few years—begun to feel that perhaps, with massive American support, defeat was not inevitable. Now they feared that the Americans would give up the fight, and they believed that without American help they could never defeat the Communist North Vietnamese.

The Tet offensive set in motion the chain of events leading to President Johnson's decision to halt the bombing and move toward negotiations. As part of that process, he had convened the "wise men" (Dean Acheson and other foreign policy venerables) to be briefed on the situation following our return to Washington, and to advise him accordingly. Habib, DuPuy, and Carver briefed them on the situation, after which the "wise men" advised the president to throw in the towel. LBJ was furious—what was the basis for their negative views? What had they been told that he hadn't? Who had "poisoned the well"? He demanded to hear the briefings they had received. Habib was not available, but DuPuy and Carver were, and they briefed the president. Before he went to the White House for this session, I urged Carver to resist the temptation to push his personal views, and to give a balanced presentation. He was still inclined, even after Tet, toward a somewhat more hopeful view of the situation than I had. I pointed out to him that this might be the most crucial briefing of his entire career, and it was important that he give the president both sides of the equation. He apparently did the right thing. Vice President Hubert Humphrey later sent Carver a note commending him for his "brutally frank" presentation to the president, and observing that the impact of his briefing was reflected in the president's announcement on March 31 favoring an end to the war and declaring that he would not run for reelection.

Some would suggest that the essentially pessimistic (or realistic) outlook that I espoused (and that was shared by others) was, in effect, a self-fulfilling prophecy. They suggest that if our negative views had been suppressed, the United States might have stayed the course in Vietnam and might have taken the appropriate measures to achieve success. There may be an element of truth in this, but I doubt it. It could be argued, on the other hand, that my "realism" should have stimulated the policymakers into considering alternative approaches to overcome the "realities" I was describing. My interest was not so much in dissuading the administration from pursuing a particular course. Throughout the war, my aim was to ensure that whatever course we followed, we did so with our eyes open, aware of the likely consequences of our actions and prepared to cope with them. I felt throughout that our leaders tended toward self-delusion, pursuing their preferred course of action while wearing blinders. As a consequence we were not quite "muddling through." It might be argued that the persistent tendency of many to discount or understate the enemy threat was a greater detriment to our success than the Cassandra-like views of the realists, that the MACV and White House Pollyannas lulled the policymakers into choosing limited options which proved inadequate to the challenge.

14
The End
of My
Tunnel

THE TET OFFENSIVE occurred during what was to be my last year of full-time involvement with Vietnam. In the fall of 1967, after the discouraging outcome of the extended controversy over the National Estimate, I requested a reassignment, or at least a sabbatical—any form of relief from my persistent focus on Vietnam. I had been at war almost continuously for eighteen years. Director Helms approved, but I was urged to stay on for one more year, after which I would be able to attend the British defense college in London. This assurance enabled me to last out the stress of that tumultuous "year of Tet," and it was with the greatest sense of relief in 1968 that I departed for London just before Christmas. I later learned that I was almost called back two weeks later when Henry Kissinger, then Nixon's prospective National Security Adviser, asked Helms to make me available for assignment to the National Security Council staff. Phil Habib later told me that he had been asked by Kissinger to suggest someone in the intelligence community who had a realistic view of the Vietnam situation, and that he had recommended me. Helms's inclination was to summon me home from London; he did not want to get off on the wrong foot with the incoming administration by rejecting one of its initial requests. Fortunately for all concerned—including Kissinger, the agency, and myself—George Carver persuaded Helms to let me have my year in London, and recommended that another CIA officer be made available to Kissinger instead. Helms earned my undying gratitude by agreeing. I don't believe I could have effectively served the Nixon administration's Vietnam policy, which allowed the fighting in Vietnam to continue for another four years before acceding to a cease-fire agreement in Paris in 1973 on terms no better than could have been obtained in 1969. Once Johnson had forgone the concept of victory, there was no real hope for an agreement that would have required Hanoi to withdraw its forces from South Vietnam.

It has been argued that time was required to "Vietnamize" the war, to develop the ARVN's capabilities to protect a non-Communist government in the South. This ignores the fact that after Johnson had conceded victory, there was no reasonable prospect for the survival of a non-Communist regime in Saigon. Unification was an inevitable conclusion to the thirty-year struggle—peacefully if the Saigon government agreed to a coalition, forcefully by North Vietnamese conquest if Saigon refused. Nixon's protracted Vietnamization program was essentially a fig leaf meant to rationalize the progressive disengagement and withdrawal of our military forces from the war. The fig leaf would not have been necessary had the Nixon administration honestly acknowledged up front the ultimate consequences of our withdrawal, and negotiated an end to the war in 1969.

As it was, the Vietnamization process unnecessarily prolonged the war. It has also been argued that it was necessary to delay the takeover as long as possible. But it would have been possible in 1969 to negotiate a settlement that would have delayed unification for a "decent interval" following the complete withdrawal of our forces. Persisting in the war while pursuing Vietnamization was a defensible course only if we intended to use the delay in some fashion beneficial to American interests.

My duties after returning from London were associated only peripherally with the Vietnam problem. I watched developments there as an observer, consulting from time to time with my former associates who continued to be involved in analysis of the war. I was in London during the 1969 Communist offensive, reading of it in the intelligence summaries to which I had access at the American embassy. I never regarded that offensive as a serious attempt by Hanoi to win the war. I saw it instead as an effort to "punctuate" the negotiations in Paris, to keep us on track, to improve the Communist position on the ground within South Vietnam, to demonstrate their continuing military potency to the Vietnamese, and to relieve pressure on the Communist position in the countryside, where the accelerated American-Vietnamese pacification program was making progress. This success in pacification stemmed from the weakening of the Communist position at the grassroots level. Their guerrilla-militia forces had been irretrievably used up in the Tet offensive, when large numbers of them had been impressed into main force and local force units and then wiped out in the attacks on population centers. Consequently their infrastructure in the countryside had lost much of its protective element and could no longer effectively counter our pacification operations. In their effort to force us to the negotiating table, the Viet Cong had sacrificed the southern "insurgency" potential; they had effectively skewed the people's war strategy in favor of a limited "fight-talk" strategy, relying primarily on the sparing use of conventional—as distinct from paramilitary—forces. They could combat our pacification program only through sporadic sapper actions and limited small-scale attacks by PAVN-augmented local force units.

From 1969 through 1973 the Communists punctuated the negotiations with massive, increasingly conventional offensive thrusts, aimed at supporting their negotiating aims and periodically applying pressure on the ARVN. This was the case with their major offensives in both 1969 and 1972. Between these actions they husbanded their main force units in remote sanctuaries and base areas generally near the borders between South Vietnam and Cambodia, Laos, and North Vietnam.

Hanoi was kept off balance by the Nixon administration's major offensives into Cambodia in 1970 and Laos in 1971, both of which gravely disrupted the enemy's logistic situation. The Cambodian thrust was aimed at destroying the enemy's main headquarters for South Vietnam (COSVN), which was known to occupy an area astride the Cambodian border northwest of Saigon, and to destroy his logistic bases in that general region. Although American and South Vietnamese forces failed to destroy the COSVN headquarters, its activities were disrupted and its elements dispersed for a time over a wide areas.

Our forces did succeed, however, in overrunning and destroying large stores of enemy supplies—weapons, ammunition, and equipment—and capturing documents which indicated that the Communists in the South had been relying far more heavily on supplies delivered by sea than had been previously believed in Washington. From 1959 through mid-1965 the North Vietnamese had used small coastal cargo ships to covertly deliver supplies to Viet Cong–controlled areas along the coast in South Vietnam. One such ship, carrying a hundred tons of first-rate arms and ammunition, was attacked by American aircraft and run onto the beach in Phu Yen Province in 1965. Its cargo was recovered by friendly forces, and documents found on the ship, along with interrogation reports of prisoners taken in other parts of the country, indicated that since 1959 there had been as many as fifty such shipments. This coastal supply system had been run by Hanoi's Group 759, which paralleled the work of Group 559, the command responsible for developing the overland logistic system of the Ho Chi Minh trail.

When American and South Vietnamese forces finally interdicted Group 759's operations, Hanoi turned its attention to developing another system to move supplies in bulk to support the war in the Mekong Delta region. This new route moved cargo covertly by sea to the Cambodian port of Sihanoukville. The system, which apparently went into operation in 1966, included more substantial deliveries by larger ships and involved secret collaboration with the Cambodian army's supply system, which moved the supplies from the port to COSVN logistical bases near the border with South Vietnam. Some of us had been conscious of Sihanoukville's potential as an entry point for supplies destined for the Viet Cong as early as 1965, when I personally lobbied in Saigon, without success, for an effort to establish some sort of clandestine "port watcher" operation there to see what might be going on.

MACV's intelligence staff in 1970 had long suspected the existence of a substantial flow of supplies through Sihanoukville, despite the lack of hard evidence. In Washington, the CIA's logistics analysts had developed a model which, as it turned out, vastly underestimated the amount of supplies required to sustain the enemy's operations in South Vietnam. Because the relatively low requirements resulting from this model could be readily moved over the Ho Chi Minh Trail, the CIA's economist-logisticians totally discounted the need for a parallel route through Sihanoukville and rejected MACV's views on its importance. The ensuing wrangle, which peaked in 1969, produced almost as much heat as had the order-of-battle controversy the year before. In this instance, however, the CIA's analysis turned out to be dead wrong. It was a long, uphill struggle for the agency to repair the resulting damage to its credibility with the Nixon administration.

In addition to grossly understating the enemy's requirements for arms, ammunition, and other supplies, the CIA's analysts had apparently overlooked the evidence regarding the earlier shipments by sea, which probably amounted to something over five thousand tons. The loss of this significant supply channel would have to be made up in some way; Hanoi had clearly found it necessary to employ this system to supplement the amount that could be delivered overland via the Ho Chi Minh Trail.

The CIA's analytical model also failed to take into account Hanoi's ongoing efforts to rearm and expand the Viet Cong, as well as its logical interest in building up substantial stocks to support major offensive operations by these larger forces. Such needs would have demanded far more tonnage than a model derived almost exclusively from estimated rates of expenditure during a period in which the enemy was mounting more sporadic operations.

Finally, the CIA's economists clearly overlooked the fundamental economies of transportation—bulk deliveries by sea were obviously less costly and more timely than trucking and manhandling supplies down the still difficult and incomplete Ho Chi Minh Trail system as it existed in 1966–1967. I was embarrassed and chagrined that the agency had not done a better analysis of this issue.

Documents captured in the Cambodian incursion of 1970 indicated that several tens of thousands of tons of weapons, ammunition, and equipment had been delivered through Sihanoukville and moved to enemy depots by the Cambodian army's supply corps. Much of this activity was related to preparations for the 1968 Tet offensive, when the Soviet-designed AK-47 automatic rifle became ubiquitous on battlefields in the Mekong Delta, even among guerrilla and militia units. The thousands of tons of enemy supplies destroyed before the allies withdrew from Cambodia represented a real setback to the enemy's operational capabilities in that region until 1972.

Our invasion of the Cambodian sanctuaries in 1970, and the widening of the war over Cambodian territory, was a major distraction to the PAVN and the Viet Cong. They were forced to move their sanctuaries farther back from Vietnam; their supply arrangements through the port of Sihanoukville were at least temporarily disrupted; and they were forced to divert many of their resources to open a new front to permit a rapid expansion of the Khmer Rouge forces now engaged in serious fighting against Cambodian government forces. To accomplish this, the Vietnamese Communists drew heavily on their already depleted infrastructure in neighboring regions of South Vietnam to assist the Khmer Rouge in establishing a full-scale insurgency.

Hanoi's quick and strong reaction to ARVN's Operation Lam Son 719 in Laos in 1971 apparently surprised both MACV and South Vietnamese intelligence. This ARVN operation, which combined helicopter-borne assaults with ground thrusts by infantry backed by mechanized columns, was intended to disrupt the movement of supplies over the Ho Chi Minh Trail, which paralleled the Vietnam border in Laos. The operation was conducted by the ARVN's elite airborne and marine corps units, and closely supported by U.S. air and artillery units (the latter firing from within South Vietnam). Because American ground units were prohibited from crossing into Laos, and American advisers were not permitted to accompany ARVN forces, the operation was, in effect, a test of the Vietnamization process.

Hanoi reacted quickly, efficiently, and with devastating effect, deploying three infantry divisions, supported by armor and a substantial number of anti-aircraft units, for a showdown battle in the area. The ARVN's drive lost momentum, and its forces were soon forced to fight a desperate withdrawal action against unrelenting enemy pressure. Both sides took heavy losses; several hundred American helicopters were damaged by the intense enemy fire, and the ARVN suffered many casualties and lost a great deal of equipment.

The operation demonstrated that the process of Vietnamization was far from complete and fraught with unanticipated problems. The absence of U.S. advisory teams with the ARVN ground combat units sharply curtailed the effectiveness of American air and artillery support. The advisory teams normally provided ARVN forces with both the communications and the expertise to call in artillery and tactical air support, including airborne resupply missions. Their absence from the operations in Laos left ARVN units with inadequate means of communicating their needs, and deprived them of the intensity and effectiveness of that air and long-range artillery support to which they had become accustomed. This shortcoming obviously contributed to their cautious and sometimes sluggish performance in Lam Son 719. On the other hand, the campaign did seriously disrupt the operations of the Ho Chi Minh Trail system, and the resulting destruction of substantial quantities of enemy supplies inhibited enemy military capabilities for several months.

Hanoi's Easter offensive in 1972 was not an attempt, as some insist, to end the war decisively but rather to improve the enemy's position in South Vietnam in anticipation of the coming cease-fire agreement. The campaign was highlighted by a massive thrust by relatively powerful North Vietnamese mechanized units driving across the DMZ, with its main weight along the axis of the coastal road. This assault caught the ARVN totally by surprise, and one of its divisions virtually disappeared in the initial onslaught; the fact that its three regiments were in the process of switching positions when the attack began led to speculation that treason may have been involved. In any event, ARVN forces in the area were clearly outgunned and outfought early in the battle. Had the newly arrived American adviser to the Vietnamese Marine Corps not been in the area on an orientation visit, the result might have been calamitous. But Colonel Gerald Turley quickly established communications with American carriers offshore and was able to piece together a system for calling in air support for the beleaguered South Vietnamese forces. The advancing enemy forces almost reached Hue before they were finally checked, largely as a result of the effective employment of American firepower which ultimately stiffened the backbone of ARVN units shaken by the appearance of substantial North Vietnamese armored units.

Coincident with—and largely masked by—this frontal assault in the far north, other PAVN units moving in from Laos mounted major attacks in Kontum Province in the northern highlands. While the ARVN was focusing on these offensive thrusts, other PAVN units were infiltrating in smaller groups from sanctuaries into rural areas to reinforce the depleted local and guerrilla forces in the countryside, hoping to improve and consolidate their position in preparation for the anticipated cease-fire agreement. Much of this latter activity—and its significance—was overlooked by U.S. and South Vietnamese intelligence, who were focused on the main force actions.

Although I was no longer directly involved in analyzing the Vietnam War, I kept in touch with developments there by reading our intelligence summaries and talking with former colleagues who were still working the problem. They occasionally sought my advice or opinion, and I shared my views freely with them. But I was quite content—and fully occupied—with my new challenges and responsibilities, and never attempted to reenter the arena of Vietnamese analysis in any serious way.

The 1973 cease-fire agreement negotiated by the Nixon administration could only delay the final outcome. It permitted the enemy to retain major military forces in control of large areas within South Vietnam, including much of the border territory with Laos and Cambodia, without effective barriers to their reinforcement. This not only gave Hanoi a pretext for a casus belli at any time of its choosing, it also ensured that the North Vietnamese would enjoy the same geostrategic advantages they had enjoyed throughout the war, with the added advantage that there would be no American ground forces in South Vietnam to oppose them. Having forced our withdrawal, they could be reasonably confident we would not return.

The cease-fire was unstable from the beginning. The Vietnamese government was understandably uneasy with it and anxious to improve its position before the inevitable Communist attempt to settle the issue. It engaged in a full-scale land grab to improve its holdings in the countryside shortly after the cease-fire took effect. This was only moderately successful, and the Communists countered by covertly bolstering their base areas, maintaining a low level of guerrilla and terrorist activity designed to improve their position at the margins.

Meanwhile, the PAVN was using the respite by developing the Ho Chi Minh Trail into a fully motorable route from Hanoi to the vicinity of COSVN headquarters. This was paralleled by a newly constructed pipeline for delivering motor fuel to PAVN and Viet Cong forces in the South. In the final campaign, some large units traveled by truck all the way from North Vietnam, their movement going undetected until their appearance on the battlefield in the South Vietnamese highlands. This contrasted sharply with the long, often agonizing trek by foot that had characterized infiltration from the North in the early and mid-1960s.

The beginning of the end in Vietnam was signaled in late December 1974 when strong PAVN and Viet Cong forces overran the town of Song Be, capital of Phuoc Long Province. The failure of the ARVN to mount a major effort to recapture this relatively isolated locale some seventy miles north of Saigon, and of the United States to react with massive air support, was taken by both sides as an omen. If the United States would not return with its B-52s to prevent the loss of a provincial capital, would it come back at all? Both sides probably drew a preliminary conclusion that we would not. The major Communist offensive begun two months later at Ban Me Thuot in the highlands was more than a second test of U.S. reactions; it almost certainly was predicated on Hanoi's assumption that we would not recommit our airpower to the war. It was in fact the beginning of a major campaign to conquer the South, which Hanoi initially believed probably would require up to two years and would pass through several phases of intense offensive action. Having clear evidence of Hanoi's strategy, the CIA estimated that the campaign would indeed last for two years. The U.S. intelligence community was stunned by the sudden collapse of the Saigon government and its military forces.

Until the fall of Ban Me Thuot in March 1975, the ARVN had continued to cling to the futile hope that the Americans might return with their military power to save South Vietnam, as President Nixon had promised at the time of the 1972 Christmas bombing of Hanoi. When the full realization struck Saigon that we would not, the South Vietnamese leadership and its military forces seemingly collapsed overnight. The North Vietnamese were probably as surprised as anyone at the suddenness and totality of the ARVN's precipitant disintegration in the face of the rapid and powerful enemy offensive in the spring of 1975; Hanoi had planned a two-year campaign. Why did the end come so quickly?

I believe that the ARVN—and the Vietnamese government—collapsed so swiftly because of their traumatic realization that American firepower would no longer be available when needed. It was the consequence of more than a decade of their reliance on American firepower as the final arbiter on the battlefield. The South Vietnamese had never believed in their own ability to meet the North Vietnamese on the battlefield and defeat them. For more than a millennium, the northerners had extended their domination over their southern countrymen. This movement was regarded by both as inexorable and irresistible, and had given rise to a fatalistic inferiority complex among southerners. In addition, they feared the harsh discipline the Vietnamese Communists would impose, and their hard-nosed, dogmatic, crusading zeal. The dynamic aggressiveness of the northerners combined with the zealous, aggressive discipline of the Communists made the enemy particularly to be dreaded and respected. Informed Vietnamese probably also saw Soviet and Chinese aid as reinforcing Hanoi's potential, and even those who were less astute were aware of the increasing power of the Communist military forces, their growing use of tanks and artillery, and the ARVN's greater difficulty in coping with the enemy main force units in combat. Even more obvious was the absence of the Americans; where there had been a half-million of them, there were now only a handful. The B-52 strikes, long punctuating the calm of the countryside, and available to support the defense of major garrisons, were gone. There were no curtains of black smoke, flame, and red soil erupting on the outskirts of Ban Me Thuot to break up enemy troop concentrations. Thieu and his colleagues almost certainly had taken at face value the reassurances of Nixon and Kissinger that we would intervene with airpower in the event that North Vietnam failed to abide by the 1973 settlement; this had been the principal purpose and message of the Christmas 1972 bombing of the Hanoi region—to demonstrate to both sides what the United States was prepared to do if the impending settlement did not hold up.

Saigon's failure to recapture the capital of Phuoc Long Province in late 1974 marked the beginning of the end. When the Communists began their attacks at Ban Me Thuot in March 1975, I told my staff at CIA's Imagery Analysis Service that the situation would unravel faster than anyone in Washington or Saigon could imagine. In the absence of massive U.S. air support, the ARVN now realized that the era of American firepower in Vietnam had ended. They were on their own now, and they would have no confidence in their ability to stand up to the forces Hanoi could throw into the battle. After the fall of Ban Me Thuot, when the B-52s remained on the ground at Guam and other bases, Thieu and his colleagues knew the end was at hand, and it was every man for himself—*sauve qui peut!*

The ensuing debacle was most dramatically depicted in a series of aerial photographs taken in mid-March 1975 from a CIA-operated aircraft flying along the ARVN escape route from Pleiku in the highlands down toward the coast. Taken from several thousand feet up, the photos show mile after mile of the mountain route jammed with uncounted numbers—certainly hundreds, if not thousands—of vehicles of all types: tanks, armored personnel carriers, and self-propelled guns intermingled with army jeeps and trucks, civilian buses, overloaded commercial rice lorries and other civilian trucks, minicars, pedicabs, motorbikes, and even bicycles as tens of thousands of people made a mad dash to safety in ARVN-held areas on the coast. Jams were occurring at almost every bridge, and vehicles fanned off to both sides of the road to look for other crossings. Some vehicles were stranded in the river beds, blocking others coming from behind. At one major town, a Communist attack was in progress, disrupting the traffic flow; shell bursts and burning vehicles could be seen. Streams of traffic were slipping around to side streets to avoid and bypass enemy fire, then reconverging on the road at the other end of town. There was no apparent escape for this fleeing mob of panic-driven civilians and soldiers, though some of them may have made it on foot days later.

We successfully urged the Office of Current Intelligence to include two pages of these photos in the national intelligence daily publication, with annotations provided by our photo interpreters. I found this an appropriate if tragic finale to my contribution to intelligence on Vietnam.

During my year in London I had an opportunity to view the world and study its major geopolitical issues from an entirely different perspective—that of the British government. The Brits were not mesmerized by the Vietnam problem, and I soon caught up with what had been going on in the rest of the world while I had been focused on Southeast Asia. It was refreshing to exchange views with brigadier-level officers and civil servants from England and the Commonwealth countries, and to wrestle with problems related to the buildup of Soviet strategic forces, the defense of NATO, and conflicts in the Middle East. When the CIA's deputy director of intelligence passed through London and asked what I would like to do when I returned to headquarters, I said "anything but Vietnam."

He was obliging. On my return from London in January 1970, I was assigned to head a division in the Office of Strategic Intelligence that was responsible for producing intelligence on current military developments in all parts of the world, specifically excluding Vietnam. In this capacity I oversaw the work of a couple of dozen keen analysts who processed information from all sources and reported on a wide variety of issues. Among other things, we closely followed the deployment of Soviet strategic missile forces, monitored the status of Warsaw Pact forces opposite NATO, kept tabs on Arab-Israeli and India-Pakistani military activities, watched the development of Chinese military forces, kept an eye on Soviet activities in Cuba, and watched third-world military movements. Our task was essentially to detect and report changes in the status quo, which meant we were constantly challenging the accepted "conventional wisdom." We had an exceptionally fine crew of competent young analysts who enjoyed being in the front line of intelligence work. Our reports were included in the agency's premier current intelligence publications; we wrote the director's briefings to the cabinet and the Congress on military matters; and we produced memoranda for the White House and senior State and Defense Department officials.

In the process I became familiar with a vast array of special intelligence collection systems and how to manage their use in order to satisfy our needs for information. I was given added responsibilities related to coordinating CIA's intelligence support for the strategic arms talks with the Soviets and was involved in guiding the development of new intelligence collection systems for monitoring compliance with anticipated arms control agreements.

After almost three years in this assignment, I moved on to become head of the agency's Office of Imagery Analysis, which was responsible for producing intelligence derived from any and all types of imagery. Working autonomously from the national photo interpretation center, our task was to focus on targets and issues in direct support of the CIA's analytical and operational interests. Our agenda extended beyond military affairs into a variety of economic and even political issues. We pioneered in developing the use of imagery to analyze foreign crop yields, oil exploration activities, electrical power distribution systems, and industrial expansion, as well as providing support for drug-control activities and a wide variety of clandestine intelligence operations.

We were also deeply involved in monitoring a variety of arms control agreements, and my growing familiarity with this process led to my assignment in June 1976 as the senior intelligence adviser to our delegation at the SALT II talks in Geneva. With the hiatus in these talks that followed our national elections in November that year, I returned to headquarters, where I filled a variety of senior staff positions, related largely to arms control matters, until the summer of 1978, when I agreed to serve as director of the CIA's Center for the Study of Intelligence.

This center, which was intended to serve as an in-house think tank on the intelligence profession, had been briefly moribund. My task was to get it back on its feet. I recruited a few "fellows" who had indicated an interest in producing research papers on issues related to aspects of the intelligence process, and held conferences on several topics. Faced with unexpected constraints placed on resources that had been promised, I chose early retirement in July 1979. For the next fifteen years I worked as an independent contractor for the CIA, producing special studies and developing courses for the agency's Office of Training and Education. Since 1994 I have occasionally lectured at agency training programs, and in 2000 I began assisting in the agency's declassification review program.

15
The U.S.
Failure
in Vietnam

THE REASONS for the failure of U.S. intervention in Vietnam will forever be enmeshed in controversy. To those involved, the generation-long conflict was many things. Franklin Roosevelt, in the spirit of Wilsonian self-determination, thought we ought to support independence for Vietnam. Truman believed we should help the French stabilize the situation on China's southern frontier. To Ed Lansdale and Tom Dooley, it was a question of our making a noble effort to secure a better life for the unfortunate people in the area. To others, like John Foster Dulles, we were engaged in a worthy crusade to contain Communist expansion. Dean Rusk saw us helping to preserve a democratic South Vietnam; Admiral Radford thought we were "stemming the tide of Red aggression" in Southeast Asia. To Walt Rostow and Robert McNamara, we were defeating Communist insurgency and the concept of wars of national liberation. To Henry Kissinger, we were attempting to create a power balance that would ensure the survival of a client state. All of these arguments, and others, were used to rationalize our involvement. We were attempting to do all these things, but most were beyond our reach.

In my own view, Roosevelt was right. It was not in the best interests of the United States for the French to reestablish their colonial rule in Indochina, and we should never have supported their efforts to do so. Our fundamental error was in not recognizing this in the 1940s, in not attempting to encourage the Democratic Republic of Vietnam to evolve as a nationalist barrier to the extension of Chinese hegemony in Southeast Asia. Our 1950 military assistance program in the Far East committed us to a sequence of actions in Indochina from which we could not extricate ourselves. Our failure to attempt to work with Ho Chi Minh, and our support for the French war in Indochina reflected a tendency to act without thinking through the consequences, without weighing the risks, without sufficiently exploring other options. With each step along the way, we found ourselves in a situation in which we had to decide later whether to reinforce (or justify) the investment we had made thus far, or to cut our losses and get out. There was little examination of the latter option; invariably the decision was to "reinforce disaster."

Progressively our commitment took on manifestations not foreseen by policymakers who had made earlier decisions. In foreign affairs and national security matters, there is no substitute for thorough, conscientious, and objective analysis of all the factors bearing on a decision, of alternative courses of action, and of a weighing of the consequences—domestic as well as foreign—of all the options available. The intelligence community should play a major role in illuminating this policy-planning and decision-making process. Most often, in recent years, domestic political factors—public opinion polls—tend to dictate the adoption of a course of action other than the one that may be in our best national security interests. When decisions are made on this basis, they should be made with an awareness of—and readiness to react to—the unfavorable international consequences of those decisions.

Between the Geneva Accords of 1954 and the beginning of the Nixon administration in 1969, I am not aware of a clear, fully agreed, comprehensive interagency expression of U.S. national interests in Indochina. In that period the Joint Chiefs occasionally expressed their views on the subject, but these were seldom circulated beyond the Pentagon and the Pacific chain of command. I recall one Joint Chiefs paper in the mid-1950s that described Laos as of "tertiary strategic significance to the United States." In the early 1950s, Vietnam's Cam Ranh Bay was generally seen as having potential strategic value—after all, it had been used as an anchorage by the Japanese navy during World War II, and it was considered important to deny its future use to an unfriendly naval power. But aside from some rubber plantations in the south, a potential for rice exports, and some first-rate anthracite coal in the north, there were no resources in Indochina of great strategic consequence. Its major geopolitical significance was as a body of land adjoining both China and the Indian subcontinent, and therefore as sitting astride routes between the two regions. Vietnam had been subject to Chinese domination for a millennium, during which it had assimilated a great deal of Chinese culture. Cambodia and Laos, on the other hand, reflected a different culture. Anthropologists have half-jokingly observed that the Vietnamese eat with chopsticks and enjoy dog soup while the Khmers and the Laotians eat with their hands and the Laotians worship the dog, along with other animate and inanimate objects.

The Viet Minh movement was perceived by policymakers in Washington in the early 1950s as part of monolithic international communism. This was particularly true during the Korean War and in the wake of the McCarthy hysteria. This outlook underlay our rationale for providing assistance to the French war in Indochina. It supported the quintessential cold war crusading attitude of John Foster Dulles, who dominated the national security decision-making process to an extent matched only by Henry Kissinger two decades later. Under Dulles, it was considered essential to our national interests to deny Indochina to the Communists, and later to deny South Vietnam to the Communist North Vietnamese. Even the existence of the massive coordinating machinery of the National Security Council under Eisenhower could not ensure rational, objective policy analysis on all issues; policies under that system were subject to domination by a single, strong-willed personality. Dulles's desire to deny South Vietnam to the Communists was not based on any value or interest inherent in the region itself—it was ideological, a reaction to the worldwide Communist threat and to an irrational fear of Chinese expansionism.

Having embraced Diem's Catholic, non-Communist regime as our instrument, we were repeatedly faced with the proposition of reinforcing our investment; protecting the "house of cards" we were building became a "national interest." Some policy analysts in 1963, however, saw our national interest as requiring an early end to political instability in the South (the Buddhist opposition and growing military dissatisfaction with Diem), and thus we modified our perception of our national interests to rationalize the overthrow of Diem. Our broader national interest, however, continued to be defined as preventing the Communist domination of South Vietnam. Lyndon Johnson never announced a change in that interest, per se; he never redefined our interests. He merely announced that we would seek to withdraw our forces under honorable conditions when our objectives were ensured.

Our national interest was thus perceived differently over the period, evolving within the broader cold war context. It probably ought to have been perceived as many see it now, in hindsight. We ought to have sought the development of stable governments in the region, free from foreign domination and committed to opposing hegemony within the region by either Moscow or Peking. Had we defined our interests this way in 1945, we would have recognized Ho Chi Minh's Democratic Republic of Vietnam and fostered his autonomy from Soviet and Chinese influence, at the same time encouraging some form of regional cooperation as a means of containing Vietnamese interests. Had we followed this course, how different history would have been.

More than a few intelligence officers in Washington felt from the beginning that our defined aims overreached our ability to achieve them. Many of us understood that the impassioned desire of the Vietnamese people for freedom from foreign domination was being effectively tapped by Ho Chi Minh's revolutionary movement. Most of us felt in the early 1950s that the Communist-led Viet Minh would outlast the will of any government in Paris for continuing what was essentially a protracted war aimed at maintaining France's colonial presence in Indochina and its posture as a world power. Some of us doubted in 1954 that the United States could develop in South Vietnam a stable government capable of resisting Hanoi's certain efforts to reunify the country. More of us doubted in the early sixties that the American people would long support a prolonged, stalemated war in South Vietnam that effectively placed us, in the eyes of the Vietnamese people, in the role of a neocolonialist power.

These attitudes obviously colored much of the intelligence produced in Washington, especially in the Department of State and the CIA. Memoranda, studies, assessments, and estimates generally contradicted the more positive views emanating from the American mission in Saigon and the hopeful mind-sets of the policymakers in Washington. U.S. policymakers consistently hoped to achieve their objectives in Vietnam through quick policy fixes involving a minimal additional commitment of American resources, so that they could go on to deal with other pressing problems, domestic or global.

Planners and decision-makers in Washington, weary of the "bad news" provided by most of the intelligence community, often looked elsewhere for information and analyses that would affirm the validity of their policies. "Beltway bandits" had a holiday as one think tank after another was asked to look for the gold at the end of the Vietnam rainbow. But many of these studies merely underscored the findings of the intelligence community.

The policy analysis process instituted by Nixon and Kissinger in 1969 provided the first full-scale opportunity since the Eisenhower administration for integrating the views of the intelligence community and those of the policy planners and decision-makers in a comprehensive review of the situation in Vietnam. And it restored some semblance of order to the development of national security policy across the board. Nixon's system wasn't perfect—no system involving human participation can be—but it certainly made more effective use of the substantial resources expended on the collection and analysis of foreign intelligence information than its immediate predecessors. Events have demonstrated that succeeding administrations have varied in their effectiveness. Only George Bush's national security process in 1989–1992 has come close to the moderately systematic Nixon-Kissinger approach.

The intelligence experience in Vietnam is not typical; it was, fortunately, an aberration. In my later incarnations on other policy issues, I found that intelligence was able to make a useful contribution. This was particularly true in the arms control process. The intelligence community was brought into discussions at the earliest stages, first to help define the nature and measure the scale and scope of the Soviet strategic arms buildup; next to analyze the potential impact on Soviet capabilities of a variety of schemes for applying mutual constraints; and then to analyze a series of "cheating scenarios" by which the Soviets might seek to avoid compliance with each type of constraint under consideration. We also analyzed likely Soviet reactions, or counterproposals, to the various options we were considering. This work was exhaustive but highly productive. It enabled us to anticipate the needs for new or refined intelligence collection systems that would permit us to monitor compliance with various types of constraints. And the thoroughness of the exercise provided assurance to the decision-makers—and ultimately to the Congress—that the arms control constraints would not redound to our disadvantage. In this context, intelligence ably served the needs of the decision-makers and justified the costs expended on it.

This is what intelligence is supposed to do. The intelligence community exists primarily for the purpose of illuminating and informing the planning and decision-making processes of our national security system. It does not *make* policy, and it should not deliberately set out to *influence* policy along any particular line. But it should be used to analyze the likely consequences and implications of various lines of policy or courses of action, especially the reactions of foreign powers. Using intelligence in this way, decision-makers can pursue policies or adopt courses of action with greater confidence in their ultimate success and greater awareness of their risks and costs.

Index

A NOTE ON THE AUTHOR

George W. Allen was born in Winthrop, Massachusetts, and grew up on military posts in Massachusetts, the Philippines, New York, Hawaii, and California. During World War II he served in the navy in the Pacific theater, and afterward studied at the University of Utah. He has been an analyst and manager for army intelligence, the Defense Intelligence Agency, and the Central Intelligence Agency, from which he retired in 1979. He is married with four daughters and lives in Williamsburg, Virginia.